D0561544

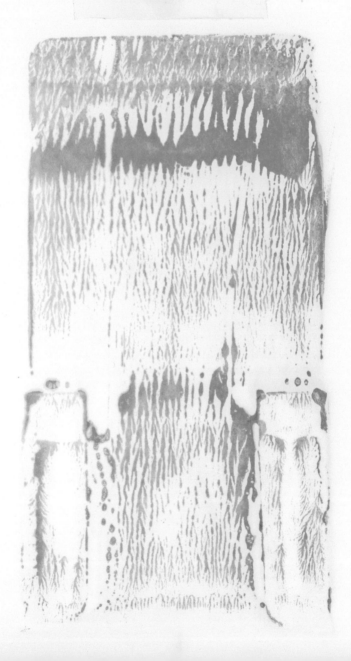

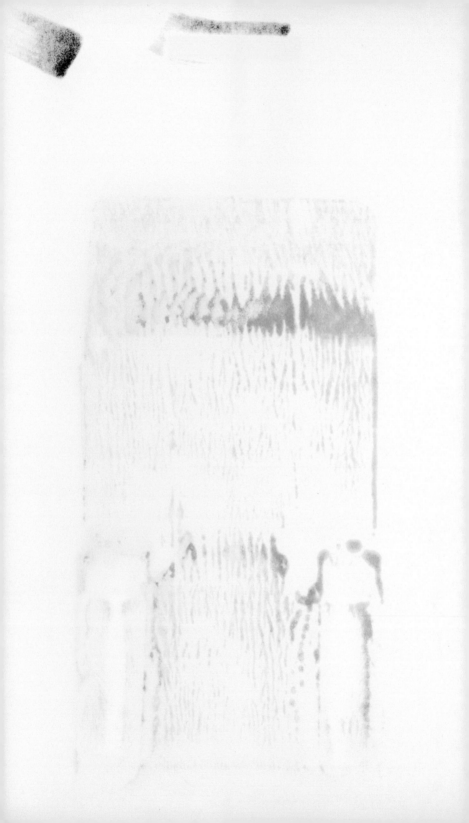

Tennyson
AND
THE REVIEWERS

Tennyson

AND

THE REVIEWERS

*A Study of His Literary Reputation
and of the Influence of the Critics
upon His Poetry 1827–1851*

By EDGAR FINLEY SHANNON, JR.

ARCHON BOOKS, 1967

To ELEANOR DUNCAN SHANNON

PREFACE

My twofold purpose in this study has been to trace the growth of Tennyson's reputation in the British Isles from 1827 through 1851 and to show the extent to which the opinions of the reviewers influenced the actual writing of his poetry.

In pursuing my first aim, I have attempted a history of Tennyson's literary career and of the critical reception of his work beginning with *Poems by Two Brothers* and ending with *In Memoriam,* the poem that established his supremacy among the English poets of his day. It may seem that ideally my account should have closed with the year 1850, which was the great year of achievement in Tennyson's professional life; but I have extended the chronological limit in order to give a fuller treatment to the reception of *In Memoriam.*

In this record of Tennyson's contemporary reputation, I have included some information contained in letters, diaries, and biographies of prominent figures of the period, and I have cited remarks on Tennyson that appeared in books published between 1834 and 1852. But I have relied chiefly upon evidence to be found in the periodical press of the time. Besides determining the critical reaction to each volume of Tennyson's poetry, I have endeavored to give some idea of the degree to which the reviewers retarded or assisted the poet's rise to fame and of the part played by political prejudice and personal bias in the tenor of the reviews.

My second aim — to examine the influence of the reviews on Tennyson's writing (and publication) — has been carried out along two lines. In view of his well-known sensitivity to hostile criticism, I have attempted to test the validity of the statement by W. E. H. Lecky, "No poet ever corrected so many lines in deference to adverse criticism"; and I have also sought to reveal how much the opinions of the critics seem to have affected Tennyson's poetic aims, his selection of subject matter, and his technical handling of that subject matter.

Thomas R. Lounsbury, in *The Life and Times of Alfred Tennyson* (New Haven, 1915), has written on certain of the points treated in this book, and to him I owe that debt which all who come after must acknowledge to their predecessors. Without his initial work my task would have been immeasurably more difficult. But recent scholarship has invalidated a number of his pronouncements; and in the light of the material that I have been able to assemble, I have found it necessary to take exception to many of his conclusions. His treatment of the influence of the reviewers is not extensive and seems to me to be for the most part misleading.

My obligation to Mr. W. D. Paden's valuable article, "Tennyson and the Reviewers (1829–1835)," in *Studies in English* (University of Kansas Publications, Humanistic Studies, VI, No. 4, Lawrence, Kansas, 1940), will be evident from the notes to Chapter I. To Miss Helen Pearce's dissertation at the University of California, "The Criticism of Tennyson's Poetry: A Summary with Special Emphasis upon Tennyson's Response to Criticism as a Factor in the Development of His Reputation" (1930), and to Mr. Walter D. Scott's dissertation at Princeton University, "Tennyson and His Age" (1934), I am indebted for references to several reviews of Tennyson's poetry that are not available in any published work. The bibliography of Tennyson in *Bibliographies of Twelve Victorian Authors* (New York, 1936), compiled by Theodore G. Ehrsam, Robert H. Deily, and Robert M. Smith, has been of great assistance to me, as has been the list of reviews of the poet's work contained in W. MacNeile Dixon's *A Primer of Tennyson* (London, 1896). To the notices of Tennyson mentioned in these volumes and in several of the books on periodicals, such as the *Spectator* and *The Times,* I have been able to add fifty-two previously unlisted articles on the poet that appeared in newspapers, magazines, and reviews between 1827 and 1851.

Except for a few of the weekly papers, such as the *Spectator,* the *Atlas,* and the *Examiner,* newspapers have been almost completely overlooked as a source of contemporary British opinion on Tennyson, and an extensive search in the files of the daily and weekly newspapers, both metropolitan and provincial, Scottish and Irish, has been richly rewarding. Since the collection of provincial newspapers in the British Museum Newspaper Library was severely damaged during the recent war and is not yet open to readers, it has been necessary for me to seek files of these papers in local archives; and I greatly appreciate the uniform kindness and efficiency that I met in municipal or university libraries and newspaper offices in Bristol, Birmingham, Liverpool, Manchester, Leeds, Sheffield, Lincoln, and Nottingham.

I am particularly obliged to the trustees of the Tennyson estate and to Sir Charles Tennyson for permission to make use of the privately printed *Materials for a Biography of A. T.*, from which Hallam Tennyson's *Memoir* evolved; and I am indebted, as all students of Tennyson will be in the future, to Sir Charles's comprehensive biography of his grandfather. I am obligated as well to Sir Stephen A. H. Lennard for permitting me to quote from two unpublished letters of Arthur Henry Hallam.

Some of the material in Chapter II appeared in *PMLA*, LVIII (1943), 181–194, and is used here with the permission of the editor.

To Professor Paull F. Baum of Duke University, from whose suggestions this book originated and who has been an inspiring counselor and guide, I wish to express my deep appreciation. I am also grateful to Professor David Nichol Smith and Colonel Cyril H. Wilkinson of Oxford University for generous assistance in the early stages of this study, to Mr. Humphry House of Oxford University for helpful criticism of the original draft of the manuscript, and especially to my revered teacher and colleague Professor Hyder E. Rollins for reading both the manuscript and the proofs and saving me from numerous errors. My thanks are due as well to the staffs of the Duke University Library, the Harvard College Library, the British Museum Library, the British Museum Newspaper Library at Colindale, and the Bodleian Library for help and innumerable courtesies. To Mr. P. D. Record of the Bodleian, I am indebted for making it possible for me to consult with great convenience the files of more than a hundred periodicals.

E. F. S., Jr.

Cambridge, Massachusetts
June 1952

Contents

Tennyson

AND

THE REVIEWERS

Chapter One

EARLY POEMS

INTRODUCTORY: *POEMS BY TWO BROTHERS* AND "TIMBUCTOO"

Alfred Tennyson's apprenticeship to poetry began in childhood; and his earliest printed verses, inspired to a considerable extent by Byron and Moore, appeared when he was not yet eighteen. They were published in the small anonymous volume, *Poems by Two Brothers,* issued by the Jacksons of Louth on April 20, 1827, under the London imprint of Simpkin and Marshall. The book was composed of one hundred and three short poems written chiefly by Alfred and Charles Tennyson, though there were a few by their elder brother Frederick. Forty-two of the pieces have been identified as Alfred's. He shared with Charles in the composition of another, two may be either his or his brother's, and four more are doubtfully ascribed to him.[1]

Acknowledged in the preface as a youthful work, *Poems by Two Brothers* created no excitement in the world of letters, though the boys were rewarded for their efforts with two short notices in contemporary periodicals.[2] On May 19, 1827, the *Literary Chronicle and Weekly Review* quoted two of the poems, introducing them with the remark, "This little volume exhibits a pleasing union of kindred tastes, and contains several little pieces of considerable merit." In June the *Gentleman's Magazine* benignly commented, "These poems are full of amiable feelings, expressed for the most part with elegance and correctness. . . . The volume is a graceful addition to our domestic poetry, and does credit to the juvenile Adelphi."

With his poems, if not his name, already in print, Tennyson went up to Cambridge in October 1827 and matriculated on February 20, 1828.[3] The following year he won the Chancellor's Medal for English verse with a poem of two hundred and forty-eight lines of blank verse entitled, as the competition required,

"Timbuctoo." It was printed in the local newspaper, the *Cambridge Chronicle and Journal*, July 10, 1829, and later in the year was published in *Prolusiones Academicae*. Owing to the poet's extreme shyness, it was read for him by his friend Charles Merivale at the exercises in the Senate House in the summer of 1829.[4]

A prize poem written in a measure other than the conventional heroic couplet was looked upon as an extraordinary work, and "Timbuctoo" made a startling impression upon some of the sanguine youths at Cambridge. Richard Monckton Milnes, a member of the "Apostles," the society of young intellectuals to which Tennyson belonged, wrote to his father, "Tennyson's poem has made quite a sensation; it is certainly equal to most parts of Milton." [5] In a letter to William E. Gladstone, then at Oxford, Arthur Henry Hallam, also an Apostle, praised the poet's "splendid imaginative power" and declared, "I consider Tennyson as promising fair to be the greatest poet of our generation, perhaps of our century." [6]

The ardor which prompted these remarks had already inspired an attempt to bring "Timbuctoo" to the notice of a wider audience than the university afforded. On July 22, 1829, the *Athenaeum* reviewed the poem with absurdly exaggerated praise. John Sterling, the editor of this struggling literary journal then less than two years old, was a former leader among the Apostles, and there can scarcely be any doubt that the criticism was written by one of the Cambridge group.[7] According to the reviewer, the poem contradicted in a decisive manner the assumption, too frequently made, that poetry in the present age "was likely to perish." Still more unusual was the discovery of such poetic promise in a prize poem. "These productions," he said, "have often been ingenious and elegant, but we have never before seen one of them which indicated really first-rate poetical genius, and which would have done honour to any man that ever wrote. Such, we do not hesitate to affirm, is the little work before us; and the examiners seem to have felt about it like ourselves, for they have assigned the prize to its author, though the measure in which he writes was never before (we believe) thus selected for honour." After quoting fifty-one lines from the poem, the reviewer ended with the question, "How many men have lived for a century who could equal this?"

There is no reason to suppose that many readers were converted to Tennyson's following by such biased opinions. He himself set no great store by "Timbuctoo"; for he wrote, about two years later, "Prize Poems . . . are not properly speaking 'Poems' at all, and ought to be forgotten as soon as recited." [8] The notice in the *Athenaeum*, however, forecast the interest which Tennyson's friends were to take in advancing his name, and at this point their zealous confidence in his powers encouraged him to try his fortunes with a volume of poems while he was still an undergraduate.

THE RECEPTION OF *POEMS, CHIEFLY LYRICAL*

The study of Tennyson's literary reputation properly begins with a chronological account of the reception by the British periodical press of his first independent poetical venture, *Poems, Chiefly Lyrical*. Published by Effingham Wilson in June 1830, when the author was not quite twenty-one, the slim duodecimo volume containing fifty-six poems appeared at an inauspicious moment.[9] George IV died on June 26, and parliamentary elections with agitation for reform occurred in England during the summer. On the Continent revolution swept triumphantly through France and Belgium, and war between these countries and the Holy Alliance seemed imminent. It was a time when the periodicals, supplied with a plethora of news, were unlikely to evince much interest in a little book of poems by an almost unknown author.

Nevertheless, the *Atlas,* a weekly newspaper with a considerable section devoted to literature, printed a brief notice of *Poems, Chiefly Lyrical* in the issue for June 27. Robert Bell, who was a friend and favorable reviewer of Leigh Hunt, edited the *Atlas* from "about 1828" until July 1842,[10] and he may have been the author of the remarks on Tennyson. Whoever the reviewer was, he found the "quaint and picturesque scraps" with which the volume was filled reminiscent of Herrick. The new book, he said, "brings us back to the pleasant times when there was a marvellous subtlety in verse, making its way through far-gathered figures and ingenious illustrations." "On the whole," he concluded, "we are greatly pleased with Mr. ALFRED TENNYSON."

Another weekly paper, the *Spectator,* edited by Robert S. Rintoul, published a generally sympathetic criticism of the book on August 21,[11] describing it as "a volume of very pleasant verses — a volume in which a good deal has been effected, and in which there is no uncertain indication of much more to be done," for the critic confidently expected "to meet the author again." Tennyson's three main faults were "a great fondness for old words," "a love for old modes of pronunciation," and "a vicious and irregular system in the arrangement of his rhymes"; yet he had "that principle of invention, the characteristic of true poetry, which can give dignity to the simple and novelty to the common." The reviewer saw "much beauty" in "The Deserted House." "Claribel," "Lilian," and "Mariana," he said, "are extremely good," as are also "The Merman," "The Mermaid," "Love and Death," and "The Kraken." At the end he printed approvingly "Nothing Will Die" and "All Things Will Die" — "a pair of little metaphysical pieces: in reading them, we could almost imagine that we had before us some recently-recovered fragment of COWLEY."

On September 25 a favorable short notice also appeared in the literary column of *Felix Farley's Bristol Journal.* The writer of the piece, who was a self-confessed friend and young contemporary of Tennyson,[12] declared, "It fortunately happens, however, in the present instance, that the sterling merit, the exquisite pathos, and undoubted genius of these productions are too manifest to subject us to the least danger of rendering ourselves obnoxious to the charge of flattery or of undue partiality, when we add our opinion that this little volume contains some of the most splendid gems of poetry we have met with for many, many years past."

The two literary weeklies, the *Athenaeum* and the *Literary Gazette,* which might have been expected to review the book, failed to comment upon it.[13] Tennyson and Hallam, who had left for the Pyrenees soon after the volume was published, returned to England in September; and on October 4 Hallam wrote to his

friend, "I cannot make out that you have been reviewed any-
where." [14] Certainly the Apostles who gathered at Cambridge for
the Michaelmas term later that month would have been informed
of the notice which had appeared in Bristol. Possibly some of them
had seen the reviews in the *Atlas* and the *Spectator* and were able
to assure Tennyson that his poems had not failed to awaken critical response. Still, it could hardly have seemed either to the poet
or to his friends that he was receiving the acclaim they had anticipated.

His work was coming to public attention in other ways, however. A few of the poems had been reprinted in at least one newspaper, [15] and three new poems — "No More," "Anacreontics," and
"A Fragment" — appeared in *The Gem: A Literary Annual* for
1831, which was actually published in October 1830. [16] The *Literary Gazette* for October 16 found the new *Gem* "a very brilliant
specimen," but of Tennyson's poems the reviewer remarked, "We
can only say, in the words of Shakespeare, 'they are silly sooth.'"
Despite this curt dismissal, the young poet's name had been mentioned, which was more than could be said for many of the contributors; and by Christmas *The Gem* would be perused in numerous drawing-rooms throughout Great Britain.

The new year, 1831, opened with a panegyrical article on *Poems,
Chiefly Lyrical* in the *Westminster Review*. Although ascribed by
Arthur Hallam to the editor, Dr. (later Sir) John Bowring, [17] the
review seems to have been written by William Johnson Fox, the
dissenting divine and editor of the *Monthly Repository*. [18] The
critic, to whom philosophical content in poetry was a *sine qua
non*, thought the little book "thoroughly and unitedly metaphysical and poetical in its spirit" and proof that "the great law" of
human progress obtained in literature as well as in mechanics.
He quoted and discussed a number of the best pieces in the volume and predicted a bright future for the poet. [19] Fourteen pages
of favorable comment in the *Westminster* was a triumph indeed,
for Allan Cunningham in his "Biographical and Critical History
of the Literature of the Last Fifty Years" (1833) listed the Benthamite journal along with its two rivals, the *Edinburgh* and the
Quarterly, as "the chief of our critical periodicals." [20] The ap-

proval of the *Westminster,* however, as will be discussed later in this chapter, was to prove a mixed blessing.

Encouraged by the recognition of such a prominent journal, Hallam sent copies of *Poems, Chiefly Lyrical* and Charles Tennyson's *Sonnets* to Leigh Hunt with a letter expressing the hope that Hunt would review them favorably in the *Tatler,* the literary and dramatic paper he was then editing.[21] The elder poet responded during the latter part of February with warm and lengthy tributes to the two Tennysons. "We have great pleasure in stating," he proclaimed, "that we have seen no such poetical writing since the last volume of Mr Keats; and that the authors, who are both young men, we believe, at college, may take their stand at once among the first poets of the day. We mean, that Mr Wordsworth and Mr Coleridge may give them the right hand of fellowship; and that all who love genuine poetry, will read them, and quote them." While Hunt did not laud Alfred's poems indiscriminately, his opening statement set the tone of his review.

At the beginning of March a very cordial notice in the *New Monthly Magazine* [22] for that month testified to the advent of a true poet:

This little book, which we read through twice before we laid it down, and which we have taken up more than twice since, is a thing not to be heedlessly passed over. It is full of precisely the kind of poetry for which Mr. Keats was assailed, and for which the world is already beginning to admire him. We do not mean that it contains any thing equal, or nearly equal, either in majesty or melody, to the "Hyperion," the "Ode to the Nightingale," or "The Eve of St. Agnes." But it does contain many indications of a similar genius; and this assurance will, we are convinced, by such a mind as Mr. Tennyson's, be accepted as a grateful and delicate compliment. Such we intend it to be. There is the same fulness of thoughts and a fervour of feeling, with much the same quaintness of expression, — an equal degree of idolatry of the old writers, mixed with a somewhat more apparent reverence for the moderns, — fewer faults, perhaps, and certainly fewer dazzling and bewildering beauties. But Nature is the same in both, and her rich and golden gifts will not be lavished in vain. She has taught Mr. Tennyson to sing as a poet should sing, — she has taught him to throw his whole heart into his harmonies.

Five months later Hallam's well-known critique was published in the August issue of the *Englishman's Magazine,* then under Edward Moxon's proprietorship.[23] Hallam argued for the superiority of poetry of sensation, exemplified by Shelley and Keats, over that of reflection, typified by Wordsworth. He identified Tennyson as a poet of sensation and enumerated five qualities of excellence in his work; namely, "his luxuriance of imagination," "his power of embodying himself in ideal characters," "his vivid, picturesque delineation of objects," "the variety of his lyrical measures," and "his elevated habits of thought." In the same issue appeared Tennyson's sonnet, "Check every outflash," which Hallam had sent to Moxon without the poet's permission. Of this number of the *Englishman's* the fashionable *Morning Post* avowed, "For the quantity and variety of its articles we hold this Magazine to be without a superior; and of its poetical department it will be enough to say that it is supplied by T. Hood, Alfred Tennyson, Leigh Hunt, John Clare, Thomas Pringle, the Hon. Mrs. Norton, &." [24]

Tennyson again came before readers of annuals in October 1831, when he contributed a sonnet each to *The Yorkshire Literary Annual* and *Friendship's Offering* for 1832.[25] But neither the *Athenaeum* nor the *Literary Gazette,* in their notices of the latter, found space or inclination to mention Tennyson's poem.[26]

All in all, 1831 was a promising year for the young poet, and interest in his volume did not cease with its passing. Professor John Wilson, better known by his pen name, Christopher North, spoke very highly of Tennyson in his monthly literary colloquium, "Noctes Ambrosianae," *Blackwood's Edinburgh Magazine,* February 1832. "Recollections of the Arabian Nights" he thought "extremely beautiful." There was "feeling — and fancy" in "Oriana." His general comment on the writer was, "He has a fine ear for melody and harmony too — and rare and rich glimpses of imagination. He has — *genius.*" Tennyson had too many affectations, North said, but he did not doubt that the young man would prove himself a poet. These were strong words of approbation in a most widely read and respected periodical. They were but the prelude to a full-length review in the May issue of *Blackwood's.*

North began this article by venting his spleen on Tennyson's eulogists, the *Westminster* critic and Hallam in particular. No doubt as much aroused by the political color of the journals in which these two reviewers had written as by some of the literary tenets which they had advanced, he castigated them in the violent and vituperative language which was too often the style of the leading critics of the time. Having lashed himself to heights of indignation, he discharged some of his fury on a number of the weaker poems in the book; but, his passion spent, he turned to quote with enthusiasm the best poems, and in one of the concluding paragraphs he paid a tribute that leaves no doubt as to his true estimate:

> Our critique is near its conclusion; and in correcting it for press, we see that its whole merit, which is great, consists in the extracts, which are "beautiful exceedingly." Perhaps in the first part of our article, we may have exaggerated Mr Tennyson's not infrequent silliness, for we are apt to be carried away by the whim of the moment, and in our humorous moods, many things wear a queer look to our aged eyes, which fill young pupils with tears; but we feel assured that in the second part we have not exaggerated his strength — that we have done no more than justice to his fine faculties — and that the millions who delight in Maga will, with one voice, confirm our judgment — that Alfred Tennyson is a poet.

Young and sensitive, Tennyson was stung by the tone of the first half of the article and reacted with his notorious squib on "Crusty Christopher" in his next published collection of poems. Later, when he wrote to North, he asserted that the review "was redeemed to me by a tone of boisterous and picturesque humour such as I love"; but he admitted that at the time he had considered it "somewhat too skittish and petulant." [27]

Hallam's appraisal was more realistic than the poet's. Instead of being "indignant," as T. R. Lounsbury says,[28] he was more amused than angry at North's treatment of his own critical remarks in the *Englishman's Magazine*. In the same undated letter to Tennyson in which he expressed this sentiment, he commented further on North: "He means well I take it, and as he has extracted nearly your whole book, and has in his soberer mood spoken in terms as high as I could have used myself of some of your best poems, I think the review will assist rather than hinder the march of your reputation." [29]

This opinion was undoubtedly correct. Both the *Athenaeum* and the *Spectator* in their notices of the magazines for the month of May called attention to North's review as the best article in the current *Blackwood's*.[30] The *Edinburgh Observer* described the critique as one "in which a well merited castigation is inflicted upon egregious nonsense — but the poet receives ample compensation in the praise awarded to a few beauties, which were in considerable danger of not being observed at all amidst the surrounding stuff." [31] The *Sun*, a London evening daily, remarked: " 'Tennyson's Poems' is a review of some early poetical effusions of a young-man who bids fair, at no distant date, to become an ornament to the literature of his country." [32] Through *Blackwood's* Tennyson's poems found their way to many readers who had previously been oblivious of their existence. For instance, on September 9, 1832, the *Oriental Observer,* a weekly newspaper and literary journal published in Calcutta, reprinted "Ode to Memory" and "The Poet's Mind," noting at the end of each that they were from *Blackwood's.* Christopher North had evidently convinced the editor of this colonial paper of Tennyson's excellence; for the succeeding issue of September 16 carried "Recollections of the Arabian Nights" and the issue of December 22 "The Sea-Fairies" and "The Sleeping Beauty."

The final mention of Tennyson's poetry before the publication of his next volume appears to have been in the *Monthly Repository,* August 1832, where Fox, reviewing James White's *The Village Poor-House,* wrote of "the rich metaphysical melodies of Tennyson" along with "the untameable vigour of Elliot" as "the first fruits of a nobler vintage than has yet been gathered in between the mount of Helicon and the plains of Marathon."

Once again Tennyson appeared as a contributor to an annual when "Check every outflash," previously published by the *Englishman's Magazine,* was reprinted in *Friendship's Offering.*[33] But no mention of the sonnet was made by the *Literary Gazette* on October 13 or by the *Athenaeum* on October 21, when these two periodicals noticed the annual.

FRIENDSHIP'S OFFERING

A brief review of the efforts of the Cambridge set on Tennyson's behalf will indicate the part played by friendship in the growth of the poet's reputation at this stage of his career. Lounsbury attributes much of the favorable reception of *Poems, Chiefly Lyrical* to the zeal of Tennyson's friends. "They began at once," he writes, "an active propaganda to spread his fame far and wide." [34] Mr. W. D. Paden has challenged this thesis and maintains that until after the *Westminster* article had appeared, more than six months subsequent to the publication of Tennyson's volume, the only probable instance of Apostolic activity — and it bore no fruit — was during the summer of 1830 when Francis Garden presented a copy of the book at Blackwood's premises with the express desire that it be reviewed in the publisher's magazine.[35] This likelihood seems to be the basis for Hallam's remark in the letter to Tennyson, October 4, 1830 (the one in which he was forced to write that he had seen no reviews), "A letter from Garden, . . . of very old date, gives hopes of *Blackwood*." [36]

Actually, the Apostles were busier than Paden realized. Southey's copy of *Poems, Chiefly Lyrical*, inscribed from James Spedding, "27 July. 1830," is extant in the Dyce Collection of the Victoria and Albert Museum,[37] and it is possible Spedding hoped that through the poet laureate the volume might be brought to public attention somewhere, perhaps in the *Quarterly* itself. Milnes was on friendly terms with Thomas Campbell and some time before the end of 1830 sent him a copy of Tennyson's work.[38] Since Campbell was editor of the *New Monthly Magazine* at the time, Milnes no doubt thought he might review the book in his journal. Coleridge had seen Charles Tennyson's *Sonnets* by early 1831; and as Hallam had called upon him in 1829 and R. J. Tennant was a frequenter of the house in Highgate, one or the other of them may have introduced him to *Poems, Chiefly Lyrical* in 1830.[39] Then there was the short notice by a friend printed in *Felix Farley's Bristol Journal*, September 25, 1830.[40]

For Lounsbury, it was "difficult not to believe that the criticism contained in . . . [the *Westminster*, January 1831] came from

the partiality of personal friendship acting either directly or indirectly"; [41] but there is every reason to believe that it was written by Fox, with whom there was no personal connection — and
we have his statement that his interest in Tennyson was aroused
by some of the poems which had found their way into a newspaper.

After the recognition from the *Westminster,* Hallam sent his
letter and the volumes of the two Tennysons to Hunt, with the
result already described. Paden also thinks it probable that
Hallam forwarded a copy of *Poems, Chiefly Lyrical,* accompanied
by a similar letter, to the editor of the *New Monthly;* [42] but this
seems doubtful, since Samuel Carter Hall, then editor of the
magazine, when he came to include Tennyson in his *Book of
Gems* (1838), had to apply to Hunt for biographical and critical
information on the poet and for copies of his two volumes.[43] It
is possible, however, that the notice in the *New Monthly,* March
1831, stemmed from Milnes's acquaintance with Campbell; for
although Campbell's editorship terminated in December 1830,
he may have made arrangements for the review of *Poems, Chiefly
Lyrical* before his connection with the magazine ceased.[44] A
letter from W. H. Brookfield to Hallam, January 15, 1831, reveals that he was preparing a review to submit to the *Sheffield
Courant* but was anticipated by the editor's publication of an
extract from the *Westminster.*[45] Whatever may have been the
foundation for Robert·Monteith's remark in his letter to Milnes,
"If we can get him well reviewed in the *Edinburgh,* it will do," [46]
nothing came of the intention.

Patently the poet's friends were doing what they could in his
behalf. Yet it is erroneous to assume that there was a fervid im-
portunity on their part. An unpublished portion of a letter from
Hallam to William Bodham Donne, written probably in the
latter part of February or the first few days of March, shows the
reverse to be true, for Hallam was the leader in matters relating
to Tennyson: "In answer to your question why I do not write
and publish some criticism of the poems, I reply that *I bide my
time.* I have no direct influence with any reviewer at present,
nor as criticisms of some kind are already bringing the book into

general notice, is there any need for hurry: I shall however very probably bestir myself in this way next summer!" [47] In an unpublished letter to Moxon, postmarked July 15, 1831, Hallam finally offered to prepare a review of Tennyson for the *Englishman's Magazine*: "Should you have room either in this number, or the next, to admit an article of mine on Tennyson's Poetry, I shall have great pleasure in writing it for you." [48] The publisher wanted the article for the August issue, and Hallam dashed it off, later acknowledging that "it was the hasty product of the evenings of one week." [49] When Edward Spedding mildly took him to task for writing abstrusely, he admitted that he had become carried away with his own thoughts and had not made the most of the opportunity to advance Tennyson's name.[50]

"Puffing," it must be remembered, was the practice of the day.[51] Publishers such as Colburn and Bentley owned or controlled periodicals in which they could be assured of laudatory reviews of the books they printed. Authors sought to launch a new work in conjunction with prearranged acclaim from prominent journals. Henry Taylor wrote frankly in his *Autobiography* of the success of *Philip van Artevelde* (1834):

> The leap was made with the advantage of a lift and a toss. The publication had been kept back so as to appear along with an article by Lockhart in the "Quarterly Review." There were one or two other plauditory articles written from personal motives; then notices, more or less slight or elaborate, swarmed in every direction; and one of my reviewers applied to me what had been said formerly of some one else (I forget of whom) that I had "awakened one morning and found myself famous." The sale was rapid, and as the edition had numbered only 500 copies, another had to be put in preparation without delay.[52]

In the light of these methods the efforts of Tennyson's companions to gain recognition for him scarcely seem immoderate. So far as can be ascertained now, three, or possibly four, of the notices of *Poems, Chiefly Lyrical* resulted from the activity of friends; and Hunt need not have responded to Hallam's request for a review if he had not been strongly convinced of Tennyson's worth. Obviously there is little justification for Lounsbury's statement that upon the publication of his first volume, Tennyson's associates "made an effort to forestall the judgment of the public." [53] Hallam did not write to Hunt until six months after the book had come out and only after the *Westminster* had eulogized Tennyson. Hallam himself was well enough satisfied with the notice that had been taken of his friend by the spring of 1831 to be in no hurry to see his own praises in print, and his article in the *Englishman's* did not appear until more than a year had elapsed from the time the volume was published. Lounsbury concedes, "Much of the warm welcome which had been extended to Tennyson's first poems had come from independent and absolutely impartial sources. There is no question that in many quarters the volume of 1830 had made a distinctly favorable impression on its own merits." "None the less," he contends, "had personal considerations played a great part in the most important notices which the work had received." [54] But the short piece printed in Bristol was of purely local significance. Both the *Tatler* and the *Englishman's* were ephemeral publications. Without doubt the reviews in the *Westminster* and *Blackwood's* were the most important, and personal considerations had figured in neither. As Paden has said, "It would seem that the influence of the Apostles on Tennyson's fame . . . has been somewhat overstated." [55]

THE RECEPTION OF *POEMS*, 1833

After the publication of *Poems, Chiefly Lyrical*, Tennyson was by no means impatient to bring out another volume, though he was busy writing and probably had a number of poems at hand. As early as August 14, 1831, Hallam commissioned Charles Merivale, afterwards Dean of Ely, to call on Moxon at 64 New Bond Street to find out if he would give Tennyson anything for the copyright of a new book.[56] Seven months later, March 30, 1832, Hallam wrote to Richard Chenevix Trench, the future Archbishop of Dublin, "I have persuaded him, I think, to publish without further delay." [57] But there was to be a delay of slightly over eight months; and when Tennyson himself wrote to Moxon, "probably in the early summer," he asked to have every proof sent "twice over": "I should like the text to be as correct as possible. To be sure this proceeding would somewhat delay the publication, but I am in no hurry. My MSS (*i.e.* those I have by me) are far from being in proper order, and such a measure would both give me leisure to arrange and correct them, and ensure a correct type." [58]

The little book of thirty poems was eventually issued under Moxon's imprint at the beginning of December 1832,[59] though it actually bore the date 1833. The response of the press to this volume, entitled simply *Poems*, was far from being as favorable as the generally sympathetic treatment accorded the previous one must have led Tennyson and his friends to expect. Still, its reception was not, on the whole, so severe as has been supposed.[60]

The new work was noticed promptly: by the middle of December it had been reviewed in four of the leading weeklies.[61]

On December 1 the *Athenaeum* informed its readers, "Mr. TENNYSON is unquestionably a poet of fancy, feeling, and imagination; gifted with a deep sense of the beautiful, and endowed with a spirit 'finely touched,' and often to 'fine issues.' " Unfortunately, he was often led from true poetry by searching for "metaphysical subtilties"; [62] he was too full of the conceits, allegories, and affectations of "our own early writers"; he was sometimes "fanciful to the verge (nay, till he is often utterly lost to us, within the precincts) of unintelligibility"; he had technical faults as well. From these general strictures the reviewer passed on to censure "O Darling Room," "The 'How' and the 'Why,' " "The Hesperides," and "The Palace of Art." But he quoted with approval from "The Miller's Daughter," "New Year's Eve," "The Death of the Old Year," and "Oenone" — the last of which he found "the poem of poems in this volume . . . wild — fanciful — chaste — and touching." After commenting favorably on "Mariana in the South," "The Lotos-Eaters," and "To J. S. [James Spedding]," the critic closed his remarks with these words: "In reverence and respect for his genius, we have not hesitated to point out the errors of the poet — his beauties will speak for themselves, and apologise for the unusual length of this article."

On December 8 William Jerdan, editor of the *Literary Gazette*, exploited Tennyson in the literary squabble over Lamb's *Album*

Verses and chastised the young writer for imitating, like Lamb, the worst faults of the "metaphysical" poets. The opening poem of the book, the sonnet "Mine be the strength," Jerdan construed so as to make it appear illogical and contradictory in sense and syntax; "Buonaparte" he found unfathomable; and he ludicrously parodied "The Lady of Shalott." In the abusive style of the period, he judged Tennyson insane and on the basis of "Who can say" and the first ten lines of "Oenone" would have committed him to a padded cell.

But Jerdan's review was not entirely disparaging. While he felt that Tennyson was misguided in his poetry, he believed that the writer had talents which, properly directed, could lead him to fame. The young author seemed to possess the impulse which makes a man a poet and to have a determination to be one. These two attributes, if not accomplishing all, could do much. Within the pages of *Poems* was a "fine perception of rural objects and imagery." There were sentiments expressed which were, "in general, pure and natural," though they were sometimes marred with affectation. Finally, Tennyson had enthusiasm — "without which there never was and never will be a poet" and which "needs only to be regulated by taste and judgment to lead the possessor on to distinction." Jerdan even cited two passages illustrative of the characteristics that he "admired," and he found aspects to praise in several poems.

A week later, on December 15, the *Spectator* printed a short notice of *Poems,* which, though not written in a caustic vein, was the least amicable of the reviews in the weeklies. The critic thought Tennyson had not added to his fame by publishing the volume. He had become more obscure; and "Eleanore," which was quoted in full, seemed to be the only poem in the new book on a par with those in the earlier one. Admittedly Tennyson excelled in "a sort of richness of words, joined with a minute taste for natural sounds and sights," but too often these seemed to be apprehended through the poetry of others rather than directly.

The day after the *Spectator,* on December 16, the *Atlas* assessed *Poems* in the first and longest review of its literary section. Possibly written by Robert Bell, the editor, the article was quiet and discriminating. While it did not fail to call attention to Tennyson's faults, it found more to approve than to censure. Although his previous poems might have been overpraised by some reviewers, his varied potentialities had not been exaggerated, for his "poetical nature is visible throughout everything he does." His style was regrettably of a school that risked spoiling its excellence with affectation, and there were "more of the faults of this style than the beauties" in this new volume. But "at the same time there is more true relish in it of that which constitutes the soul of genuine poetry than in a thousand such books as are daily published under its name. Mr. TENNYSON is rich enough to afford a large fine to censure: he can suffer the penalty to be estreated, and still maintain high credit with the world." After reproving him for an excessive use of the compound epithet and a tendency to lose sight of the whole design in the pursuit of particulars, the reviewer quoted enough of "The Miller's Daughter" to give the story and judged "Rosalind" "one of those happy conceptions in which Mr. TENNYSON appears to have the field to himself." "The Palace of Art," "Oenone," and "The Hesperides" he considered "exquisite morsels."

Throughout the month of December Tennyson's work attracted attention in various parts of the British Isles. On December 6 the London *Albion* printed five stanzas of "New Year's Eve." The *Sheffield Mercury* for December 8 quoted the full text of the same poem.[63] Toward the end of the month the Belfast *Northern Whig,* the Edinburgh *Scotsman,* and the *Liverpool Albion* reprinted "The Death of the Old Year." [64]

The magazines responded as quickly as the weeklies to the publication of *Poems.* Notices of the book appeared in the January numbers of the *Metropolitan, Tait's Edinburgh,* the *New Monthly,* and the *Monthly Repository.*

The *Metropolitan,* edited by Captain Frederick Marryat, printed brief remarks on current books at the end of each issue. In a short evaluation of *Poems,* which has previously been unnoticed, the critic for this journal was restrained but sympathetic. He found the verses "productions of one who has a deep feeling for poetical beauty" and continued, "We do not pretend to say that all the poems are equally good; yet are none of them so bad that the author might not be proud to own them."

Tait's Edinburgh Magazine was cursory: "Mr. Tennyson's new volume contains many good and a few beautiful poems; but it scarcely comes up to the high-raised expectations of the author of *Poems chiefly Lyrical.* We must return to it at more leisure." The leisure never came.

The *New Monthly*, in a review probably by Edward Bulwer,[65] set upon Tennyson's defects as exemplary of the faults of recent poets. He had their "besetting sin" of affectation; and for this reviewer, affectation meant imitation of "the worst conceits of the poets of the time of Charles II., and the most coxcombical euphuisms of the contemporaries of Elizabeth." Also, Tennyson was censured for following the style of Shelley and Keats. "O Darling Room" and "To Christopher North" were treated with derision, and the critic harped on his belief that the poet had been flattered and misled by the reviews of his previous volume.[66] Nevertheless, Bulwer's attitude (if Bulwer's it was) was not really hostile, and he expressed more hope for Tennyson than for the majority of his contemporaries. He called "The May Queen" and its sequel, "New Year's Eve," "two very sweet and natural poems," adding, "If Mr. Tennyson would lean more to the vein manifest in these poems, he would soon insensibly detach himself from his less wholesome tendencies, and would be in everybody's mouth." The reviewer also referred to "The Death of the Old Year" as "another poem of remarkable beauty" and quoted it in full, saying that he did so "in justice to Mr. Tennyson," though he could "ill afford the space."

W. J. Fox, who probably had praised *Poems, Chiefly Lyrical* so extravagantly for the *Westminster* two years before, accorded Tennyson much the same treatment in the *Monthly Repository*:

The true poet is compounded of the philosopher and the *artiste*. His nervous organization should have internally the tenacity which will weave into the firmest web of solid thought, and in his sense, externally, be tremulous as the strings of the Æolian harp, that quiver in every breeze, but ever tremble tunefully. The author has a large endowment of both these qualities, yielding, perhaps, among poets of modern fame, only to Wordsworth in the one, and only to Coleridge in the other; and affording, by their combination, a promise which the world requires and needs of him.[67]

This high opinion of the poet was matched by a fervid reviewer for the *True Sun*, probably John Forster,[68] whose hitherto unrecorded encomium filled more than a column of that London daily newspaper on January 19. He advocated that Tennyson at once be assigned a high place in the poetic hierarchy and fearlessly predicted that his position would "hereafter surely be the most high, if his maturity answer to the promise of his youth. He has the true spirit of poetry in him, and words fit to enshrine it. He has feeling in its widest range, — he has delicacy, and a fervid sympathy, — he has imagination at will, — an exuberant fancy, — and, when it pleases him, a most exquisite simplicity. We could point to no living poet, with such a luxuriously intense feeling of beauty, as is observable in some of the writings of Mr. Tennyson." To be sure, he was not faultless. His profusion of imagery sometimes wearied and offended; his rich flow of "truth and sentiment" too often evaporated "into a thousand glittering and fantastic shapes of conceited rhapsody." He had a predilection for roughness of versification and "a royal disdain of pronunciation when it suits him." But the purpose of the article was to enjoy "some of the beauties of this rich little volume," and the critic proceeded to admire "The Lady of Shalott" — "a fine glowing piece of mysticism, studded with pearly bits of field landscape, and scenic picturing"; "Mariana in the South" — "exceedingly lovely in her desertion, with the scenery around in keeping with her heart"; and "The Miller's Daughter" — "exquisite throughout — full of the calm beauty of contented happiness, reflecting back a youthful passion — of heart-affection — of simplicity and homely truth." He cited a number of beautiful passages from "Oenone" and "The Palace of Art" ("a truly great one") and, after commenting upon several other pieces, concluded: "We could have dallied on through another column. We bid Mr. Tennyson, for the present, a reluctant farewell. May his youthful spirit never grow old — while it ripens with coming years. His faculty is a great and happy one

— and planted in a fertile soil. It will assuredly produce a most rich and abundant harvest."

Tennyson was mentioned in the April issues of two monthly magazines. While reviewing the poems of William Motherwell for *Blackwood's*, North revealed his irritation over the lines to "Crusty Christopher" and with some justice said that the poet should have accepted both the blame and praise without retort. Fox, discussing Browning's *Pauline* in the *Monthly Repository*, thought Tennyson and Browning were probably fellow worshipers at the same shrine.

These asides on Tennyson were obscured, however, by the review in the April *Quarterly*, now proved beyond doubt to have been the work of John Wilson Croker.[69] Written with scathing irony throughout, it made cruel sport of Tennyson's new volume, and some biographers have assumed that it checked completely his growing reputation.[70] The influence of the *Quarterly*, which to many was "the next book to God's Bible," [71] is certainly not to be disregarded, but its effect in this instance seems to have been overestimated.

Moxon, who thought a review "even with a sprinkling of abuse in it . . . worth a hundred advertisements," [72] was reported by Hallam as having said that the *Quarterly* had "done good"; and in a day when a review in a prominent periodical was supposed to make or ruin the sale of a book,[73] Hallam wrote to Tennyson that his volume continued "to sell tolerably." [74] If the accuracy of Hallam's testimony is open to question because he would indubitably wish to encourage the poet, at least the second Lord Tennyson in his *Memoir* of his father says that other friends believed the review would prove far from disastrous, since the *Quarterly* "was known in London to be the organ of a party, both in politics and literature." [75] Besides, the Tory party was in the minority at the time. Hallam also wrote to his friend, "Rogers defends you publicly as the most promising genius of the time." [76] The importance of this succor from the aging poet whose breakfast parties were the delight of a large and influential circle is not to be minimized.

As for the periodicals themselves, Mr. Harold Nicolson has said that after the "universal guffaw" which followed Croker's sarcasm, only John Stuart Mill in the *London Review* had the courage to protest, two years after the event.[77] But Mill was not alone in braving the scorn of the Tory mouthpiece. Three days after the *Quarterly* had been published,[78] the *Sun* took issue with the "stinging review of the productions of a young man, who, whatever may be said of his eccentricities and errors of taste — a fault by no means of unfrequent occurrence among young writers — is unquestionably not devoid of the 'vision and the faculty divine.' Mr. Tennyson has the *raw material* of poetry about him; but time, perseverance, and familiarity with the best models, are necessary to render it available. We know of no other modern writer who could have penned the beautiful stanzas entitled 'Mariana at the Moated Grange.' " [79] At the end of the week the *Athenaeum* also spoke out in behalf of the author: "The article on Tennyson in the *Quarterly* is strangely provocative of comment. No sane man imagines that Tennyson is the Homer which the *Westminster* affected to believe; but he has much fine poetry about him; and if we are to give the name of poets only to those whose works are illustrated by Turner and Calcott then Wordsworth is no poet, neither is Wilson." [80]

Other judges were not blinded by Croker's savagery. During the autumn of 1833 Allan Cunningham wrote as follows in the *Athenaeum*: "ALFRED TENNYSON has a happy fancy; his originality of thought is sometimes deformed by oddity of language; and his subject has not unfrequently to bear the weight of sentiments which spring not naturally from it. He has lyrical ease and vigour, and is looked upon by sundry critics as the chief living hope of the Muse." [81] An article entitled "A Few Words on Reviewing" in the first number of the *Oxford University Magazine*, March 1834, deplored the lack of fair, unbiased, competent literary criticism and compared the flagrant review of Tennyson in the *Quarterly* with the one in *Blackwood's*. In the former was "virulent — even coarse — abuse; no mitigation — no praise of any sort"; in the latter there was "ridicule where ridicule was due — praise in its right place; the best things extracted for commendation — the worst for blame; all fair and above board. No one now doubts which one was the fairer." [82]

The last of the rejoinders to the *Quarterly* was John Stuart Mill's fair and penetrating article in the *London Review*, July 1835, referred to by Nicolson. Mill specifically set out to refute Croker's estimate and maintained that *Poems, Chiefly Lyrical* "gave evidence of powers such as had not for many years been displayed by any new aspirant to the character of a poet. This first publication was followed in due time by a second, in which the faults of its predecessor were still visible, but were evidently on the point of disappearing; while the positive excellence was not only greater and more uniformly sustained, but of a higher order."

It has been said of the *Poems* of 1833, "Seldom indeed has the critical community been so unanimous in condemnation." [83] But, as the foregoing discussion shows, the volume was not received without approbation; and one must bear in mind that some of the best poems were in a far different form from the polished versions read today and were accompanied by several distracting pieces of inferiority and banality that were subsequently suppressed. The *Monthly Repository* and the *True Sun* both printed lengthy and detailed appreciations of Tennyson's work, and his talent and poetic promise were recognized by many of the critics. Croker, it is true, dealt the young poet a vicious blow; but it was not fatal, for defenders rose to his side and the remarks on his behalf in the *Sun* and the *Athenaeum* alone show that the authority of the *Quarterly* was not overwhelming. While some of the comments Tennyson received were severe enough to make his sensitive nature writhe, it cannot be said that his genius went unappreciated.

RADICAL ASSOCIATIONS

The reason for much of the asperity that was directed against Tennyson is to be found in the political and personal prejudices of certain editors and critics, for the truth is that he was thought of as a radical throughout his early career. Hallam, alert to this danger, tried to clear him of the charge by declaring in the

Englishman's, "He has also this advantage over that poet [Keats], and his friend Shelley, that he comes before the public, unconnected with any political party, or peculiar system of opinions." [84] But a French critic, writing in *L'Europe littéraire* two years later, seems to reflect the prevailing conception when he describes Tennyson as "a young man from the ranks of the utilitarian school, brought up among the followers of Bentham, who has cherished the idea that the Benthamite philosophy — with its axioms, corollaries, and dogmas, with its oracular and abstract style — need not prevent him from being a poet." [85]

In the first place, as the poet of the Cambridge intellectuals, Tennyson would inevitably be suspect in certain quarters. When Hallam went up to the university in October 1828, he found Utilitarianism the "ascendant politics" of the Cambridge Union; and although he understood that their poetical beliefs had suffered many fluctuations, he wrote to Gladstone, "At the present day *Shelley* is the idol before which we are to be short by the knees." [86] The influence of the Union at Cambridge is attested by Hallam's observation, in the same letter, "[It] is very much felt here, extending even among reading men, who have actually no share in it, but are modified in one way or another by its spirit." Members of this body a year later were debating with the Oxford Union on the greatness of Shelley's poetry and publishing *Adonais* for the first time in England in book form.[87] Although the actual divisions in the Cambridge Union from 1828 through 1832 indicate that the sentiment of the house was not extreme, it disapproved of the administration of the Duke of Wellington and favored free trade, abolition of the rotten boroughs, and extension of education to the lower orders of society.[88] These opinions were enough to convince many an Englishman that radicalism prevailed at Cambridge.

Two outstanding Cantabrigians who had preceded Tennyson at the university — Frederick Denison Maurice and John Sterling — were ardent liberals (the latter a most vociferous one) in the London Debating Society, of which John Stuart Mill and a number of the Philosophic Radicals were members.[89] As editors of the *Athenaeum* from 1828 to 1830, Maurice and Sterling staunchly supported the cause of the Spanish revolutionists.[90] Several of the Cambridge men were actively involved on the side of the Constitutionalists; and the plot, directed by Sterling, to send General Torrijos and fifty of his followers to Gibraltar by a special ship loaded with supplies and ammunition was discovered and the ship seized by the British government.[91] Tennyson's own participation in the conspiracy through his expedition with Hallam in the summer of 1830 to the Pyrenees to carry money to the insurgents may not have been wholly unknown.[92] Neither can it have helped the poet's reputation that his uncle, Charles Tennyson (later Tennyson d'Eyncourt), a Member of Parliament of some years' standing, though not definitely a member of any party, worked "always with a Radical bias." By 1829 he was "recognized as one of the leaders of the movement for Electoral Reform." [93]

Besides these associations, the fact that the publisher of *Poems, Chiefly Lyrical*, Effingham Wilson, had been connected with Bentham and was still engaged in Radical publishing ventures would have tended to strengthen Tory misgivings.[94] The paeans of praise from the *Westminster Review*, the Benthamite journal and instrument of the Radicals, made it distinctly appear that Tennyson was the protégé of the extremists; for, according to Mr. G. L. Nesbitt in his study of the *Westminster*, "Blind partisanship . . . is the outstanding characteristic of the review in the early thirties." [95] Leigh Hunt's paper, the *Tatler*, was a vehicle for his unorthodox views. The spirit of the *Englishman's* was definitely liberal; [96] and Hallam admitted to Edward Spedding, to whom he wrote soliciting contributions, that in view of the policy of the magazine "conservative principles cannot be *openly* maintained." [97] The critiques in the *Tatler*, the *New Monthly*, and the *Englishman's* linked Tennyson with Shelley, the atheist and revolutionary, and Keats, the detested "Cockney." That North spoke so highly of the poet in a Tory journal attests his critical integrity.[98]

The publication of *Poems*, 1833, intensified the young writer's connection with radicalism. Although Edward Moxon was to become the respected and respectable "publisher of poets," the appearance of Tennyson's new book under the imprint of the man whose first venture had been Lamb's *Album Verses* in 1830, who had published the crusading *Englishman's Magazine* in 1831, and who in 1832 brought out Hunt's collected works and Shelley's long-unpublished *Masque of Anarchy*,[99] could hardly have been reassuring to conservatives.

The *Athenaeum*, the first periodical to notice the second volume, was liberal in tone; and the proprietor-editor, Charles Wentworth Dilke, considered himself a Radical.[100] The reaction of the *Literary Gazette* the next week was to be expected, since its editor, William Jerdan, was strongly conservative and was still smarting from the replies to his attack on Lamb's *Album Verses*.[101] Here was another book issued by the same publisher and by an author associated with the Cockneys. Moreover, it had been handled sympathetically by the *Athenaeum*, the independent journal that had come to Lamb's rescue and had declared war on Jerdan's own "puffing" practices.[102] The *Spectator* had announced for Reform.[103] Its coolness toward *Poems*, which contrasted with its pleasure over the first volume, may have resulted from the friendship of the editor, Rintoul, with Blackwood and a growing conviction on his part of Tennyson's association with the Cockney School. On November 11, 1828, he had written to Blackwood, "There is at least one feature of resemblance between the 'Spectator' and 'Maga' herself — straightforwardness, and the preference of plain strong sense to affected finery or Cockney simplicity." [104] The *Atlas*, which gave Tennyson much credit as well as considerable censure, was founded, according to H. R. Fox Bourne, "as an organ of the Benthamite school"; and in 1835 Hunt wrote of it as a "Reform paper." [105]

All the magazines that noticed Tennyson about January 1 — the *New Monthly, Tait's Edinburgh*, the *Metropolitan*, and the *Monthly Repository* — were liberal or radical. The *New Monthly* and *Tait's Edinburgh* found more·to blame than to praise in the new volume, but that they reviewed it at all was tantamount to a free advertisement. The *New Monthly*, under the editorship of Bulwer, had become notorious in advocacy of political change.[106] *Tait's Edinburgh*, in Walter Graham's description, carried on "in the Northern capital, the political work of the *Westminster Re-*

view in London . . . contributed to by John Stuart Mill, Richard
Cobden, and John Bright." [107] The *Metropolitan* at the beginning of its first bound volume (1831) had declared, "We are the
unflinching advocates of a Reform in State and Church . . . a
rational reform which shall give back to the people of England
those rights, furtively abstracted from them and grossly abused."
Furthermore, it went on record as sympathizing with the cause of
freedom in Poland, France, and Belgium. Probably most odious
of all in Tory eyes was the *Monthly Repository,* which had given
Tennyson extensive praise. Originally a Unitarian journal which
"through most of the years of the first series" (1806–1826) had carried as a motto on its title page a quotation from Bentham, it
was owned and edited by Fox after 1831 and had been launched
upon an outspoken crusade for political and social reform.[108]
Fox himself, as a member of the Political Union, whose represen-
tatives were in danger from the law, fearlessly addressed the people
in Leicester Square when the agitation for the passage of the Reform Bill was in progress.[109]

Nothing more than the association of Tennyson with radicalism
and the Cockney poets was needed to incite Croker to the attack
that appeared in the *Quarterly*. Recent scholars are assuredly right
in abandoning Lounsbury's theory that the squib on "Crusty
Christopher" instigated this article and that but for the lines to
North it would have been of a different nature.[110] With Tennyson
appearing to be of the same poetical school and political stamp as
Keats, Shelley, and Leigh Hunt, there is little likelihood that any
other tone would have been adopted in the *Quarterly*. Croker's
letters to young John Murray, the son of the publisher of the
periodical, clearly reveal his attitude. On January 7, 1833, he
wrote, "Tell your father and Mr. Lockhart that I undertake
Tennyson and hope to make another Keats of him." That evening he sent a second note saying, "I should have begun on Tennyson tonight but wanted to read the old articles on Keats and
Leigh Hunt, and lo! discovered that I had not my *Quarterly*." [111]

The encomium of Tennyson in the *True Sun,* which appeared
after Croker had already determined to victimize the poet but
more than two and a half months before his review was published,

gave further evidence that the young man was the darling of the extreme political faction; for the *True Sun,* founded by Patrick Grant to campaign for more drastic action than the Whig *Sun* would countenance, was known as "an ultra Radical affair." [112] Mill's sympathetic article in the *London Review* continued Tennyson's unpropitious connection with the Radical press.[113] It is not surprising that he was still being written of in France in 1839 as the Homer of the Benthamites.[114]

TENNYSON'S REPUTATION, 1834–1842

A common misconception concerning Tennyson's reputation during his so-called ten years' silence between 1832 and 1842 is that "mourning the loss of Arthur Hallam, and discouraged by criticisms of his early poems, [he] kept silent and allowed himself to be forgotten." [115] Although his recognition was undoubtedly retarded through his refusal to publish another book, his name was by no means lost to the public following Croker's attempt to destroy his pretensions as a poet. As has already been shown, replies to this attack appeared in periodicals during 1833, 1834, and 1835. References to him continued in *Blackwood's,* though "Maga" did not deign to review *Poems.*[116] In August 1835, in a review of John Clare's *The Rural Muse,* North referred to Shelley, Keats, Hunt, and Tennyson as "all poets." In September, reviewing Trench's *The Story of Justin Martyr and Other Poems,* he called Alfred Tennyson and several others writers of good sonnets.[117] In December of the same year a writer on "The Philosophy of Poetry," who signed himself S., cited "Oriana" in a footnote as "an instance of a singular effect produced by the passionate repetition of a name."

In a critique of the dramas of Joanna Baillie, February 1836, North turned aside to comment on Tennyson whom he had "delighted to praise." But he scoffed at the folly of a debate which was said to have occurred at Cambridge on the question, "Is Alfred Tennyson a GREAT POET?" North's reply was, "He has yet written but some beautiful verses — a few very charming compositions, that are in truth little poems — not great ones — his feeling is exquisite, and so is his fancy — but oh! how feeble too often

his Thought!" He called "Alfred" a "wilful fribble" made worse
by the flattery of his followers. But the professor was not entirely
acrimonious, for he expressed the belief that Tennyson had the
power to be the "*true* poet" he was "designed . . . to be." Three
months afterward North returned to Tennyson in a review of
Henry Alford's *The School of the Heart,* where he spoke with
scorn of the lines to "Crusty Christopher," the "midge" which
Tennyson had commissioned to drive him to Hades. Two years
later he made a passing allusion to Tennyson; and finally in
"Christopher in His Alcove," April 1839, he mentioned, among
contemporary young poets, the Shelley and Tennyson schools.

Other Tory journals, less willing to admit Tennyson's talent,
failed to see that the surest way to commit him to oblivion was to
cease referring to him. *Fraser's Magazine,* July 1836, published
a mock version of a Cambridge examination. The fifth question
read in part as follows: "What is Professor Smythe's opinion of
the Nebulous and Incomprehensible in poetry? Illustrate your
explanation by extracts from Tennyson's *Timbuctoo.*"

When the *British and Foreign Review,* edited by John Mitchell
Kemble, a former Apostle, noticed Richard Monckton Milnes's
Poems of Many Years and *Memorials of a Residence on the
Continent* in October 1838, the reviewer, very likely Kemble
himself and certainly one of the Cambridge set, expanded upon
his views concerning didacticism and beauty in poetry with these
words:

> We are intitled to expect from a true poet that he should have faith
> in his art, faith in the good which is inseparable from its genuine exer-
> cise, in its essentially noble and elevating tendencies.
>
> He should not perpetually vex the goddess who inspires him, with
> that most vexatious question, *Cui Bono?* who will be the wiser for
> what you are now saying? Let him recollect that high truth, expressed in
> its entirety by the great poet whose intuition pierces and whose prac-
> tice realizes that harmonious co-operation of the presiding genii, to
> [n]one of whom he would yield an exclusive allegiance:
>> "That Beauty, Good, and Knowledge, are three sisters,
>> That dote upon each other, friends to man,
>> Living together under the same roof,
>> And never can be sunder'd without tears."   — A. TENNYSON.[118]

But Milnes's poems elicited from Lockhart in the *Quarterly*, June 1839, a different kind of observation concerning Tennyson. Continuing the disparaging note struck by Croker, Lockhart predicted that Milnes would "regret few sins of his youth more bitterly than the homage he has now rendered at the fantastic shrines of such baby idols as Mr. John Keats and Mr. Alfred Tennyson." In March 1842, on the eve of Tennyson's new poetical venture, the *Quarterly* made a final depreciatory comment in a review of a collection of translations entitled *Arundines Cami*. It praised Lord Lyttelton's translation of "Oenone" into Latin hexameters, while superciliously belittling the original: "The translator has caught very happily the wild and fanciful tone of Mr. Tennyson's poem, and quietly dropped its affectations. He has not, perhaps, quite subdued it to classical purity; it still reads considerably below the Virgilian age. We must be considered, indeed, as quoting Lord Lyttleton [*sic*], not Mr. Tennyson, who, however, might study with advantage how much his language must be filtered, and its exuberance strained off, before it can be transfused into classical verse."

The two poems that Tennyson was induced to publish between 1832 and 1842 — "Saint Agnes" and "Stanzas" ("O that 'twere possible"), the nucleus of *Maud* — brought him considerable attention from the press. "Saint Agnes," which appeared in *The Keepsake* for 1837, was reviewed by the *Athenaeum*, November 5, 1836.[119] Among contributions by the popular Letitia E. Landon, Miss Boyle, H. F. Chorley, and others, Tennyson's poem was quoted by a critic who was pressed for space. Apparently aware of the contempt with which its author was regarded in some quarters, he justified his selection by saying, "[It] is withal so perversely fantastic, that we extract it as much for its curiosity as its beauty." This was grudging recognition, but the word-painting and originality of the poem could not fail to make an impression amid the mediocrity that surrounded it.

"Stanzas" was printed in *The Tribute* (London, 1837), an anthology projected by Lord Northampton to raise money for the indigent and deserving Reverend Edward Smedley, who died before the book reached the public. The *Athenaeum*, which noticed this collection on September 2, 1837, complained, "The task even of selection from a volume like this — containing contributions by Southey, Joanna Baillie, Bernard Barton, Tennyson, and probably a hundred others more or less known to fame — is a somewhat invidious duty." The *Literary Gazette* reviewed the volume in the leading article of the issue for September 2. The critic did not list Tennyson in such prominent company as the *Athenaeum* had, but he included him among the better-known contributors, indicating that the poet's name was becoming more familiar to the public. The *Metropolitan* mentioned him along with Wordsworth, Southey, Landor, Moore, Horace Smith, Milman, Bowles, and several others, as "a few of the many contributors" to this collection of miscellaneous poetry.[120]

The *Edinburgh Review,* October 1837, printed a seven-page article on *The Tribute.* The Whig quarterly had first taken cognizance of Tennyson the year before (January 1836) in a review of Henry Alford, where he was described as the "most known of any of the young Cambridge poets who have lately taken wing." [121] But the *Edinburgh* had then considered him inferior to Alford. Now it gave him more approbation. While bits of poetry by such famous writers as Wordsworth, Southey, and the others already enumerated were published in *The Tribute,* the reviewer advised his readers, "Our selections shall, in general, be made from the poetical effusions of those with whose compositions . . . the public is less familiar than with those of the more distinguished contributors to the undertaking." He quoted fifty-eight lines of Tennyson's poem, first remarking: "We do not profess perfectly to understand the somewhat mysterious contribution of Mr Alfred Tennyson, entitled 'Stanzas;' but amidst some quaintness, and some occasional absurdities of expression, it is not difficult to detect the hand of a true poet — such as the author of 'Mariana,' and the 'Lines on the Arabian Nights' undoubtedly is." Here was conformity to the stock charges of obscurity, silliness, and affectation that had dogged Tennyson from the beginning; but here also was a generous recognition of his ability. Yet, in spite of this, two years later (July 1839) in a review of Shelley, the *Edinburgh* spoke of the "unbearable coxcombry of the 'intense' and mystic school of versifiers, who made him their model — including both the Shellites [sic] of the old connexion, and those of the new, or Tennysonites."

Three books published during the thirties also brought Tennyson's name before literary readers. The first was *The Sister's Tragedy* (1834) by Charles T. Thurston, a dramatic work based on Tennyson's ballad "The Sisters."[122] In his preface, Thurston acknowledged his debt to Tennyson and evinced his admiration for this poem:

> The powerful ballad of the Sisters, by Mr. Alfred Tennyson, is the ground work on which this play has been founded —
>
>> "We were two sisters of one race,
>> She was the fairest in the face."
>
> An attempt to retain the graphic force, and harrowing interest of those stanzas, if expanded through five acts, must necessarily be hopeless. But the story is eminently dramatic, and I thought that, if I were fortunate enough to combine judiciously the elements of tragedy, a sufficiently strong interest, though a modified and more varied kind, might still be elicited from it.

A short notice of this closet drama in the *Athenaeum*, November 22, 1834, failed to mention that it was an expansion of Tennyson's plot. It does not seem to have been reviewed by the *Literary Gazette*; but *Fraser's Magazine*, March 1836, spoke cordially of it in an article entitled "Asinarii Scenici," which included comment on *Paracelsus* and the second edition of Taylor's *Philip van Artevelde*. Joanna Baillie had brought the play to the attention of the reviewer, who said, "Her good opinion is sufficient to bear the author up bravely; nor has it been without warrant discernible in the merits of his play, which is founded on the powerful ballad of *The Sisters,* by Mr. Alfred Tennyson."

Some remarks on the young poet appeared in *Specimens of the Table Talk of the Late Samuel Taylor Coleridge* (1835).[123] Although Coleridge did not believe that Tennyson understood the principles of versification and prescribed an apprenticeship of several years in "well-known and strictly defined metres, such as the heroic couplet, the octave stanza, or the octo-syllabic measure of Allegro and Penseroso," he thought there were "some things of a good deal of beauty" among the poems that he had seen.

In 1838 Samuel Carter Hall, former editor and long-time sub-editor of the *New Monthly,* published the third of his anthologies of the British poets under the title *The Book of Gems.* This volume, subtitled *The Modern Poets and Artists of Great Britain,* contained selections from forty recent poets with introductory biographical and critical remarks on each. The biographical data on Tennyson, for which Hall cited Leigh Hunt as the source, included little more than the information that he was the son of a clergyman, was educated at Cambridge, and was related to Mr. Tennyson d'Eyncourt, M.P. for Lambeth.[124] Hall further stated that he was "of the school of Keats" and after the fashion of that poet delighted "in the same brooding over his sensations — and the same melodious enjoyment of their expression." But he was quick to admit that Tennyson had his own genius and would have written poetry if Keats had never lived. In such poems as "A Character" and "Supposed Confessions of a Second-rate Sensitive Mind," he credited the younger poet with having a psychological subtlety lacking in Keats. While he pointed out faults in Tennyson's work, Hall was not unsympathetic. For reprinting he selected "Buonaparte," "Mariana," "The Merman," "The Mermaid," "Lilian," and "Love and Death."

Although only three hundred copies of *Poems* had been sold by 1835, Tennyson's gradually growing prestige is indicated in a letter from Leigh Hunt, dated July 31, 1837.[125] Hunt had begun his brief editorship of the *Monthly Repository* with the July number.[126] Among other matters about which he wrote to Tennyson, he asked, "Will you . . . look into your desk and see if you can oblige me *with a few verses and your name to them,* for my new adventure?" The italics were Hunt's, and he explained, "I want my magazine to be such a magazine as was never seen before, every article worth something, though *I* say it that shouldn't, and I believe you know my gallant wish to be a sort of Robin Hood of an editor, with not a man in my company that does not beat his leader. A sonnet — a fragment — anything will be welcome, most especially if you put your name to it; and therefore for the sake of poetry and my love of it, again I say, *oblige me if you can.*" Hunt was eager to put out a magazine of unusually high quality and to make it financially successful. His insistency upon a contribution from Tennyson (which he did not get) and his emphasis upon the signature leave no doubt of the value he attached to Tennyson's name in 1837. By early 1840 James Spedding could write to Macvey Napier that the edition of *Poems* had been exhausted "for some time" and that the demand continued.[127]

Chapter Two

SILENCE AND WORK

Tennyson's almost morbid sensitiveness to criticism, which in the eyes of his friends and acquaintances contrasted extraordinarily with his rugged physical appearance, is so well known that it scarcely requires documentation. Sir James Knowles, his friend, unofficial literary agent, and the architect of Aldworth, tells us that a

frequent subject of his talk was the criticism on his own work, *when unfavourable*. All the mass of eulogy he took comparatively little notice of, but he never could forget an unfriendly word, even from the most obscure and insignificant and unknown quarter. He was hurt by it as a sensitive child might be hurt by the cross look of a passing stranger; or rather as a supersensitive skin is hurt by the sting of an invisible midge. He knew it was a weakness in him, and could be laughed out of it for a time, but it soon returned upon him, and had given him from his early youth exaggerated vexation.[1]

In view of this temperament, which must be constantly kept in mind, the question arises as to the part played by the reviewers in Tennyson's ten years' silence from 1832 to 1842, in the revisions and suppressions of the poems of his first two independent volumes, and in the style and subject matter of the new poems published in 1842.

It is evident that he saw a number of the reviews of both volumes. The *Memoir* refers to the notices in the *Westminster,* the *Tatler,* and the *Englishman's.*[2] Tennyson was at Cambridge for part of the Lent term that began on January 13, 1831.[3] If he had not read his praises in the *Westminster* before he returned from the Christmas vacation, he would certainly have had the opportunity to do so upon his arrival; for Hallam had seen the review prior to the opening of term; and from Cambridge, Monteith wrote to Milnes of it, before Tennyson left the university.[4] Hallam sent the number of the *Tatler* containing Hunt's remarks on Alfred and Charles to their sister Emily at Somersby, where his friend must have seen them and the copy of Fox's review in the *Monthly Repository* that Hallam forwarded to Emily at a later date.[5] There can be no question about Hallam's own article in the *Englishman's*, since he wrote to Tennyson that he had arranged for Moxon to send it to him.[6] We know from Tennyson's letter to North that he read the critique in *Blackwood's* and that he saw Croker's abuse in the *Quarterly*. Hallam Tennyson testifies that the latter disturbed his father's "equanimity of . . . mind" and that Mill's article "was a great encouragement." [7] The poet probably read the *New Monthly* review of 1833 as well. When *The New Timon* appeared anonymously in 1846, he guessed that it was by Bulwer, since he thought the attack on him was a continuation of Bulwer's animosity displayed in the notice of the preceding decade.[8] As for the others, there is no proof, but it is quite possible that he saw most, if not all, of the reviews published in the United Kingdom.[9]

In the light of Tennyson's hypersensitiveness to the "gadfly" of hostile criticism, the accepted hypothesis that his failure to publish another volume until 1842 sprang largely from a fear of exposing himself to further attack seems correct.[10] Corollary reasons, which influenced him for a time, there may have been. Hallam's death, of course, paralyzed him at first; but less than five months afterward, January 22, 1834, Trench wrote to Donne that he heard Tennyson had "so far recovered from the catastrophe in which his sister was involved, as to have written some poems, and, they say, fine ones." [11] There were also family difficulties to distract him — Septimus' distressing mental condition, Charles's return to opium and the deterioration of his marriage, the plight of the fatherless family and the eventual necessity of moving them from the rectory at Somersby. He was not always in the best of health or spirits.[12] Furthermore, he may have wanted time for revision of the old poems, though as early as June 22, 1833, Kemble wrote to Donne complaining bitterly of new readings already effected; [13] and the next year Tennyson informed Spedding, "I have corrected much of my last volume, and if you will send me your copy I would insert my corrections." [14] Possibly all of these considerations, plus the time to produce a greater bulk of new poems, contributed to Tennyson's delay in publishing; but they could not have been responsible for his protracted refusal to bring out a new edition with additional poems. As he later confessed, "he had been almost crushed" by the *Quarterly*; [15] and with most of the critics finding faults in the poems of 1833, he believed for a time that English readers could never care for his verse and felt the atmosphere of England to be so inimical that he thought seriously of living abroad.[16] His only wish was to keep out of public notice. Evidence of his anxiety on this score is apparent from his letter to North in 1834, begging that his poems not be "dragged forward once more," and from another to Spedding, asking him to deter Mill from his intended critique. In the second letter he wrote with underscored words, *"I do not wish to be dragged forward again in any shape before the reading public at present."* [17]

Although he broke his vow of silence by contributing "Saint Agnes" to *The Keepsake* (1836) and "Stanzas" to *The Tribute* (1837), in both instances the poems were earnestly solicited; and through Milnes's irritation over his letter of refusal at first, he was almost forced into appearing in *The Tribute*.[18] As has been seen, the *Athenaeum* was impressed by the beauty of "Saint Agnes" and the *Edinburgh Review* regarded "Stanzas" as indicative of the "hand of a true poet," but the qualifications with which both hedged their praise could hardly have given a sensitive man encouragement. Also, as previously noted, the prevailing tone of references to him in Tory journals would have led him to expect little mercy at their hands in the event of a new volume. An unpublished letter from Spedding to Napier, editor of the *Edinburgh*, February 26, 1840,[19] unmistakably reveals the poet's attitude. After explaining that Tennyson's poems were out of print and still in demand, Spedding continued, "His bookseller as well as his friends are urgent with him to publish another edition of the old ones, and a volume of new — but from some doubt as to the value or the probable reception of them he will not be persuaded. He w^d be willing, however, to publish, *if I could under-*

take to review him.'' Spedding assured Napier that the article would be "no puff — but an honest criticism," and the editor agreed to take it if it was not too fervent. But when Tennyson was finally about to venture before the public two years later, his friend was called out of the country; and the author was still so apprehensive of what his fate with the reviewers might be that he wrote to Edmund Lushington, "I have not yet taken my book to Moxon. Spedding's going to America has a little disheartened me, for some fop will get the start of him in the *Ed. Review* where he promised to put an article and I have had abuse enough." [20]

REVISIONS AND SUPPRESSIONS

How far the critics were responsible for Tennyson's alterations and suppressions in the collective first volume of *Poems,* 1842, is a disputed question. His contemporaries were convinced of his attention to the reviewers. Browning wrote to Elizabeth Barrett in 1845, "Tennyson reads the *Quarterly* and does as they bid him, with the most solemn face in the world — out goes this, in goes that, all is changed and ranged.[21] The same year Charles Astor Bristed wrote in the New York *Knickerbocker Magazine,* "Of all the passages assailed by the reviewer [Croker], there is but one which has not been either entirely expunged or carefully re-written." [22] Hallam Tennyson says that his father "kept up his courage, profited by friendly and unfriendly criticism, and in silence, obscurity, and solitude, perfected his art." [23] Nevertheless Lounsbury, after discussing the problem at considerable length, reaches the conclusion that "there is no evidence that anything, whether coming from favorable or unfavorable sources, determined, save in occasional instances, his own conclusions. On the contrary, the evidence is overwhelming that it did not. . . . Hostile criticism had no perceptible effect in dictating the omissions or alterations which were found in the edition of 1842." [24] In view of this division of opinion, a second descent to Lounsbury's "dreary realm of statistics" seems warranted.

To be complete, a statistical analysis of Tennyson's debt to his periodical critics must be based on a study of both the poems condemned as a whole and of specific passages censured. Some poems were summarily condemned, others were condemned but with special criticism of certain passages, and even in some of the poems that were praised, lines were cited which might, in the critics' judgment, be changed to advantage.

Of the fifty-six pieces in *Poems, Chiefly Lyrical,* twenty-four were condemned as a whole.[25] Of these twenty-four, fifteen or slightly over three-fifths were not reprinted in 1842. The other nine were printed unchanged, except "The Poet's Mind," in which there were two unimportant changes and the omission of one stanza which might have appeared rather egotistical. A comparative list of the twenty-four unfavorably criticized poems will facilitate the discussion.

Reprinted 1842

The Poet's Mind	The Merman
A Dirge	The Mermaid
Claribel	Song — The Owl
Recollections of the	Second Song — To the Same
Arabian Nights	The Dying Swan

Reprinted Later

The Sea-Fairies (1853)	We Are Free (1872)
All Things Will Die (1872)	Elegiacs (1884)
Nothing Will Die (1872)	National Song (1892)
The Kraken (1872)	

Never Reprinted

English War Song	Sonnet ("Shall the hag Evil")
Lost Hope	The Grasshopper
Love and Sorrow [26]	The "How" and the "Why"
Love, Pride, and Forgetfulness	The Tears of Heaven

Only one of the seven poems reprinted after 1842 was allowed to appear in less than thirty years. Five of these were in collective editions. "The Sea-Fairies," reprinted in 1853, was materially changed throughout. The "National Song" was introduced after fifty years as a song in *The Foresters* with the last four lines of each of the two stanzas rewritten.

On the other hand, it is true that Tennyson did not republish in 1842 seventeen poems of the 1830 volume that had not been censured. This fact might be considered evidence of independence of the critics, but it is not so clear as Lounsbury seems to think; for some of these poems are examples of certain general strictures. These were: (1) too many short poems "about the length of one's little finger," which are the result of making poems of "all the fancies that fleet across the imagination"; [27] (2) use of antiquated words and obsolete pronunciation; [28] (3) irregularities of measure. Also, Tennyson was always irritated by the charge of imitation. Several critics, complaining of his conceits, had likened him to writers of the seventeenth century.[29] The *New Monthly* had observed, "The newer aspirants to Parnassus . . . draw their inspiration now from Keats, and now from Herrick, or copy one line from the Sonnets of Shakespeare, in order to pillage the next from the Fragments of Shelley." [30] Tennyson "has filled half his pages with the most glaring imitations, and the imitations have been lauded for their originality." Such accusations may have conditioned his judgment in the suppression of a number of poems.

Lest one fall into special pleading, it must be admitted that "The Deserted House" and "Song" ("I' the glooming light") were not published in 1842 despite North's and Hunt's belief that the first was "perfection" and "affecting" and Mill's opinion that the latter was "beautiful." Although Hero was among the ladies with whom North declared he was in love, "Hero to Leander" was never included in an authorized edition, nor did the "Supposed Confessions of a Second-rate Sensitive Mind," which Hallam, Fox, Hunt, the *New Monthly,* and the *Westminster* had mentioned favorably, reappear until 1884. But Tennyson's statement, *"I remember everything that has been said against me, and forget all the rest,"* [31] must be borne in mind in connection with these poems.

A survey of the volume of 1833 shows that thirteen of the thirty poems were condemned as a whole or charged with special faults.[32] Seven of the thirteen were not reprinted in 1842 — the seven which had received the most severe criticism. The following is a tabular list of these thirteen poems, all of which were criticized in reviews that Tennyson assuredly saw:

Reprinted 1842

The Lady of Shalott	The Palace of Art
The Miller's Daughter	A Dream of Fair Women
Oenone	The Lotos-Eaters

Reprinted Later

To — ("All good things"), 1865 and 1871	Sonnet ("Buonaparte"), 1872
	Sonnet ("Mine be the strength"), 1872

Never Reprinted

O Darling Room	To Christopher North
The Hesperides [33]	Song ("Who can say")

The six reprinted poems were the longest and best poems in the volume, and Tennyson could hardly have been expected to suppress them. While Croker had ridiculed them at considerable length, he could not dismiss them as mere "drivel," as North had done with some of the short poems of the earlier volume. All six poems, however, were much rewritten or rearranged. Although the two criticized passages in "A Dream of Fair Women" were not changed in 1842, six of eight in "The Lady of Shalott" were omitted or altered in the second version, four of eight in "The Miller's Daughter," one of two in "The Palace of Art," and four of twelve in "Oenone." [34] The metrical recasting of these poems, which will be discussed below, is even more remarkable. And it is not unlikely that the accusation of similarity to Keats figured in the revision of some of the poems, especially "The Palace of Art." [35]

The two sonnets, "Buonaparte" and "Mine be the strength," were finally inserted in a collective edition without change; but "To —," the third censured poem omitted in 1842 and later reprinted, distinctly shows the effects of Croker's review. The last two stanzas, which contained four condemned passages, were deleted, and one of the other four points of attack was altered.

Absurd as was Croker's ridicule of endowing the jay with human qualities in the lines,

> And through damp holts, newflushed with May
> Ring sudden laughters of the jay!

Tennyson changed "laughters" to "scritches."

Seven poems in the volume of 1833 that had not been adversely criticized were suppressed.[36] With these added to the seventeen from *Poems, Chiefly Lyrical,* one might say that Tennyson was making a selection from his early poems for the first volume in 1842 and accept Lounsbury's cavalier statement, "The poems appearing in his first two ventures which he failed to republish there would have been thrown out in any case." [37] But would he have been at such pains to make a selection if the poems had passed relatively unchallenged? Is it reasonable to affirm that these poems would have been discarded "in any case," when he wrote to North in 1834, "I could wish that some of the poems there broken on your critical wheel were deeper than ever plummet sounded. . . . I never wish to see them or hear of them again"? [38]

One of the commonest charges of the early critics, and one to which Tennyson paid most heed, was the affectation they found in his excessive compounding of words, especially in his writing them together without a hyphen and in his constant use of the accented *-ed.* He himself late in life admitted that as a youth he "had an absurd antipathy to hyphens." [39] Taking the reviewers' strictures to heart, he hyphenated his compounds in 1842 and continued to do so in his subsequent poems. He removed a number of compounds, particularly in "The Lady of Shalott" and "Oenone," dispensed with many accented endings, and deleted the diacritical marks.

But it is from a study of the words, phrases, and lines singled out for criticism by the reviewers that we gain the most conclusive evidence of Tennyson's reaction. In all, including both volumes, there were eighty-seven passages that drew specific adverse comment or were tacitly censured by being italicized.[40] Of these, fifty-six were in poems reprinted, and twenty-two of the fifty-six were corrected or omitted. The other thirty-one of the eighty-seven were in poems not reprinted in 1842. It is valid to consider these along with the twenty-two, since in every case except one ("Kate," which I shall not count) there can hardly be any doubt that the number of the passages cited or the stricture on one integral passage was the main reason for the suppression of the poem, rather than that the passages accidentally happened to be in a poem not reprinted for some other reason.[41] Thus altogether, fifty-two out of eighty-seven or 60 per cent of the passages that the critics censured did not reappear in 1842 as they had originally stood.[42]

The final disposition of the thirty passages in poems not reprinted in 1842 seems to show the effects of criticism carried over to a later date. Five of these passages were changed or omitted when the poems were finally reprinted, and twelve were in poems never reprinted.

It might be argued that since it is not absolutely certain that Tennyson saw all the reviews, my figures are not beyond the pale of coincidence. But the percentages based on reviews he is known to have read are even higher. If we use only passages criticized by Hunt, Hallam, North, Croker, and Mill, whose articles he undoubtedly knew, we find that fifteen of thirty-six passages in poems reprinted were altered or omitted and twenty-six were in poems not reprinted — a total of forty passages (I except "Kate") out of sixty-two (65 per cent) corrected or suppressed. With Croker's review alone the tally is thirty-five out of fifty (70 per cent).

A few examples of the alterations will show how clear the effect of the critics often is. Arthur Hallam had written in the *Englishman's Magazine* that the word "unrayed" in the lines from "Recollections of the Arabian Nights,"

> Dark-blue the deep sphere overhead,
> Distinct with vivid stars unrayed,

did not convey "a very precise notion"; and Tennyson changed the word to "inlaid." After Croker had noted with derision that the name, *The Lady of Shalott,* was "below the stern" of the boat, Tennyson made the reading "around the prow." Mill rightly judged the last stanza of "The Lady of Shalott" "a lame and impotent conclusion," and Tennyson substituted the vastly superior stanza which now ends the poem. In "Eleanore" the *Literary Gazette* found a "confused metaphor . . . of sleeping *waves* having glorious dreams," and the poet deleted the objectionable line. The passage originally stood:

> As waves that from the outer deep
> Roll into a quiet cove,
> These fall away, and lying still,
> *Having glorious dreams in sleep,*
> Shadow forth the banks at will.

The revised form is:

> As waves that up a quiet cove
> Rolling slide, and lying still
> Shadow forth the banks at will.

Testimony of the reviewers' influence almost as striking as these verbal alterations seems to lie in Tennyson's modifications of his prosody. Only through reading J. F. A. Pyre's painstaking study, *The Formation of Tennyson's Style,* can one fully appreciate the extensive and salutary effect of criticism upon his technical advancement. It is necessary here merely to point out the nature of the reviewers' strictures and to outline the development presented in detail by Pyre.

Familiar as we are with the metrical virtuosity of the mature Tennyson, it is difficult for us to realize that his versification was ever faulty, since the record has been modified by his revisions and suppressions. But one need only read the early poems in their original form to recognize the validity of Coleridge's comment that Tennyson began "to write verses without very well understanding what metre" was.[43] So partial a friend as J. W. Blakesley wrote in November 1830, "The worst of Tennyson's poetry is that it is necessary to hear him read it before you can perceive the melody, at least for ninety-nine men out of a hundred." [44] As Pyre says,

The 1830 poems are, as a whole, strangely and rashly anarchic. There is, throughout, the most admired disorder of wild and irregular metres.

Scarcely any two poems are in the same metre with each other, and only a small proportion of the individual poems are systematically strophied throughout. . . . It is not altogether accidental that in two or three conspicuous instances in this volume where the poet adopted and adhered to a systematic and comparatively simple pattern of verse, he was rewarded for his faithfulness by an unusual and lasting success, as in the case of *Mariana*. But in a large proportion of the individual poems, the metre is quite unregulated except by the caprice of the poet's ear, and even when a provisional strophe has been adopted, it is no uncommon occurrence for it to be violated in some unsystematic or unexpected manner.[45]

It is not to be laid to stupidity on the part of the reviewer, then, that the *Spectator*, August 21, 1830, listed as one of Tennyson's faults "a vicious and irregular system in the arrangement of his rhymes." Even the enthusiastic critic, probably Fox, in the *Westminster Review*, January 1831, wrote: "We must protest against the irregularities of measure. . . . There are few variations of effect which a skilful artist cannot produce, if he will but take the pains, — without deviating from that regularity of measure which is one of the original elements of poetical enjoyment; made so by the tendency of the human frame to periodical movements."

These remarks may not have gone entirely unheeded, for there were "far fewer really 'wild' metres in the 1833 volume." [46] Still, even in the new work, instead of employing an accepted strophic form, Tennyson tended to originate the arrangement of lines in every poem, though, once he had adopted a stanzaic pattern, he was much more likely to conform to it and to a basic meter throughout than he had been in 1830.

The *Athenaeum*, the first periodical to review *Poems*, 1833, remarked, "We must just advert, also, to his broken and irregular measures, for the sake of observing, that he gives himself a licence in that respect, which, with his obvious sensibility to melody and finely-toned ear, has the effect of carelessness." The *Literary Gazette* said that both Lamb and Tennyson had imitated the worst faults of Donne and Cowley whose "rich veins of original thinking" were "hid under rugged phrases and impracticable metre." It also mentioned the "queer versification" in "Eleanore." The appreciative reviewer in the *True Sun* declared, "Mr. Tennyson is often most wilful in his verse — prefers roughness and discords for their own sakes." It remained for John Stuart Mill in the *London Review* to expatiate upon Tennyson's metrical deficiencies:

> We will not conclude without reminding Mr. Tennyson, that if he wishes his poems to live, he has still much to do in order to perfect himself in the merely mechanical parts of his craft. In a prose-writer, great beauties bespeak forgiveness for innumerable negligences; but poems, especially short poems, attain permanent fame only by the most finished perfection in the details. In some of the most beautiful of Mr. Tennyson's productions there are awkwardnesses and feeblenesses of expression, occasionally even absurdities, to be corrected; and which generally might be corrected without impairing a single beauty. His powers of versification are not yet of the highest order. In one great secret of his art, the adaptation of the music of his verse to the character of his subject, he is far from being a master: he often seems to take his metres almost at random. But this is little to set in the balance against so much excellence; and needed not have been mentioned, except to indicate to Mr. Tennyson the points on which some of his warmest admirers see most room and most necessity for further effort on his part, if he would secure to himself the high place in our poetic literature for which so many of the qualifications are already his own.

From the record of his life it is abundantly evident that Tennyson was nothing if not a craftsman. The critics had asserted that he had not mastered the basic principles of his art; and, as was to be expected, the man who about this time thought "only the concise and perfect work . . . will last" [47] set about to remedy his lack. The results of his amazing technical revisions are to be seen in such poems as "The Lotos-Eaters," "Mariana in the South," "The Palace of Art," "A Dream of Fair Women," "The Miller's Daughter," "Oenone," and "The Lady of Shalott." [48] Weak measures, initial inversions, syllabications, juxtaposed sibilants, and the like were eliminated, as well as excrescences of imagery, feeble expressions, and faulty diction. The result was the melodious perfection, the variety within order, the felicitous phrasing that we know in the standard versions of these poems. There can scarcely be any doubt that the rigid discipline to which Tennyson subjected himself and his poems was to a great extent inspired by the reviewers.

Metrical considerations seem to have entered also into his choice of poems for republication in 1842. While those reissued, according to Pyre, "furnish still a sufficient variety of stanzaic forms and though these stanzaic forms are for the most part of the poet's own invention . . . there is nevertheless a tendency toward the adoption of *some* stanzaic system and an adherence to it. Further, unquestionably, a larger proportion of the poems are in a comparatively simple form and a uniform metre, and the process of selection has tended to bring these poems into a relatively greater prominence." [49]

THE NEW POEMS FOR 1842

The effect of the reviewers on the style, subject matter, and treatment of the poems that appeared for the first time in the volume of 1842 is less conclusively demonstrable than it is in the revisions and suppressions of the early poems. The ground here is uncertain, and it is easy to fall into dangerous generalizations. Nevertheless, there is a striking agreement between the advice of the critics and the work of the poet.

Even the casual reader cannot fail to remark the conventional versification of the new poems. Pyre's analysis fully confirms this impression:

Practically every new poem in the 1842 edition was in some standard and well-known metre and observed a definite stanzaic order of construction. The conventional form was usually modified in some minute particular, but this modulation was always simple, organic, and consistently observed. . . . Of these 36 poems, 9 are in blank verse; two are in free-syllabled ballad movements; two are anapestic; two are trochaic; only one, *The Vision of Sin*, has any radical change of metre, and all the rhymed poems, with this exception, are in fixed strophic or couplet forms. Twenty of the poems are consistently iambic and, of these, all but two are in the simple quatrain arrangements of four-stress or four-and-three-stress verses.[50]

Tennyson's willingness to mold his thoughts in regular and familiar patterns corresponds significantly with the reviewers' strictures on the anarchy of his measures and with their general charges of striving too much for idiosyncrasy and individuality.

While not so readily apparent, perhaps, as the modification

in style, there is a noticeable change of tone in the new poems. As his son wrote, "My father's comprehension of human life had grown: and the new poems dealt with an extraordinarily wide range of subjects, chivalry, duty, reverence, self-control, human passion, human love, the love of country, science, philosophy, simple faith and the many complex moods of the religious nature." [51] Spedding in the *Edinburgh Review*, April 1843, found "the interest deeper and purer; — there is more humanity with less image and drapery; a closer adherence to truth; a greater reliance for effect upon the simplicity of nature. Moral and spiritual traits of character are more dwelt upon, in place of external scenery and circumstances. He addresses himself more to the heart, and less to the ear and eye."

Tennyson's swing away from the fanciful and pretty to ideas and themes more concerned with the interests of the day and closer to the hearts of men cannot be laid entirely to external influences. Some of the poems, such as "The Two Voices" and "Ulysses," are known to have sprung from his despondency over Hallam's death and his effort to combat it. There are possibly autobiographical associations in "Love and Duty." And these poems must have been written more for himself than to preach to or inspire his readers. Also, some of the poems were not a new departure. He had essayed patriotic verses in 1830.[52] He had started to moralize with "The Palace of Art" and the speech of Pallas in "Oenone." With "The Miller's Daughter" he had begun the tender stories in rhyme that were conspicuous in the new edition.

Neither was the shift in emphasis in the later poems out of harmony with the poetic role he had envisaged for himself in some of the poems in the earlier volume. In these the conflict between opposing conceptions of the poet's function — what Professor Douglas Bush calls "the problem of the poet" [53] — is patent. Shall the poet aspire to be one of Shelley's "unacknowledged legislators of the world"? Shall he, metaphorically speaking, mix and mingle with humanity in an attempt to provide leadership and inspiration, or shall he retreat into his own imaginative land

of sensation, content to influence his fellow men only so far as
their response to beauty is ennobling?

Tennyson enunciated in a clarion voice the first of these ideals
in "The Poet," where Freedom is portrayed as shaking the world
with "one poor poet's scroll." The sonnet "To Poesy," included
in the *Memoir*,[54] expressed, in even more Shelleyan terms, a personal hope of participating in the great conquest when Poetry
shall overcome Falsehood:

> O God, make this age great that we may be
>   As giants in Thy praise! and raise up Mind,
> Whose trumpet-tongued, aerial melody
>   May blow alarum loud to every wind,
>   And startle the dull ears of human kind!
> Methinks I see the world's renewed youth
>   A long day's dawn, when Poesy shall bind
> Falsehood beneath the altar of great Truth:
> The clouds are sunder'd toward the morning-rise;
>   Slumber not now, gird up thy loins for fight,
> And get thee forth to conquer. I, even I,
> Am large in hope that these expectant eyes
> Shall drink the fulness of thy victory,
>   Tho' thou art all unconscious of thy Might.

"Mine be the strength," the first poem in the volume of 1833,
declared, not too successfully but manifestly, the poet's desire to
influence his contemporaries.

In contrast to these poems is "The Poet's Mind," where Tennyson likens the mind of the poet to a garden in which the singing
bird will drop dead and the melodious fountain will cease if the
"dark-browed sophist" comes near.[55] Here is an exalting of the
poetic imagination and poetic faculty and the assertion of their
need for aloofness from the chilling and deadening contact with
the unpoetical world. In "The Hesperides," also, the poetic imagination may be embodied in the golden apple which Father
Hesper, the dragon, and the sisters three are guarding warily,
"Lest one from the East come and take it away." If Mr. Lionel
Stevenson is right in his association of the Lady of Shalott with
the poet's psyche,[56] her experience seems to reflect the poet's
dilemma. The Lady weaves her web of mirrored images. When

love enters her heart, she rejects her imaginary world; but death
is the result of her first contact with reality.

In "The Palace of Art" the poet attacked the problem directly
and declared unequivocally for human sympathy instead of artistic isolation. Yet even in this poem, the conclusion is more thought
than felt. The poet's obvious delight in describing the pleasures
of the palace, in the original version of the poem, and his dwell-
ing upon sensuous imagery and detail in many of the poems of
1833 lead one to doubt that he had actually disassociated himself
from the realm of fancy for which he had shown such an affinity.

Tennyson's failure to eschew the dream world of mermaids and
lotus-eaters in spite of the lip service he paid to opposing principles in "The Palace of Art" has led scholars to account for his
attempting to write on more catholic subjects as the result of
external forces that conditioned his thought and attitude. Sir
H. J. C. Grierson saw the change evidenced in 1842 as springing from "the high seriousness of Hallam and his Cambridge
friends." [57] Nicolson, echoing the same belief, writes:

> On leaving the intensive domestic atmosphere of Somersby for a Cam-
> bridge in which the new generation, under the fomenting influence of
> men like Hare and Connop Thirlwall, were convinced that to them
> alone had been entrusted the enlightenment of a dull lethargic age,
> Tennyson fell, inevitably also, under the influence of the Trinity
> "Apostles," and the strength that was in him was diverted into ethical,
> and not, as one might have wished, into emotional channels. By the
> time he left Cambridge the harm had been done. The great lyric poet
> who had been born up there among the Lincolnshire wolds had been
> already tamed, controlled, labelled, and given a function unnatural to
> his genius; the wild, unhappy animal that lurked within him had been
> caged and shackled, and the real intention and meaning of the man
> had been for ever veiled — even from himself.[58]

Certainly there was an intense belief in the moral and instructive aspect of literature among the group in which Tennyson
moved. Before he published his first volume, he had received a
letter from Blakesley, calling upon him to cease dallying in the
groves of fancy and to address the world with strength and vigor:

> I trust that you have taken advantage of the inspiration derived from
> seeing Miss Kemble, and the leisure afforded by the vacation to in-

gratiate yourself yet more with the Muses; and it is the earnest wish of me and all the rest of your friends, that you will desist from flirting with each of them alternately, and declare at once "what your intentions are" to some one of them. The present race of monstrous opinions and feelings which pervade the age require the arm of a strong Iconoclast. A volume of poetry written in a proper spirit, a spirit like that which a vigorous mind indues by the study of Wordsworth and Shelley, would be, at the present juncture, the greatest benefit the world could receive. And more benefit would accrue from it than from all the exertions of the Jeremy Benthamites and Millians, if they were to continue for ever and a day.[59]

On February 18, 1830, Trench, then in Rome, wrote to Donne with approval of Sterling's *Arthur Coningsby* and Maurice's *Eustace Conway,* saying, "They will both, I doubt not, do a great deal of good." In the same letter he asserted, "You in England have a great task in hand, the greatest that could be offered to men, viz. the exaltation of the tone of our literature." On June 23 of the same year, Trench, then in England, in another letter to Donne, referred specifically to Shelley, Keats, Wordsworth, and Byron and deplored the subjective nature of modern poetry:

When, except in our times, did men seek to build up their poetry on their own individual experiences, instead of some objective foundations, common to all men? Even we, who inhabit their own age, suffer by their error. Their poems are unintelligible to us, till we have gone through that very state of feeling to which they appeal; as, for instance, none can entirely comprehend "Alastor" who has not been laid waste by the unslaked thirst for female sympathies; and so with the rest.[60]

In the next paragraph he spoke of the newly published volumes of Alfred and Charles Tennyson and expressed a fear that the adulation of his Cambridge friends would injure the former, if he was not careful. Another Apostle, Henry Alford, recorded that his wish in composing the poems which were published as *The School of the Heart* had been "to undertake a work for God, and to promote his glory." [61] Hallam, analyzing "Mariana in the South" for Donne early in 1831, wrote, " 'An artist' as Alfred is wont to say, 'ought to be lord of the five senses,' but if he lacks the inward sense which reveals to him what is inward in the heart, he has left out the part of Hamlet in the play." Again, on

July 26, 1831, he wrote to Tennyson, "You say pathetically, 'Alas for me! I have more of the Beautiful than the Good!' Remember to your comfort that God has given you to see the difference. Many a poet has gone on blindly in his artistic pride." [62]

In the face of the ideas of his associates and his implied contrition over having more of the Beautiful than the Good, Tennyson went right on leaving Hamlet out of the play. Except for "The Palace of Art" and "Oenone" the poems of 1833, presumably the fruit of the Cambridge period, are strangely lacking in traces of the Apostles' creed. Among the unpublished poems of the period, since given to the public by Sir Charles Tennyson, the single one evincing a spirit of didacticism is the unfinished allegory, "Sense and Conscience." [63]

Although the influence of his friends seems to have been slight at the time when he was closely associated with them at Cambridge, the seed there sown may have borne fruit later when he was more willing to heed advice. At any rate, the suggestions of some of the friends, written in letters during the period of silence, seem to have had considerable effect. George Stovin Venables wrote that "his poems had too much concentrated power and thought, were too imaginative and too largely imbued with the 'innermost magic,' easily to excite popular interest, or to be read at once by those whom he specially wished to influence." In another letter of the period, Venables outlined his belief that success for a modern artist lay in a synthesis of opinions and a combination of the real and ideal: "The great Catholic painters could express what was at the same time ideal and real in the minds of the people; but the modern artist has hardly ever found similar objects of high imagination and intense popular feeling for his art to work upon. If . . . an artist could only now find out where these objects are, he would be *the* artist of modern times." According to Hallam Tennyson, "Venables affirmed they were not to be sought in any transient fashions of thought, but in the 'convergent tendencies of many opinions' on religion, art, nature, — of which tendencies he and others believed, he said, that my father, with his commanding intellect, and conspicuous moral courage, ought to be the artistic exponent and unifier." [64]

Another force acting upon Tennyson may have been the success of the poetry of his Apostolic friends, Henry Alford and Richard Trench, which was heavily larded with instructive thoughts and pious sentiments. Alford's *The School of the Heart* was published in 1835 and cordially reviewed by the *Athenaeum*, the *Literary Gazette*, and Christopher North in *Blackwood's*, who said: "We love the Poet, though to us personally unknown, for the sake of his poetry, which flows on sincere as any stream in a pastoral land. . . . Here we have no affected raptures — no fantastic or distorted passions — no simulated sorrows — no carefully got up agonies — no elaborate despair. Natural feelings, pure and high and good, find for the most part appropriate expression, and always expression animated and eloquent. . . . He is a Christian indeed." The *Edinburgh Review* criticized more than it praised Alford's work, but at least it treated him to a lengthy article, which it had denied Tennyson.[65]

Trench's *The Story of Justin Martyr and Other Poems* also came out in 1835. It fared so well that before the year ended a second edition was necessary;[66] and the author was thus encouraged to bring forth another collection, *Sabbation; Honor Neale, and Other Poems*, in 1838. Indicative of the welcome accorded Trench are the opening words of *Blackwood's* review of his first book: "This is a delightful little volume, bearing throughout the indisputable impress of genius, and breathing throughout the spirit of religion. Every composition it contains charms by its sincerity and the most artless of them are poems by the mere force of truth."[67]

The poetic doctrine advanced by Henry Taylor in the preface to *Philip van Artevelde* — that closet drama which produced such an immediate sensation — seems also to have affected Tennyson. Lockhart was unrestrained in his praise in the *Quarterly*, writing that "years and years have passed since it came in the way of our office to call attention to the appearance of a new English poem at once of such pretensions and such execution."[68] This young man of approximately Tennyson's age had opened the gates of fame. What was the key to his success?

In his preface Taylor struck at the poetry of the Romantics,

typified to him specifically by Byron and Shelley. He attacked
the roots of the tradition in which Tennyson was writing:

> These poets were characterised by a great sensibility and fervour, by
> a profusion of imagery, by force and beauty of language, and by a
> versification peculiarly easy and adroit, and abounding in that sort of
> melody, which, by its very obvious cadences, makes itself most pleasing
> to an unpractised ear. . . . But from this unbounded indulgence in
> the mere luxuries of poetry, has there not ensued a want of adequate
> appreciation for its intellectual and immortal part? . . .
>
> So keen was the sense of what the new poets possessed, that it never
> seemed to be felt that any thing was deficient in them. Yet their de-
> ficiencies were not unimportant. They wanted, in the first place, sub-
> ject matter. A feeling came more easily to them than a reflection, and
> an image was always at hand when a thought was not forthcoming.
> Either they did not look upon mankind with observant eyes, or they
> did not feel it to be any part of their vocation to turn what they saw to
> account. It did not belong to poetry, in their apprehension, to thread
> the mazes of life in all its classes and under all its circumstances, com-
> mon as well as romantic, and, seeing all things, to infer and to instruct:
> on the contrary, it was to stand aloof from every thing that is plain and
> true; to have little concern with what is rational or wise; it was to be,
> like music, a moving and enchanting art, acting upon the fancy, the
> affections, the passions, but scarcely connected with the exercise of the
> intellectual faculties. These writers had, indeed, adopted a tone of
> language which is hardly consistent with the state of mind in which a
> man makes use of his understanding. The realities of nature, and the
> truths which they suggest, would have seemed cold and incongruous,
> if suffered to mix with the strains of impassioned sentiment and glowing
> imagery in which they poured themselves forth. Spirit was not to be
> debased by any union with matter, in their effusions; dwelling, as they
> did, in a region of poetical sentiment which did not permit them to walk
> upon the common earth, or to breathe the common air. . . . Poetry of
> which sense is not the basis, though it may be excellent of its kind, will
> not long be reputed to be poetry of the highest order. It may move the
> feelings and charm the fancy; but failing to satisfy the understanding, it
> will not take permanent possession of the strongholds of fame.[69]

In the execution of his dramatic poem Taylor had attempted to
appeal more to the mind than to the emotions and to strip his
lines of unessential imagery.

Tennyson read both the poem and the preface, and his reaction is preserved in a letter to Spedding: "I close with him

[Taylor] in most that he says of modern poetry, tho' it may be that he does not take sufficiently into consideration the peculiar strength evolved by such writers as Byron and Shelley, who, however mistaken they may be, did yet give the world another heart and new pulses, and so we are kept going. . . . But 'Philip is a famous man' and makes me 'shamed of my own faults." [70]

Not the least of the external pressures influencing Tennyson must have been the reviews, which emphasized the ideas that came to him from other sources. The man so sensitive to the critics that their opinions lingered in his mind, sometimes for years, can hardly have failed to take their words into account. The grounds for his advance along a new line may be found in the review of *Poems, Chiefly Lyrical* by Hallam,[71] who was a connecting link between the opinions of friends and those of the press. Undoubtedly he and Tennyson had discussed theories of poetry before his death; his written word was a lasting token for the poet.

Hallam attempted to make a strong case for the type of poetry that Tennyson had written in *Poems, Chiefly Lyrical.* In recent times he saw ordinary life and poetic conception moving in different directions, in contrast to an earlier day when they were confluent. Among the divergent types of modern poetry, he delineated poetry of sensation, of reflection, and of passionate emotion. He also described a kind of poetry that dealt primarily with the simple human emotions such as love, friendship, ambition, and religion without transforming them by high imagination. Classing Tennyson among the poets of sensation, with Shelley, Keats, and Hunt, Hallam declared that theirs was the highest type of poetry. Of the poetry dealing with simple and common emotions, he said, "We are very far from wishing to depreciate this class of poems, whose influence is so extensive, and communicates so refined a pleasure. We contend only that the facility with which its impressions are communicated, is no proof of its elevation as a form of art, but rather the contrary." Yet Hallam was quick to realize the objection to which he was open. How did he account for Homer, Dante, and Shakespeare, unquestionably great poets, who were popular and conveyed pleasure with great facility? To this he would reply, "Shall we not say, after all, that the difference is in the power of the author, not in the tenor of his meditations? Those eminent spirits find no difficulty in conveying to common apprehension their lofty sense, and profound observation of Nature. They keep no aristocratic state, apart from the sentiments of society at large; they speak to the hearts of all, and by the magnetic force of their conceptions elevate inferior intellects into a higher and purer atmosphere." He argued also that these authors lived in an active time when readers were more susceptible to "stirring influence," when there was more "reciprocity of vigour between different orders of intelligence."

But the age in which we live comes late in our national progress. That first raciness, and juvenile vigour of literature, when nature "wantoned as in her prime, and played at will her virgin fancies," is gone, never to return. . . . Those different powers of poetic disposition, the energies of Sensitive, of Reflective, of Passionate Emotion, which in former times were intermingled, and derived from a mutual support an extensive empire over the feelings of men, were now restrained within separate spheres of agency. . . . In the old times the poetic impulse went along with the general impulse of the nation; in these, it is a reaction against it, a check acting for a conservation against a propulsion towards change.

By his reasoning and defense Hallam admitted that Tennyson's was a specialized kind of poetry and little likely to appeal to the generality of readers. This poetry embodied only one of the elements combined in the poetry of England in its prime. Also, the greatest poetic geniuses were able to be highly imaginative and at the same time to appeal to common interests and raise less intelligent readers to their level. Could a poet with the high ambition of Tennyson fail to appreciate the challenge? Furthermore, Hallam tried to extenuate the divergence of Tennyson's early poetry from the common feelings and the life of the period. He was seeking an apology for this characteristic of poetry of sensation — a characteristic which he was simply stating as a fact and not necessarily as an estimable one. Here, then, lay an inference for Tennyson. If, as Hallam had said, poetry was more healthy in an elder age, might not modern poetry be more wholesome that responded to the motivation of the nation, championing change instead of reacting against it?

Other reviewers left nothing to implication. Urging him to use his gifts to the highest purpose, the *Westminster* declared, "A genuine poet has deep responsibilities to his country and the world, to the present and future generations, to earth and heaven. He, of all men, should have distinct and worthy objects before him, and consecrate himself to their promotion." Tennyson, the reviewer said, has a "facility of impersonation . . . by which he enters so thoroughly into the most strange and wayward idiosyncrasies of other men" that he must be careful lest he become merely "a poetical harlequin."

> He has higher work to do than that of disporting himself amongst "mystics" and "flowing philosophers." He knows that "the poet's mind is holy ground;" he knows that the poet's portion is to be
> > 'Dower'd with the hate of hate, the scorn of scorn,
> > The love of love;'
> he has shewn, in the lines from which we quote, his own just conception of the grandeur of a poet's destiny; and we look to him for its fulfilment. It is not for such men to sink into mere verse-makers for the amusement of themselves or others. They can influence the associations of unnumbered minds; they can command the sympathies of unnumbered hearts; they can disseminate principles; they can give those principles power over men's imaginations; they can excite in a good cause the sustained enthusiasm that is sure to conquer; they can blast the laurels of tyrants, and hallow the memories of the martyrs of patriotism; they can act with a force, the extent of which it is difficult to estimate, upon national feelings and character, and consequently upon national happiness.[72]

North did not scruple to inform Tennyson what he must do if he would be a great poet:

> That day will never come, if he hearken not to our advice, and, as far as his own nature will permit, regulate by it the movements of his genius. This may perhaps appear, at first sight or hearing, not a little unreasonable on our part; but not so, if Alfred will but lay our words to heart, and meditate on their spirit. We desire to see him prosper; and we predict fame as the fruit of obedience. If he disobey, he assuredly goes to oblivion.
>
> At present he has small power over the common feelings and thoughts of men. His feebleness is distressing at all times when he makes an

appeal to their ordinary sympathies. And the reason is, that he fears to look such sympathies boldly in the face, — and will be — metaphysical. What all the human race see and feel, he seems to think cannot be poetical; he is not aware of the transcendent and eternal grandeur of common-place and all-time truths, which are the staple of all poetry. All human beings see the same light in heaven and in woman's eyes; and the great poets put it into language which rather records than reveals, spiritualizing while it embodies.[73]

The *New Monthly* and Fox in the *Monthly Repository* directed Tennyson toward more serious aims than he had yet undertaken. The former was the first to call upon him to portray the spirit of his age:

We have been thus harsh with our young poet because we have more hopes of him than of most of his contemporaries. And it is time for a POET once more to arise; . . . how magnificent the objects which surround him! The elements of the old world shaken — the mine latent beneath the thrones of kings, and the worm busy at their purple — the two antagonist principles of earth, Rest and Change, mightily at war! — Every moment has its history; and every incident in the common streets of men is full of the vatication of things to come. *A poet, rapt in the spirit of this age, will command the next!* What themes and what fame may be reserved for one whose mind can be thus slowly nurtured to great thoughts by great events; steeped in the colours of a dread, yet bright time; elevated with the august hopes that dawn upon his species; and standing on the eminence of one of those eras in the records of the world in which —

"WE SEE, AS FROM A TOWER, THE END OF ALL!" [74]

Fox demanded more moral purpose from the young poet: "His power must have a more defined and tangible object. It were a shame that such gifts as his should only wreathe garlands, or that the influences which such poetry as his must exercise, should have no defined purpose, and only benefit humanity (for, any way, true poetry must benefit humanity) incidentally and aimlessly. Let him ascertain his mission, and work his work." [75]

Mill as well, in his comment on "The Palace of Art," contributed to the idea that Tennyson should present ethical verities. He did not think the poem "wholly successful," but in its attempt to render "not only vivid representations of spiritual states, but [also to be] symbolical of spiritual truths" he considered it a

"most favourable augury for Mr. Tennyson's future achievements." Mill also called for intellectual development on the part
of the poet: "It rests with himself to see that his powers of thought
may keep pace with" his "powers of execution." And Mill added:
"To render his poetic endowment the means of giving impres-
siveness to important truths, he must, by continual study and
meditation, strengthen his intellect for the discrimination of such
truths; he must see that his theory of life and the world be no
chimera of the brain, but the well-grounded result of solid and
mature thinking; — he must cultivate, and with no half devotion,
philosophy as well as poetry." [76]

Some of these critical precepts seem to have been digested by
the Tennyson who appeared in 1842 appealing to human sympathies and common feelings in "Dora" and "The Gardener's
Daughter," prophesying the future, sounding the clarion hopes
of the day, and singing of progress and change in "Locksley Hall,"
moralizing in "The Vision of Sin," and presenting topical discussions in "Walking to the Mail" and "Audley Court."

Finally, it should be pointed out that the *Atlas* had introduced
the sixteen stanzas quoted from "The Miller's Daughter" as "pure
verse that will outlive the memory of his affections." The *Athenaeum* had extracted a great many lines of it for approval, and the
True Sun had called the poem "exquisite throughout — full of the
calm beauty of contented happiness, reflecting back a youthful passion — of heart-affection — of simplicity and homely truth." The
New Monthly had stated that to be popular Tennyson had only
to lean "more to the vein manifest" in "The May Queen" and
"New Year's Eve"; and Mill had praised the latter as "fitted for
a more extensive popularity" than any other piece in the two
volumes. Is it to be laid to coincidence alone that Tennyson
added to these poems the mawkish "Conclusion" and sprinkled
through the edition of 1842 such sentimental stories as are to be
found in "The Gardener's Daughter," "Dora," "The Talking
Oak," "Edward Gray," "Lady Clare," "The Lord of Burleigh,"
"Sir Launcelot and Queen Guinevere," and "The Beggar Maid"?

In addition to the agreement between the opinions current at
the time and the new type of poetry that Tennyson was writing,

we have direct testimony of external influence from the poet's son. After quoting Venables' opinion that Tennyson's poetry was too full of the "innermost magic" to appeal to the masses and saying that the *Quarterly* failed to realize he could influence many people indirectly, Hallam Tennyson wrote in the privately printed *Materials for a Biography of A. T.*:

> Yet to a certain extent he took advice and was now inclined to rest [his poetry] more on the "broad interests of the time and of universal humanity," although no doubt it was harder to idealize common associations than things that never acted but upon the imagination. . . . My father pondered all that had been said, and after a period of utter prostration from grief, his passionate love of nature and of humanity drove him to work again, with a deeper and more real insight into human nature and the *requirements of the age.*[77]

Tennyson himself maintained that his poetry was all the public needed in the way of biographical information; and though modern scholars are grateful to have available other sources of knowledge concerning him, several poems written during this period provide glimpses of the author's emotional response to the criticism he had received. In "What Thor Said to the Bard before Dinner" [78] we find him determined to write unflinchingly of the abuses of the age and to win recognition for his muse. We see him rebuilding his self-esteem, so completely undermined by the reviewers, in two lines of "Will Waterproof's Lyrical Monologue": "I grow in worth and wit and sense, / Unboding critic-pen." In "The Moral," one of the pieces added to "The Sleeping Beauty" in 1842, he betrays both a defensiveness that the poem expresses no practical teaching and an impatience that anything more than the moral implicit in beauty should be expected. Most revealing of all is the poem "An Idle Rhyme," [79] in which we discover a reaction to the pressure brought to bear upon him. There is a momentary assertion of his right to make verses with no other aim than pleasure and to revel in the realm of the senses. Ironically as well, there is a sensible awareness that poetry too much concerned with contemporary matters loses its appeal with the passage of time.

In view of the evidence here presented, it seems legitimate
to say that the reviewers had a profound effect upon the young
Tennyson. He may at first have wished to remain silent in order
to improve his poems; he may for a time after Hallam's death
have been so mentally and physically depressed that publication
was out of the question; he may have been harassed by domestic
difficulties; he may even have wished to wait until he had a large
body of poems written. But most of all he was plagued by an
underlying fear of again putting himself at the mercy of the
reviewers, and he would not have revised so thoroughly or been so
selective in reprinting had he not been so severely censured. With
his self-criticism aroused, he went beyond the reviewers and produced incomparably superior work in the second versions of such
poems as "Oenone" and "The Lady of Shalott"; but in these instances he was often correcting along lines the critics had indicated. Still, in most of the poems there were many more verbal
changes and omissions than were suggested by his censors, and
mere altering of criticized passages would not have accomplished
what he did. When he could not agree with the reviewers, he
ignored them. Yet both in his revisions and in the suppression of
poems he accepted the opinion of the critics in more than half of
their strictures. Finally, in the new poems of 1842, in both style
and content, there is a significant concurrence with the advice
of the reviewers. The periodicals expressed representative opinion; and more important than that, they had a large share in
forming the literary taste of the public. An attentive consideration
of the judgments of such organs was in order for a young poet
who was determined to win recognition of his talents.

Chapter Three

THE CORNERSTONE OF FAME: *POEMS*, 1842

THE RECEPTION OF *POEMS*, 1842

The new edition that Tennyson was finally induced to publish appeared on May 14, 1842.[1] Entitled simply *Poems*, it was issued in two volumes under Moxon's imprint. The first volume was composed chiefly of poems published in 1830 and 1833, though several new pieces, all but one of which had been written in 1833, were included.[2] The second was made up of previously unpublished poems with the exception of· "St. Agnes" and "The Sleeping Beauty."

Poems, 1842, was no *Philip van Artevelde*. Contrary to the assurances of Robert Horton and Arthur Turnbull, the success of the volumes was not "immediate and unbounded."[3] Nor were they launched in conjunction with an effusive tribute from a powerful journal, as Taylor's work had been; for Hallam Tennyson is inaccurate in saying that "Milnes and Sterling led the chorus of favourable reviews."[4] Nevertheless, *Poems* made a name for Tennyson, and his recognition by the press was neither tardy nor slight.

Lounsbury, whose account of the reception of the volumes of 1842 has long been the accepted one, proclaims with characteristic vehemence the reluctance of the reviewers to acknowledge Tennyson's achievement in 1842. He further asserts that the poet's reputation was forwarded by public approval in the face of recalcitrant critics. "Professional criticism," he says, "followed and followed reluctantly, and almost protestingly, popular appreciation. Tennyson's reputation advanced against a sullen opposition which insinuated a depreciatory estimate which at last it did not venture to proclaim openly." He even insists that the reviewers waited for public opinion to manifest itself ·before daring to commit themselves, instead of taking the lead in guiding and molding the literary taste of their readers.[5] But Lounsbury's statements are based on only eight reviews, while, in point of fact, there were at least ten others published during 1842.[6] These ten reviews must be taken into consideration if anything like an accurate conception of the critical reaction to the new edition is to be reached. In addition, Lounsbury's interpretation of several reviews will bear revision.

The first notice seems to have appeared in the *Examiner* on May 28, two weeks after the publication of *Poems*. Now under the proprietorship of Albany Fonblanque, the *Examiner* was vehemently Whig in its politics and had a high reputation for its pronouncements on literature.[7] The article on Tennyson was undoubtedly written by John Forster.[8] FitzGerald complained of its quietness; but apart from a blatant "puff," the poet could hardly have asked for more kindly treatment. Lounsbury, while depreciating the review, concedes that it "might fairly be called cordial"; [9] and cordial it assuredly was. Instead of being a mixture of censure and praise, the critique was almost entirely an encomium. In the second paragraph, Forster said that by publishing "The Goose," "Walking to the Mail," and "The Skipping Rope," Tennyson had provided ammunition for his foes, but that he himself had no inclination to turn them against their author. He then devoted most of his review to commending fifteen of the new poems.

At the beginning he traced the history of Tennyson's literary career, admitting that there were faults and foibles in the early volumes; but of the poetry between 1832 and 1842 he wrote, "It is, we suspect, to be confessed that we have had nothing new, in this Decade of years, comparable to the best passages of the poetry of those same two, small, much praised, much carped-at volumes." Although the poet had not outgrown all his faults, in the new poems he showed "matured taste and greatly strengthened power."

From the reading of these poems [Forster declared] we rise with a conviction that Mr Tennyson has not only redeemed the promise of his early writings; but given forth a new pledge, to be hereafter yet more worthily redeemed. He is acquiring one of the most valuable arts a poet can master: that of selection and compression. His imagery is less profuse; his "lavish lights and floating shades" are scattered with more discrimination. His sense of the beautiful, which his earliest poems at once proved him to possess in so eminent a degree — luscious, gorgeous, delicate — has become more chastened, more intellectual, less alloyed. . . . His descriptive passages have a sharper and more definite outline. His verse too, always most musical and sweet, is stronger and more varied. In a word, we think that he would find himself able to fly a higher flight than lyric, idyl, or eclogue, and we counsel him to try it.

Nor was Forster sparing in his praise of the individual poems. He knew of "nothing more complete" than the "Morte d'Arthur" for "exact adaption of beautiful words to beautiful thoughts. . . . In this poem, the simplicity of the action, the picturesque truth of the language, the grand cadence of the verse, and the rich colouring of old romance which gradually steals into the reader's mind and heart — show how thoroughly Mr Tennyson's imagination identifies itself with a subject, and what power of expression he has to do perfect justice to both." "The Gardener's Daughter" is "a more simple but not less lovely pastoral." "Dora" has "the homely beauty, without the trivial detail, of one of Wordsworth's ballads," though "its severe simplicity is perhaps too sudden a contrast to the gorgeous richness that surrounds it." "The Talking Oak" is "filled with quaint fancy and voluptuous beauty"; "Locksley Hall," "a piece of strong, full-blooded, man's writing . . . is not unlikely to be the favourite piece of the whole collection, with most readers. It is full of daring conception, and most bitter passion, and the verse rushes on with a wild solemn flow, in splendid unison with the theme." After quoting "Godiva" in its entirety, Forster said that with a "rapture, as though we had newly discovered an exquisite old Greek gem, did we welcome that lovely and most perfect poem."

This then is FitzGerald's "quiet" and Lounsbury's "somewhat colorless" review. One can scarcely refrain from wondering how much more enthusiastic than rapturous a reviewer can become.

On the same day that Forster's review appeared, another was printed in the evening edition of the *Sun*, a London daily news-

paper with pronounced Whig sympathies and an extensive country circulation. Its literary criticism "enjoyed considerable respect." [10] The attitude of the unknown reviewer was not entirely
amiable.[11] Some of his opening remarks about "affectations" and
"puerilities" were an echo of the criticism of the earlier volumes.
He linked Tennyson with Shelley and complained of frequent
obscurity. "The Palace of Art" was full of "far-fetched conceits,
and quaint, hazy imagery" as well as evidences of laborious craftsmanship. But in "Mariana" "every line is instinct with the truest
feeling." In "Locksley Hall," which attracted this critic's chief
attention, "strength and earnestness of purpose are visible
throughout, relieved and softened off by occasional touches of
infinite tenderness." His final comment to a large extent made
amends for his introductory strictures and was far from reluctant
praise: "We entertain so high an opinion of the elegance, the
variety, the alternately reflective and impassioned spirit, which
characterise this poem, that we unhesitatingly give it the preference over the majority of those that have appeared within the
last ten years." This, it must be remembered, was not written
after the readers had forced the critic's hand but two weeks
after publication.

Two days later, on May 30, the *Morning Post*, the Tory, High
Church journal of the *beau monde*,[12] reprinted "Godiva" in a
section headed "Tennyson's Poetry." The prefatory comments
gave a hint of the enthusiasm that was to well over in a full-
length review some weeks later.

The *Spectator*, which reviewed *Poems* on June 4, still associated Tennyson with the Cockney School. A good many of the
strictures, like those in the *Sun*, harked back to previous years.
Tennyson, the critic said, too often approached the "namby-
pamby"; the truths he mirrored tended to be special or particular
rather than general. His "most obvious defect . . . is his
diction . . . piebald with the spots of various times" after the
Cockney fashion. His versification, "sometimes made purposely
irregular," only served in the short poems to divert "the attention from substance to form"; his style was often reminiscent
of his predecessors. Yet the reviewer admitted that Tennyson

possessed powers "which properly cultivated would place him among the first rank of living poets. He has a keen eye for the beauties of nature . . . he has a perception and a relish of the natural and the homely, whether in manner or in feeling; his affections appear to be genial . . . his ken is extensive, and he can read, we fancy, both past and present with a more judging eye than belongs to the tribe of poetasters."

According to Lounsbury, after the review in the *Spectator* there was an "ominous silence" in the leading periodicals which was finally broken on August 6, more than two months later, by the *Athenaeum*. To bear out his statement, he quotes FitzGerald as writing in a letter of August 16 that he had seen no reviews except the one in the *Examiner*.[13] But FitzGerald's reading of periodicals during the summer of 1842 cannot have been very extensive, for the press was far from silent. Four reviews of *Poems* appeared before the one in the *Athenaeum*, and still another was published prior to the date of FitzGerald's letter. The attention of readers was also drawn to the volumes by short comments in three other periodicals.

As evidence of the lack of importance with which Tennyson was regarded, Lounsbury cites the failure of the *Atlas* — "one of the three leading politico-literary weeklies" — to review the *Poems*.[14] As a matter of fact, the *Atlas* not only noticed the new poems in its issue of June 25 but commended them warmly for their indications of poetic growth.[15] The poems in the second volume, the reviewer said, left the impression "that the mind of the author is undergoing a very important process of transition, from the twilight fantasies of his earlier pieces to the broad daylight of sound feeling and pure taste." Although there was some diminution of the imaginative luster of the early poems, it was more than compensated for by "the increase of sincerity, of real power, and of solid thoughtfulness manifested in these his later productions." They were "nearer to our sympathies, and more frequently" touched "the heart." In the versification there was "a great advance." He quoted seven stanzas of "The Sleeping Palace," writing, "Here is a fragment from a larger piece called the 'Day-Dream.' It is a beautiful picture of a luscious and drowsy fancy."

Critiques of Tennyson appeared in the July numbers of the *Monthly Review* and the *Christian Remembrancer*, which came out about the first of the month. While the *Monthly Review* did not like everything about the new poems, it displayed great appreciation of Tennyson's achievements.[16] He was characterized as "a person largely gifted with the poetic temperament, and giving the highest early promise of mastery in the poet's art," who had "husbanded and cultivated his talents, with patience, judgment and success." In the new poems, Tennyson appeared to have fulfilled the promise of his early work. He had overcome a number of his peculiarities of style and had made a decided advance "in the great essentials of his art." He was sometimes reckless in "thought and expression" and occasionally indulged "a talent for wanton and wilful vagaries of words as well as of images and ideas." "But still," the reviewer rhapsodized, "what an amount of manly and right English thought swells in these new poems, — how much that is pure and picturesque, — simple and overpowering! The mere expressions are often seeped as it were in a poetic fount of delicious sweetness and surpassing richness of flavour." "Locksley Hall" was called "a poem full of genuine passion and powerful thinking, uttered with a commanding music," and nineteen couplets from it were quoted. Both "Godiva" and "The Lord of Burleigh" were reprinted in entirety with approving comments.

Francis Garden, one of Tennyson's Cambridge associates, was coeditor of the *Christian Remembrancer*, a High Church organ;[17] and possibly he himself wrote the review of his friend's work. The magazine was running a monthly series of articles entitled "Poetry of the Year 1842." Wordsworth and Campbell had been discussed in June; in July the entire section was devoted to Tennyson, who, said the critic in the opening paragraph, "is pretty generally acknowledged to hold the foremost place" among the poets of "the rising generation." And Tennyson was thus described only six weeks after the publication of *Poems*.

The review was sympathetic. There were words of praise for

the "Recollections of the Arabian Nights," "Oriana," and "Mariana." To the question, Had the poet's mind progressed? the critic's answer was a qualified Yes. There were finer poems in the second volume: they showed "greater depth and body of thought"; the "effervescence" of the early style had been "tamed down"; the "mannerisms" had "nearly all disappeared." Moreover, the author was writing "on the whole such genuine and vigorous English." Still, his progress was not so great as desired or expected because he had not yet "become *human* enough." The reviewer suspected Tennyson of having derived from Hallam a belief that the poet must remain aloof from the ordinary world of men. But Tennyson was not uniformly remote. "The May Queen," "New Year's Eve," and now the "Conclusion" were "singularly human and touching" and had become, therefore, the most popular of his poems. The entire "Conclusion" was quoted, and there were excerpts with favorable comments from "The Lord of Burleigh," "The Talking Oak," and "The Gardener's Daughter." "The Two Voices" was described as "the longest and most powerful . . . of all Mr. Tennyson's poems," and readers of the *Remembrancer* were urged to "acquaint themselves with" it.

The *Westminster Review* for July, the first number of that quarterly to appear after the publication of *Poems*, did not let the volumes go unnoticed. They headed the list of new publications in the field of poetry and drama that was printed near the end of each issue. In a short paragraph in italics at the foot of the column, the *Westminster* directed *"the especial attention of our readers"* to the *Poems* of Tennyson and those of Robert Nicoll, *"both works of high merit,"* and promised to find an opportunity to do justice to them in a succeeding number.[18]

On July 27 the *Morning Herald*, a London daily with conservative leanings,[19] reprinted "Godiva" and spoke of Tennyson's "two small modest but most rich volumes."

Tait's Edinburgh Magazine for August, which appeared at the end of July, gave Tennyson unstinted praise.[20] On July 30 the *Morning Advertiser*, a London daily newspaper, called *Tait's* "one of the best magazines of the day" and mentioned among the articles of the August number "a Criticism on Tennyson's *Poems,* as worthy to attract very general attention." Commenting on the same issue, the *Leeds Times*, August 6, declared, " 'Tennyson's Poems' are reviewed in a masterly manner; and such as greatly to excite the reader's desire to cultivate an acquaintance with the work itself."

The review in *Tait's* is indeed worthy of attention, for it was ardent in its exposition of Tennyson's "very high powers." The reviewer advanced several main points of excellence in the poetry and illustrated them profusely with quotations. One of the poet's "most peculiar gifts" was his "power of making the picturesque delineation of external nature illustrate the mood of mind portrayed." His descriptive ability was excellent and his fusion of poetic artistry and moral sentiment estimable. There was a long paragraph on the development in thought, human interest, and power of language displayed by the new poems.

The review by Henry Chorley published in the *Athenaeum*, August 6, seems cool after the warmth of the *Tait's* panegyric. Yet it was by no means so cautious and reserved as Lounsbury makes it appear.[21] At the outset Chorley objected to some of the alterations in the old poems. He also dissented from those who maintained that Tennyson had overcome "the crotchets which distinguished his earlier efforts." With the introduction to the "Morte d'Arthur," "Walking to the Mail," "Amphion," "The Skipping Rope," and "Will Waterproof's Lyrical Monologue," he thought Tennyson had added as many silly things as he had suppressed. "But," he continued, "these allowed for, the new volume is so thickly studded with evidences of manly force and exquisite tenderness — with feelings so true, and fancies so felicitous, clothed in a music often peculiar in its flow, but never cloying — as to substantiate Mr. Tennyson's claim to a high place among modern poets. Let us prove what we say by the extracts we shall offer." Thus, having briefly entered his points of dissidence first, Chorley devoted the remainder of his review (and it was the major part) to confirming his high opinion of the poet. In the course of his remarks, he commented on Tennyson's "lyrical power" and judged him as having asserted in his new poems "his claim to be crowned as chief of the modern *minne-singers.*"

The last of the reviews to appear before FitzGerald's letter of August 16 was a most significant and hitherto unnoticed one in the *Morning Post* of August 9. The enthusiasm of this reviewer was boundless and must have been of no little consequence in advancing Tennyson's name. The *Post* catered to the fashionable world, where the greatest sale of poetry was still to be expected. At the same time, its literary department was considered by a contemporary writer describing the newspapers of 1842 to contain "much vigorous writing and unconventional thought." [22] In addition, it addressed itself to a clientele which might still have been harboring notions of Tennyson inculcated by the *Quarterly*.

The *Morning Post* filled three and a half full-sized newspaper columns with eulogistic comments and extensive extracts. The introductory observations on the poems of the second volume are indicative of the review as a whole:

Speaking with all reserve and moderation, they exhibit a strength, a brilliancy, a truthful earnestness of sentiment — a perfect mastery of language — an unerring power and discretion in adapting it to the most effective forms of versification — which, beyond the possibility of a doubt or question, must entitle Mr. Tennyson to take his stand at once amongst the most famous of our living poets. This we say advisedly and deliberately, for the merit of these poems is so great as to make mere cavilling on details quite contemptible. The reader is carried, from beginning to end, in one stream of sweet enthrallment. A quiet, pleasing, and not overdone pathos is the author's favourite vein; but whatever be his humour, the reader is sure of falling in with it, and has so little time or inclination for picking quarrels about minor defects, that he has not even an opportunity to stop and think of admiring the author, so entirely are the senses enslaved by the strong spell which the wand of genuine poesy has flung over them.

This reviewer thought "Morte d'Arthur" "alone sufficient to make the reputation of a young poet. . . . English literature contains nothing more perfect of the kind — more rich and overflowing in all the charms of thought and language — than this fragment." With great difficulty he desisted from quoting the poetry and finally referred his readers to the edition itself, in the belief that they would "one and all allow that the commendations we have bestowed on it are richly merited."

One more notice of *Poems* was printed in a newspaper during the month of August. The *Weekly Dispatch* discussed it briefly on August 21. The critic believed that the "two volumes might much better have been condensed into one, for a vast number of the poems are extremely trifling." He accordingly approved of the pruning that some of the old poems had undergone. But from generalizations, he quickly passed on to give "as long extracts as our space admits of, in order that our readers may have an idea of the author's conceptions." He then quoted from "The Vision of Sin" and "The Day-Dream," prefacing the selection from the latter with the comment, "The following poem is really beautiful."

Short and rather equivocal as it was, this article is noteworthy for early bringing Tennyson to the attention of an extensive class of readers far removed from those of the *Morning Post*. The *Weekly Dispatch* was a radical paper addressed to "artisans and operatives" and dedicated to the denunciation of abuses. Owned by Alderman James Harmer and coedited at this time by him and Joseph Wrightson, the paper had a circulation of over 66,000 — a vast figure for 1842 and triple that of the *Sunday Times*, its nearest weekly competitor in numbers of readers.[23]

During the summer, several of Tennyson's poems were reprinted in the columns of provincial newspapers. "The Lord of Burleigh" appeared in the Belfast *Northern Whig*, June 4, and in the *Manchester Chronicle*, July 16. "Godiva" was reproduced on June 11 by the *Sheffield and Rotherham Independent*. "The Sleeping Palace" was printed in the *Manchester Chronicle*, August 13; and on September 3 parts of "Locksley Hall" and "Oenone" were quoted by the *Leeds Times*.

On September 8, 1842, Tennyson wrote with obvious delight to Edmund Lushington, "500 of my books are sold: according to Moxon's brother I have made a sensation!"[24] As poetry sold in 1842, and especially in comparison to his earlier volumes, the number was an appreciable one. Nor can it be said that this figure was reached unaided by the press. At the time, instead of only three notices — in the *Examiner*, the *Spectator*, and the *Athenaeum* — ten reviews and numerous references to the *Poems* had been published. Two of the articles had been outspoken in their eulogy, and none had been really inimical.

In September came John Sterling's critique in the *Quarterly Review* — the first of the articles that appeared in the three leading quarterlies. It was followed by Milnes's in the October number of the *Westminster* and Spedding's in the *Edinburgh*, April 1843. The months that each of these periodicals allowed to elapse before they noticed Tennyson are not evidence of a hesitancy to commit themselves or a reluctance to recognize the new genius. The *Edinburgh* was delayed by Spedding's trip to America as private secretary to Lord Ashburton, head of the commission on the Maine boundary dispute, and by his having to postpone the article on Tennyson after he had returned, in order to produce a timely review of Dickens' *American Notes*; for the editor had agreed to accept a review by Spedding before the poems had gone to press.[25] The other two journals actually showed considerable alacrity in bringing Tennyson's volumes to public attention. The first issue of the *Quarterly* after they were published was brought out in June, too soon for a review to have been included unless it had been arranged for well in advance. That the *Quarterly* reviewed *Poems* in the next issue is somewhat remarkable, since even Taylor and Macaulay, men whose names were already well known, were allowed to wait longer before *Edwin the Fair* and *The Lays of Ancient Rome* were noticed.[26] As previously mentioned, the *Westminster* had commended *Poems* to its readers in July; and its pledge to review them as soon as possible was redeemed in the very next number.

Sterling's critique in the *Quarterly* was not so extremely laudatory as has sometimes been assumed. The questionable critical thesis with which he approached Tennyson's poetry — that great poetry must reflect the life of the time — prejudiced his view of some of the best pieces in the volumes. Certainly he voiced some strange judgments on particular poems, and he had an annoying tendency to praise in one clause and damn in the next. But he had a warmer admiration for Tennyson than appears in his article,[27] and he was laboring under a serious handicap. Lockhart, the editor, out of deference to Croker, would not allow express commendation of any poem that had been ridiculed in the *Quarterly* of 1833.[28] Sterling wrote to Mill, "As to Tennyson I am persuaded you would not have thought our differences of opinion nearly so great if you had seen my *Review* at first." In another letter to Mill he no doubt correctly estimated his service to the poet: "The article says as much in praise of Tennyson as could be admitted after their former abuse; and though desiring to say more in praise of the first volume I thought it better for him & for Poetry to get so much eulogy inserted rather than perhaps a second attack." [29]

As it was, Sterling managed to say a good deal in Tennyson's behalf. In the first part of the review, after advancing his theory and citing Chaucer and Shakespeare as great poets because they reflected their age, he wrote: "Mr. Tennyson has done more of this kind than almost any one that has appeared among us during the last twenty years. And in such a task of alchemy a really successful experiment, even on a small scale, is of great worth compared with the thousands of fruitless efforts or pretences on the largest plan, which are daily clamouring for all men's admiration of their nothingness." Sterling also thought the new poems "far advanced" over the old ones. "There is more clearness, solidity, and certainty of mind visible . . . throughout: especially some of the blank-verse poems . . . have a quiet completeness and depth, a sweetness arising from the happy balance of thought, feeling, and expression. that ranks them among the riches of our recent literature." He found Tennyson's lyrical poems full of beautiful word painting. With truth he said, "As minstrel conjurations, perhaps, in English, 'Kubla Khan' alone exceeds them. The verse is full of liquid intoxication."

For Sterling, the English idylls, such as "The Gardener's Daughter," "Dora," "Locksley Hall," "The Lord of Burleigh," were "a real addition to our literature." "In all," he wrote, "we find some warm feeling, most often love, a clear and faithful eye for visible nature, skilful art and completeness of construction, and a mould of verse which for smoothness and play of melody has seldom been equalled in the language." There was certainly no stinting here, and a little further on he spoke of Tennyson as "the most genial poet of English rural life that we know."

In his works there has been art enough required and used to give such clear and graceful roundness; but all skill and labour, all intellectual purpose, kept behind the sweet and fervid impulse of the heart. Thus, all that we call affection, imagination, intellect, melts out as one long happy sigh into union with the visibly beautiful, and with every glowing breath of human life. In all his better poems there is this same character — this fusion of his own fresh feeling with the delightful affections, baffled or blessed, of others — and with the fairest images of the real world as it lies before us all to-day. To this same tendency all legend and mystery are subordinate — to this the understanding, theorizing and dogmatizing, yet ever ministers, a loyal giant to a fairy mistress.

Although it has seemed valuable to go into the background of Sterling's review and to attempt to establish the actual tenor of his remarks, their unfavorable extent, which Lounsbury is so concerned to demonstrate, is largely irrelevant to the contention that Tennyson's name gained ground against the opposition of the critics and unaided by their pens. The point to be determined is how the critique appeared to contemporary readers, and there can be no doubt of the way in which it was construed by the literary world of 1842. Croker was so incensed by what he considered to be a complete repudiation of his judgment that he wrote a heated protest to Lockhart, vowing that he had refrained with the greatest difficulty from severing his connections with the *Quarterly*. It required a most persuasive letter from Lockhart to mollify him.[30] The *Observer*, in a review of the September number of the *Quarterly*, called the article on Tennyson a "eulogised" critique. The *Sun* described it as "favourable" and Tennyson as "the most promising young poet of the day." The *Inquirer* said of the article that "amidst a variety of matter which may by no means all of it secure" the reader's "approbation, he will find deserved praise of Tennyson, and specimens that will be very likely to send him to the volumes, if he has not already enjoyed them." [31] It was not necessary for the public to read Sterling's review to know that the *Quarterly* had recanted. The particular strictures on various poems might never be seen by a great number of persons, while the approving attitude of the *Quarterly* became general knowledge through the medium of the newspaper press. That the Tory journal did not handle Tennyson roughly, as was to have been expected, was notice to those who had accepted Croker's estimate to revise their opinion.[32]

Milnes's article in the *Westminster* for October was lacking in force and sometimes in continuity. Nevertheless, there could be no mistaking that his intent was friendly; through extensive quotations, he presented much of the best from the *Poems* for the reader's perusal.[33] He closed with a challenge to the poet to show that he had substance to match his exquisite command of diction and accurate harmony of verse. His final reminder was that "the function of the poet in this day of ours" was "to teach still more than he delights." It is to be feared that Tennyson took this dictum too much to heart.

Three reviews in addition to Milnes's appeared in the periodicals for October. Although Leigh Hunt's critique in the *Church of England Quarterly Review* [34] was not so enthusiastic as might be expected, he clearly considered Tennyson a poet of no mean ability. As the *Sheffield Iris* said of the article, it "good naturedly criticises Tennison's [*sic*] poems and allots to him no scanty meed of praise, with no sparing selection of passages to show that the praise is well deserved." [35] Hunt's favorite poem was "The Two Voices," which, he felt, contained "genuine, Christian, manly, and poetical philosophy." The poem was too long, he said, to extract in entirety; [36] and he urged the reader "to buy the work, if it were only for this single poem, though his money would be well laid out were it not among the contents." He concluded that Tennyson was "at present a kind of philosophical Keats." While he lacked some of the latter's fine qualities, he was "a genuine poet"; and Hunt thought it highly possible that he might gain as great a name as Keats through a class of poetry, entirely his own, which exceeded Keats's in thought and was "more pleasurable and luxuriant" in feeling than Wordsworth's.

The *Christian Teacher*,[37] a Unitarian journal which three years later became the *Prospective Review*, exhibited an unfeigned delight with much of Tennyson's work. Its only objection was to the poet's "Muse, either in her bitterer or in her more jocular moods." The critic began by saying that upon the publication of the poems, "It was seen at once that they distinguished themselves from the daily outpourings of imitative insipidity or extravagance." There was originality and power disclosed in them. The power was not that of a Homer, a Shakespeare, a Milton, or a Burns; but the reviewer "willingly and cordially" enrolled himself among those who "were disposed to welcome" the appearance of Tennyson's volumes. "One characteristic of Mr. Tennyson's poetry," he approvingly remarked, "is a keen and unslumbering perception of the Pure, the Graceful, the Lofty and the Lovely in Womanhood." He regarded Tennyson as "fortunate in his reproductions from classical fiction" and felt that poetic efforts of this nature were not to be deplored, as they were by some. The poet's rendering of classical themes, he thought, entitled him to a place in the "brotherhood" of Shelley, Wordsworth, and Keats, who had produced "memorable" works from the same materials. Finally, he believed Tennyson "particularly excellent, and particularly qualified to excel" in one department: "He can write a real simple and natural *ballad*. This is no light, and no vulgar praise. It indicates a power, which we consider very uncommon; and the degree of it, in the present instance, is such as to make it still more so."

The third review was published in the October issue of the *Cambridge University Magazine*, a periodical conducted by undergraduates that made a substantial name for itself during the brief years of its existence (1840–1843) through many articles on literature, described by Walter Graham as "notable." [38] It very legitimately regretted Tennyson's publication of poems such as "The Goose" and "The Skipping Rope" as "wilfulness, in mixing his pearls with pebbles." [39] But this censure was merely an opening cavil. "To speak generally," the reviewer remarked, "we would say that high and holy feelings, an earnest love of all that is beautiful and true, a keen sympathy with every nerve that vibrates in humanity, an affectionate observance of nature in her outward manifestations, an accurate discernment of the human passions and affections, great imaginative powers, perfect mastery over the English language, and an almost unrivalled melodiousness in versification — all these elements of the true poet are abundantly manifested in Tennyson." [40]

On November 19, 1842, William Jerdan finally reviewed Tennyson in the *Literary Gazette*. His notice was a tardy one for a weekly literary journal, but this delayed response to the publication of *Poems* was the exception and not the rule. Jerdan's main thesis was a lament over the changes made in the old poems. To illustrate, he printed beside each other the original and later versions of lines from "Mariana in the South," "The Miller's Daughter," "Oenone," "The Lotos-Eaters," and "Eleanore." He was so much concerned with these that he failed to mention any of the new poems individually, though he said, "There *are* poems in these new volumes excelled by none in the present day." He grumbled about Tennyson's love of strange epithets, his straining after compounds, and his predilection for exotic description and imagery. Yet he ranked him "among the foremost of our young poets."

The year 1842 closed with a review in the December issue of the *London University Magazine*.[41] A companion piece to the article in the *Cambridge University Magazine*, it praised Tennyson somewhat more eloquently. At the conclusion the reviewer, who signed himself W. A. C. (possibly William Arthur Case),[42] mentioned "in a friendly spirit the errors into which . . . [Tennyson] is apt occasionally to fall." The poet could have omitted several more of the old poems to advantage and deleted more lines. He was sometimes obscure. Poems like "The Mermaid," "The Merman," and "The Dying Swan" were lacking in appeal to human sympathies. Regrettably, his writings had been "*too few*, and *too short*." The reviewer's purpose, however, was set forth in these words: "We hope to bring forward from his writings passages of such sweet beauty, and to show in them such depth of feeling, originality of conception, and elegance of fancy, as will induce those of our readers who have not yet met with them, to make themselves immediately acquainted with the poems of this interesting and amiable writer." Quoting from a number of the poems in both volumes, the young critic carried out his intention at some length.

The last review of *Poems* to appear before the publication of the second edition was Spedding's in the *Edinburgh*, April 1843. A gesture of friendship, it requires the closest attention, for in it are advanced the opinions of one of Tennyson's most intimate associates and of the literary adviser who previously had made suggestions to him about some of the poems reviewed.[43] Moreover, the article reflects the literary climate in which Tennyson worked while preparing the poems for his new edition; and it undoubtedly expresses many of his own ideas about his poetry — or at least ideas which he had accepted.

Lounsbury's description of Spedding's review, which he says was more cordial than those in the other quarterlies though it was not allowed to be too much so,[44] gives little notion of the appreciative warmth that pervades it. Although partisanship was kept in check by the editor's stipulation that Spedding should make no predictions,[45] he was able to achieve a master stroke in Tennyson's behalf. His explanatory and interpretive criticism was thorough and extensive. Like the methodical editor and apologist of Bacon that he was to become, he systematically countered the general criticisms which had been advanced by previous reviewers. And he asseverated for the Victorians the high seriousness of Tennyson's attitude toward poetry and life.

Spedding's first concern was to trace the maturing of Tennyson's powers; in so doing, he refuted the assertions of Leigh Hunt and the *Christian Remembrancer* that the poet's progress was slight or of a negative kind. The excesses of *Poems, Chiefly Lyrical* he defended as wholesome signs of the freedom and scope of a youthful fancy. Yet even among the "vague melodies," the "bevy of first-loves," and the "delineations of every state of mind," there flashed occasionally "a genuine touch of common humanity," as in "A Character" and "Circumstance." The *Poems* of 1833, he thought, showed a great step forward not only in poetic technique but also "in the general aim and character." In these poems "the moral soul was beginning more and more to assume its due predominance," though there was still a superfluity of imagery and too much appeal to the "luxuries of the senses."

The decade of silence had brought about a notable decrease in these excesses. In direct rebuttal of Chorley and Jerdan, the poet's advocate began to illustrate his contention with some of the alterations in the poems previously published. The suppressions and revisions were indicative "of improving taste and increasing power." The latter were made "always with a view to strip off redundancies — to make the expression simpler and clearer, to substitute thought for imagery, and substance for shadow." The divestment of the Lady of Shalott's pearl garland, royal robes, and other finery, for instance, was a vast improvement in taste. The introduction of the boy's mother in "The Miller's Daughter" greatly enriched that poem; and though many might regret the loss of some of the former stanzas, they had been "displaced, to make room for beauty of a much higher order." Some of the additions to "The Lotos-Eaters" were of deep significance, and the "Conclusion" to "The May Queen" was "another instance . . . of Mr Tennyson's growing tendency to seek deeper for sources of interest."

Having testified to Tennyson's progress in thought and execution and having explained and approved the principles governing the changes in the old poems, Spedding took up in earnest the matter of Tennyson's appeal to human sympathies, which he had glanced at earlier in his references to *Poems, Chiefly Lyrical.* He subscribed to and restated the axiom advanced by previous critics: "All that is of true and lasting worth in poetry, must have its root in a sound view of human life and the condition of man in the world; a just feeling with regard to the things in which we are all concerned." Yet, he asserted, as if to contradict the *Christian Remembrancer,* which had found Tennyson not human enough, "In this requisite Mr Tennyson will not be found wanting. The human soul, in its infinite variety of moods and trials, is his favourite haunt; nor can he dwell long upon any subject, however apparently remote from the scenes and objects of modern sympathy, without touching some string which brings it within the range of our common life." The last clause seems to be a rejoinder to Sterling's criticism.

The heart of Spedding's critique lay in its exposition of "The Palace of Art," "St. Simeon Stylites," "The Two Voices," and "The Vision of Sin." In these were to be found indications of Tennyson's "moral theory of life and its issues, and of that which constitutes a sound condition of the soul." He explained in detail the moral of each poem — "*selfish* enjoyment" in "The Palace of Art"; "pride of asceticism" in "St. Simeon"; the "history of the agitations, the suggestions, and counter-suggestions of a mind sunk in despondency, and meditating self-destruction" in "The Two Voices"; and "the end, here and hereafter, of the merely sensual man" in "The Vision of Sin." In his interpretation of "The Palace of Art" he answered effectively the complaints of Sterling and the *London University Magazine* that the lesson of the poem was a mistaken one. He admitted that poetically there were weaknesses in "The Two Voices," but insisted that it was the moral aspect of the poem with which he was concerned.

Here was the key to Spedding's approach to Tennyson's poetry — and, for that matter, the key to the early-Victorian critical approach in general. In his summing up, Spedding frankly stated that he had spent more time on these four poems than they merited as poetry in order to show that Tennyson was no mere versifier enthralled by beauty but a man with "a heart accustomed to meditate earnestly, and feel truly, upon the prime duties and interests of man." His friend here cast Tennyson in the role of Thinker and Teacher from which he was never to escape, and Spedding's final words were an exhortation of the poet to produce the great and sustained work of which he was capable. The insight this review provides into Tennyson's poetic development can hardly be overestimated.

From the preceding discussion of the reception of *Poems*, 1842, it is apparent that Lounsbury's version needs considerable readjustment. It is highly misleading to characterize the critical reaction as "adverse" and to describe it as "disdainfully set aside by" the "great body of intelligent readers." [46] As a matter of fact, it seems safe to say that the critical reception of the first edition of the *Poems* was largely favorable. True, there were no pane-gyrics except in *Tait's Edinburgh Magazine* and the *Morning Post*, and a number of the reviews found considerable fault; but there was no hostility. No more friendly critic than William Jerdan wrote, in his review in the *Literary Gazette*, which appeared after all but two of the other reviews had been published, "Critics of all denominations admit him as a true and sterling poet . . . all are for him; none against him." As the *Cambridge University Magazine* remarked in October 1842, "Certainly he has no right to complain of the degree of attention and favour with which the present edition has been welcomed." Within a very few months, Tennyson had been placed in the front rank of poets. In July the *Christian Remembrancer* had spoken of him as "pretty generally acknowledged to hold the foremost place" among the new generation of poets. The *Morning Post* in August had said that he could "take his stand at once amongst the most famous of our living poets." On September 21 the *Sun* had dubbed him "the most promising young poet of the day," while the *Literary Gazette* in November spoke of him as "among the foremost of our young poets." He had been reviewed by period-icals of all types and complexions, by daily and weekly news-papers, by literary weeklies, by magazines, both secular and religious, by student publications, by the great quarterly reviews, and by organs of all parties catering to all classes of readers from lords to laborers. As if by common consent, the critics had passed over the poems that would have been the obvious butt of ridicule and had concentrated on Tennyson's finer things. In fact, the majority of the strictures leveled against him resulted from the admission of his excellent qualities. His contemporaries took themselves, their age, and their poetry so seriously that they required something more of Tennyson than he had accomplished.

Clearly, the story of critical neglect and popular acclaim in the face of recalcitrant reviewers is a myth. Rather than trying to counteract the people's acceptance of Tennyson by hostile crit-icism, the reviewers — even some who made adverse comments on individual poems — urged the public to become better acquainted with him through the volumes themselves. No fewer than five directed their readers to the text for a fuller comprehension of Tennyson's beauty and strength,[47] while the *Westminster* took pains to call attention to the poems before it had an opportunity to review them.

A third misconception fostered by Lounsbury is that there was a general disapproval of the alterations in the early poems republished in the new edition. Of the *Literary Gazette* he writes, "Most of its article was given up to the task of finding fault — which had now begun to grow wearisome — with the changes which had been made in the poems previously printed." And again of Sterling's review in the *Quarterly*, "For one thing in particular we may be thankful. He refrained from echoing the cuckoo cry which had been going on of deploring the alterations which had been made in the poems previously published." [48]

So far as the British reviews of the first edition were concerned, there was no cuckoo cry. Among the thirteen periodicals that mentioned the changes, the *Literary Gazette* was the only one that objected to them categorically. Two others, the *Christian Remembrancer* and the *Athenaeum*, equivocated, approving a few of the alterations while objecting to others.[49] Of the remaining ten reviewers, however, eight approved of the alterations wholeheartedly, a few wishing that the poet had gone even further, while two accepted them as reasonable concessions to criticism.[50] Favorable reaction to the changes was thus overwhelmingly in the majority.

A number of the reviewers also subscribed to the belief in Tennyson's poetic progress. Leigh Hunt in the *Church of England Quarterly Review* was the least willing to admit that the poet had advanced, saying that the progression was only of a negative sort. There was merely less "fantasticism and whimsicality." He was inclined to admit even less development when he realized that "The Two Voices" bore the date 1833. The *Christian Remembrancer* said that Tennyson's poetry still contained too much pure gold of imagination and, as a whole, was lacking in human sympathy. Yet it admitted, "There is much positive progress. The poems in the second of the two volumes before us are unquestionably . . . greater and finer performances than those in the first." This reviewer found a great improvement in depth and thought. There were fewer mannerisms; the style was less flamboyant, and the diction was more robust. Spedding's detailed analysis of Tennyson's growth has already been noted. The *Examiner,* the *Atlas,* the *Monthly Review, Tait's Edinburgh Magazine,* the *Quarterly Review,* and the *London University Magazine,* all, in one respect or another, bore witness to the poet's maturing taste and power, his increased concentration of thought, vigor of expression, grasp of language, and metrical skill.

With the *Poems* of 1842 Tennyson seems largely to have effaced the stigma of radicalism. He was still linked with Shelley and Keats; but only in the Whig *Sun,* where he was compared with Shelley, and in the *Spectator,* where he was tagged as a "Cockney," was there any suggestion of political animosity. He was cordially reviewed by prominent organs of all three factions — the *Examiner,* the *Morning Post,* and *Tait's Edinburgh,* for example — before the heavy artillery of the parties took up their position on the firing line. That he was well handled by all three of the powerful partisan reviews was, perhaps, his greatest triumph at this stage of his career. Quite patently, it was not achieved unassisted.

His friends made certain that he would not be attacked by any of the chief party organs, and in this respect they played a major part in the reception of *Poems,* 1842. In spite of Lounsbury's disgust with what he considers the tepidity of the critiques in the *Quarterly,* the *Westminster,* and the *Edinburgh,* they performed a valuable service for Tennyson's reputation. At the same time, these articles were not mere "puffs" designed to anticipate independent judgment. Numerous appreciative reviews had been published and five hundred copies of the *Poems* had been sold before any one of the three appeared.[51]

TENNYSON'S REPUTATION, 1843–1847

As extensive and as favorable as had been the reception of the first edition of *Poems,* 1842, Tennyson was still far from the summit of his fame. While he was extravagantly admired in some quarters, his progress during the mid-forties with the public at large was gradual. But beyond question, he was steadily gaining recognition. Before the publication of *The Princess* in December 1847 his twin volumes had passed through four editions, each numerically greater than its predecessor.[52] A number of articles and references to him in books and periodicals from 1844 through 1847 sustained his growing reputation.

In January 1844 the *Foreign and Colonial Quarterly Review* printed an article headed "Modern Poets — Tennyson, Marston, and Browning." Although the periodical was designed for the colonies, it was published in London and later in the same year became the *New Quarterly Review*, under which title it existed until 1847. This review expressed a high admiration for Tennyson and printed "Ulysses" entire, complaining of its neglect by previous critics and calling it "one of the most exquisite . . . poems in this or any other language."

Richard Hengist Horne's *A New Spirit of the Age*, published in March 1844 and consisting of two volumes of critical essays on the literary figures of the day, contained a cordial appraisal of Tennyson's poetry.[53] Early in his remarks the essayist said, "We are about to claim for Alfred Tennyson — living as he is, and solely on account of what he has already accomplished — the title of a true poet of the highest class of genius."

Between March and June of the same year Tennyson figured prominently in the protracted discussion of modern poetry carried on in the *Athenaeum* by its correspondents "Beta," "Sigma," and "Theta." [54] On July 12, 1845, *Chambers's Edinburgh Journal*, a weekly periodical devoted to fiction, poetry, and criticism, published an appreciative essay on "The Poetry of Alfred Tennyson." And the following month the *British Quarterly Review* [55] introduced him to its audience of Dissenters as the writer of "some of the most charming verses these later times have produced." The article mingled blame and praise, but the approach to Tennyson was amicable.

Bulwer's attack on him in *The New Timon*, a satirical poem, which appeared early in January 1846,[56] and the subsequent comments and rejoinders in the periodicals gave Tennyson considerable notoriety. A chapter in William Howitt's *Homes and Haunts of the Most Eminent British Poets*, published in December 1846,[57] George Gilfillan's critique in *Tait's* for April 1847,[58] and an article in *Hogg's Weekly Instructor* on December 25, 1847, continued to keep Tennyson before the public until the very day of publication of his next work. Howitt's opinion of the poet was couched in glowing phrases; Gilfillan was more critical but not unsympathetic; and *Hogg's Instructor* was, in the main, ecstatic.

In these notices from 1844 through 1847 there is specific testimony of the status of Tennyson's reputation at the time. By early 1844 he had made his mark in cultured circles. The *Foreign and Colonial Quarterly Review* felt that he needed no introduction to its subscribers: "To every reader of highly cultivated taste and feeling for poetry it cannot now be requisite that we should do more than express our admiration for the fine genius of Mr. Alfred Tennyson, and our sympathy with his efforts to elevate the tone of modern poetry by that ideal beauty, the divine presence of which we recognize in almost every poem he writes." Horne declared, "It may fairly be assumed that the position of Alfred Tennyson, as a poet of fine genius, is now thoroughly established in the minds of all sincere and qualified lovers of the higher classes of poetry in this country." Furthermore, said Horne, "The name of Alfred Tennyson is pressing slowly, calmly, but surely . . . from the lips of the discerners of poets . . . along the lips of the less informed public, 'to its own place' in the stony house of names." [59]

Tennyson's name was indeed reaching the less-informed classes. In an address to the Liverpool Mechanics' Institution, February 26, 1844, Dickens quoted a stanza from "Lady Clara Vere de Vere" and referred to its author as "a great living poet, who is one of us, and who uses his great gifts, as he holds them in trust, for the general welfare." [60] W. J. Fox devoted a lecture to Tennyson in a series entitled "Living Poets; and Their Services to the Cause of Political Freedom and Human Progress," delivered before the Working Men's Association of Holborn early in 1845.[61]

In July of the same year *Chambers's Edinburgh Journal* began its article on Tennyson by citing his "popularity" as a refutation of the common lament that the age of poetry was past and that men were too much occupied with material pursuits to be interested in poetry. "Suddenly," this writer stated, "it has become the fashion to consider Alfred Tennyson as a great poet, if not as the 'poet of the age.' "

But acquaintance with Tennyson's work was still limited. Only a month after the article in *Chambers's*, the critic in the *British Quarterly Review* felt free to quote liberally from the poems, since he did not suppose that they were very well known to a large portion of his readers. At the end of 1846 Howitt confessed, "We are often surprised to find Tennyson still wholly unread in quarters where poetry is read with much avidity." [62]

Nevertheless, the stature which Tennyson had achieved by 1846 is illustrated by the reaction of the press to Bulwer's attack in *The New Timon*:

> Not mine, not mine, (O Muse forbid!) the boon
> Of borrowed notes, the mock-bird's modish tune,
> The jingling medley of purloin'd conceits,
> Outbabying Wordsworth, and outglittering Keates,
> Where all the airs of patchwork-pastoral chime
> To drowsy ears in Tennysonian rhyme!
>   .   .   .   .   .
> Let School-Miss Alfred vent her chaste delight
> On "darling little rooms so warm and bright!"
> Chaunt, "I'm aweary," in infectious strain,
> And catch her "blue fly singing i' the pane."
> Tho' praised by Critics, tho' adored by Blues,
> Tho' Peel with pudding plump the puling Muse,
> Tho' Theban taste the Saxon's purse controuls,
> And pensions Tennyson, while starves a Knowles,
> Rather, be thou, my poor Pierian Maid,
> Decent at least, in Hayley's weeds array'd,
> Than patch with frippery every tinsel line,
> And flaunt, admired, the Rag Fair of the Nine!
>   (Part II, lines 60–85; omitted in the
>   third and all subsequent editions)

The *Athenaeum* was scornful of the poem as a whole and rallied stoutly to Tennyson's defense. The *Eclectic Review* asserted:

"Little dogs at the foot of Mount Parnassus, as here manifest, will still bark at the moon. This writer before venting his bile at Tennyson or bragging of himself, should first have presented us two poems, we ask no more, equal to 'The Two Voices,' and 'Locksley Hall.' . . . There is just one little difference between his [Tennyson's] poetry and the New Timon, one is for all time, the other for a day." *Lowe's Edinburgh Magazine* expended two pages in Tennyson's behalf, saying that besides his manifold beauties "he has an imagination for feelings and sublimities in human nature which transcend the ken of all the mere muscular poets" such as the author of *The New Timon*. *The Times* called the remarks on Tennyson in Bulwer's satire "ill-natured and unjust." [63]

The reference in *Chambers's Edinburgh Journal* in 1845 to Tennyson as "the poet of the age" brings up an important aspect of the notions about his work then current. The question of Tennyson's claim to this title had already been raised the preceding year in the *Athenaeum*. [64] In the first of the series of letters on "Modern Poetry," "Beta" complained that modern poetry was of the "emasculated school . . . cold and unimpassioned." The poets of the day were not "in relation to their age." Their poetry was not infused with "the circumstances and wrongs of the age," nor was "the progress of our social system" reflected in it. "Sigma" replied that modern poets *were* expressing the thoughts and feelings which impelled the age. He quoted sixteen lines from "Locksley Hall" beginning "For I dipt into the future" through "a cycle of Cathay" and asked, "When did ever poet more eloquently express the hopes and efforts of his age than Tennyson, in these gorgeous and heart-stirring lines?" But "Beta," in a succeeding letter, thought that the poets were not "kindling that generous and sublime enthusiasm of the heart." They wrote for a coterie, not for the masses, when what was required was "something that the generality of men may read — the millions; those engaged in active scenes of life" and in the building of the empire. As for Tennyson, "Sigma's" extract was exceedingly "unhappy." It was "simply 'gorgeous' nonsense, and anything but 'heart-stirring.'" "Beta" said that he was "the last to limit the conquest of science. But pilots of purple twilight, dropping down bales of wool, and the heavens filled with commerce, and nations' airy navies grappling in the central blue, and plunging through thunder-storms, are really only adapted to the audience so loved by the critics — Fit though Few."

This controversy over Tennyson's success as a reflector of his times was symbolic of the conflicting opinions that continued to be voiced about him. By July 1845, when the article in *Chambers's Edinburgh Journal* appeared, the idea that he was "the poet of the age" had apparently become widespread and persistent enough for the critic to be at some pains to refute it. "Hope," he said, is the spirit of the age, and after this quality come "action," "enterprise," "inquiry," "energy," and "material prog-ress." Tennyson's poetry is not fashioned out of these elements. His inspiration comes from the past; his muse is contemplative, not active. "He has a deep knowledge of the human heart, great earnestness of mind, a consummate mastery of the art of versification, and sympathies that are ever on the side of the multitude; but too deeply impressed with the beauty of the classics, and with the exquisite poetical mythology of the Greeks, he has become the poet of scholars, and not, as he might have been . . . the poet of the people." At the end of his article, however, the writer held out hope for Tennyson: "Though not yet the poet of the age, he may perhaps become so."

Late in 1846 Howitt rendered just the opposite verdict. After quoting long sections of "Locksley Hall," he queried, "Who shall say, after this, that Alfred Tennyson wants power? There speaks the man of this moving age. There speaks the spirit baptized into the great spirit of progress." [65] Yet George Gilfillan, analyzing "Locksley Hall" in *Tait's*, April 1847, called it a poem, not of hope, but of despair and bitterness. Of the poet he said with considerable perspicacity, "He is not the poet of hope, or of action, or of passion, but of sentiment, of pensive and prying curiosity, or of simple stationary wonder, in view of the great sights and mysteries of Nature and man. . . . His genius is bold, but is waylaid at almost every step by the timidity and weakness of his temperament." Gilfillan thought him "on the whole . . . less a prophet than an artist."

The derogatory implication of this last pronouncement is one of the curious aspects of the Victorian criticism of Tennyson. It was not enough that he was an artist; he must be a seer as well. The critics almost perversely censured him for not being what they wanted him to be. The opinions that Gilfillan had advanced erupted in a petulant outburst, childlike with inconsolable peevishness, in *Hogg's Weekly Instructor*, December 25, 1847. The greater part of the critique was a eulogy of Tennyson; and it closed with the words, "Long may he live . . . and wider may his fame spread! We are not singular in believing him to be one of the greatest of living poets." But in the concluding paragraphs, the critic said that Tennyson's poetry was not of its age and denounced him for failing to assume the prophet's mantle:

His poems . . . hardly allude to the era of their birth, and they certainly are not coloured with the light of that era. He suffers, and he knows that *we* suffer; but he only developes himself in the spasmodic throes of his doubt, or in the mnemonical glory of his innocence; he does not speak to us in the language of sympathy, and of hope. He is indeed what George Gilfillan calls him — an "artist, but no prophet."

Genius is a rare gift, and it is given to man for a high and holy purpose; it will shine of its own native lustre, and it will illumine all who recognise it; but it depends upon its possessor whether it will be expended in phantasmagoric displays that merely minister to the senses and the educated imagination, or whether it will glide before man like the pillar of fire, leading him on towards a new region of life. The poet has his mission to perform as well as the more prosy portion of his brother men; he has duties devolving on him, and he is responsible for the performance or intromission of those duties. If the impulse of the world is forward, he is the first to feel and know so. . . . He has no excuse, therefore, for expending his precious hours, his glowing thoughts, and his sweet-toned voice, in painting the hues of the peacock's tail. . . . We have had enough of the past; we have had enough of description, and passion, and cold reflection; we now want sympathy, and hope, and direction. Alfred Tennyson was born and lives at a time when men are shouting in the wilderness of the world, "Oh, for a better time!" He might have been the herald of a new era; the prophet-preacher of a "good time coming." He has a right appreciation of human nature; knows man to be what nature says he is. . . . But he wanted courage to become a teacher, and left to far less capable men the direction of the mind of the masses. He rests upon the downy couch of his study, with a pension of two hundred pounds per annum, to assist in preserving his dream-langour; and the images of an elegant but too ethereal fancy flit round his brow. He is content to be styled "Tennyson, the star of the new poetic era;" we had rather that he had chosen, with his fine genius and magic song, to have been "Tennyson, the poet of a new and better moral era." He has capacities for such a position, and he knows that he has; "but, sickening of a vague disease," he is too tremulous to attempt to preach. . . . The Hebrew prophet led the children of Israel from a Goshen of slavery and toil to a better land. . . . He sympathised with his people, and, leaving the land of his exile and seclusion, he came and wept with and encouraged them. Why does not Alfred Tennyson leave the Midian of his retirement to point the people's way to the coming Canaan?

Hogg's Instructor, in emphasizing the poet's mission and social responsibility, reiterated the criticism of 1833. Tennyson had done his best to "ascertain his mission, and work his work," [66] but there was a strong current of feeling that he had not achieved the goal. The critic also gave violent expression to other misgivings about Tennyson harbored by some of his contemporaries. His poetry was not full of "the manly courage, the cheerful faith and hope," the "triumphs over material obstacles, and all the generous struggles with social injustice" [67] that they required. They suspected him of being indolent. Horne in *A New Spirit of the Age* had regretted that Tennyson displayed an "absence of any marked and perceptible design in his poetical faith and purposes." He is "sure of his power, sure of his activity, but not sure of his objects. . . . There appears to be some want of the sanctification of a spiritual consistency; or a liability at intervals to resign himself to the 'Lotos-Eaters.' " [68] *Chambers's Edinburgh Journal* had said, "He must not linger too much upon the memories of the past, neither must he eat of the lotos nor stray in the gardens of the Castle of Indolence, in which we hear he takes more delight than becomes a man so gifted as he is." [69]

THE EFFECT OF THE REVIEWERS, 1843–1847

The fear of critical onslaught that had harassed Tennyson while he was preparing his poems for publication in 1842 continued to plague him two months after his volumes had been launched. On July 13, 1842, Browning wrote of him to Alfred Domett, "I have been with Moxon this morning, who tells me that he is miserably thin-skinned, sensitive to criticism (foolish criticism), wishes to see no notices that contain the least possible depreciatory expressions — poor fellow!" [70] Yet Browning's statement should not be taken as proof that Tennyson isolated himself from much of the criticism of 1842. Whether or not he actually read the reviews, he undoubtedly became acquainted with the tenor of a number of them. He spoke unreservedly of his reaction to Sterling's opinion of the "Morte d'Arthur," of which more will be said later. Through conversations, if by no other means, he must have been familiar with the criticisms of friends and acquaintances, such as Milnes, Leigh Hunt, and Forster. For Spedding's ideas, he need never have glanced at the *Edinburgh Review*, though it is not unlikely that he saw his adviser's article at some stage in its production.

Although Tennyson professed to be no reader of periodicals,[71] it is quite probable that he read them more than he would lead one to believe; for in January 1843 he wrote to Spedding from Mablethorpe reminding him to send the *Athenaeum*, and from the same place to Moxon, "If you have any stray papers which you do not know what to do with, as you once told me, they would be manna in the wilderness to me." [72] Also, Aubrey de Vere has recorded Tennyson's reading of criticisms and his reaction to them in 1845.[73] On April 17 De Vere set down in his diary, "I called on Alfred Tennyson, and found him at first much out of spirits. He cheered up soon, and read me some beautiful Elegies, complaining much of some writer in 'Fraser's Magazine' who had spoken of the 'foolish facility' of Tennysonian poetry." The following day, when De Vere again saw him, Tennyson was still growling about the remark in *Fraser's*, saying that "he would willingly bargain for the reputation of Suckling or Lovelace" and that "he was dreadfully cut up by all he had gone through." Three months later, on July 16, 1845, De Vere wrote that he had found Tennyson "much out of spirits."

He was very angry about a very favourable review of him. Said he could not stand the chattering and conceit of clever men, or the worry

of society, or the meanness of tuft-hunters, or the trouble of poverty, or
the labour of a place, or the preying of the heart on itself. . . . He complained much about growing old, and said he cared nothing for fame,
and that his life was all thrown away for want of a competence and
retirement. Said that no one had been so much harassed by anxiety and
trouble as himself. I told him he wanted occupation, a wife, and orthodox principles, which he took well.

However annoyed the poet may have been by the reviews of
his two volumes, he remained unmoved by the censure accorded
certain poems and passages. Fourteen of the poems that had previously been published received general adverse comment from
at least one reviewer.[74] Sterling in the *Quarterly Review*, for
example, judged the two songs to the owl "not worth doing";
the *London University Magazine* thought "The Sisters" "very
revolting (or else very silly)" and wished that "both the Merman
and the Mermaiden [had been] expunged from the volume."
This time, however, Tennyson had made up his mind. He had
painstakingly selected from his early work what he wanted to
stand, and he would not be shaken from his decision. None of
the fourteen poems was dropped from succeeding editions.

If "The Epic," as the introduction to "Morte d'Arthur" is
designated, be considered a separate poem, thirteen of the new
pieces were criticized as a whole.[75] The *Christian Remembrancer*
thought "Will Waterproof's Lyrical Monologue," "The Vision
of Sin," and "St. Simeon Stylites" "great disfigurements of the
collection." Milnes in the *Westminster* would have been glad
to see "St. Simeon" "altogether out of the volume." The *Cambridge University Magazine* declared that "The Goose" was "absurd" and that the "puerility" of "The Skipping Rope" was
"atrocious." But here again Tennyson was adamant. Only "The
Skipping Rope" was dropped, after nine years, in the edition of
1851. Furthermore, there were very few changes of any kind in
the new poems for later editions.

With regard to the passages singled out for stricture, Tennyson
was equally firm. One of them — the fourth stanza of "Sir Launcelot and Queen Guinevere," where Sterling found a harshness of
recurring *r*'s — was in a new poem. Twenty, including seven in-

stances in which the critics objected either to excisions or to new readings, were in the old poems. All twenty-one passages remained unchanged in later editions.

It must not be supposed, however, because of this evidence, that Tennyson was at last prepared to disregard the reviewers entirely. The influence of criticism on him from 1842 through 1847, while manifesting itself in a different manner, was scarcely less far-reaching than it had been during the previous ten years. Its first effect was to prevent him from writing an Arthurian epic in twelve books. He told William Allingham, in 1867, that Sterling's comments on the "Morte d'Arthur" had stopped him. Knowles and the poet's son corroborate the testimony of Allingham, who reports the poet as saying, "I had it all in my mind, could have done it without any trouble. The King is the complete man, the Knights are the passions." [76]

Sterling in the *Quarterly* had written that there was "less costly jewel-work, with fewer of the broad flashes of passionate imagery" in the "Morte d'Arthur" than in some of Tennyson's other poems and that its "inferiority" was not compensated for "by any stronger human interest." "The miraculous legend of 'Excalibar,'" he declared, "does not come very near to us, and as reproduced by any modern writer must be a mere ingenious exercise of fancy." The criticism was not harsh; but it provides an index of Tennyson's sensitivity. It had touched him on an exposed nerve. Attracted by the elements of poetry inherent in the subject of Arthur and his mystical death, he had originally written the poem without its introduction or conclusion. The excuse "for telling an old-world tale," later added according to FitzGerald,[77] and the concluding apology, "Perhaps some modern touches here and there / Redeem'd it from the charge of nothingness," reveal the poet's apprehension over taking, without some extenuation, a mere poetic journey into fairyland. Whether he had already accepted the dictum that poetry must be a reflection of contemporary life and felt that he must justify his poem on Arthur, or whether he was merely attempting to placate those who subscribed to that view, it is impossible to determine. But his awareness of the theory which Sterling made the criterion of his review is evident. He had already had misgivings about the matter. Sterling's assertion that the legend of Excalibur told by a modern poet could be no more than an ingenious exercise apparently convinced Tennyson that an Arthurian epic could have no hope of critical or even general approval. Perhaps, as well, he was persuaded that it would be a retreat from his poetic duty.

Tennyson's decision in 1842 not to proceed with his epic of Arthur changed the whole pattern of his literary career and may well have affected seriously the position he is to hold in English letters. Knowles, freely admitting the reviewers' hand in Tennyson's development, asserts, "For once, at any rate, the interposing critics did art good service, for they deferred till the experience of life had given him, as it were, many lives, a poem which could not have been produced without wide acquaintanceship with the world and human nature." [78] But modern readers may be more inclined to suspect that the reviewers (especially Sterling) perpetrated a lasting disservice to poetry. Some would willingly exchange the ornate and evil-heavy *Idylls of the King*, a product of the poet's heightened craftsmanship yet growing pessimism, for an earlier version, infused, as it might well have been, with more vigor and enthusiasm.[79] Although Tennyson finally turned to the Arthurian subject, as Allingham says, it was "not as with the first inspiration." [80]

The positive effect of the criticism on *The Princess* seems to be no less remarkable. Seldom has a poem owed so much to contemporary literary doctrines.

The reviews of *Poems*, 1842, had brought out five points concerning poetry in general or Tennyson in particular: (1) modern poetry must idealize and mirror contemporary life and thought; (2) the highest type of poetry must be concerned with human existence; (3) the poet's primary duty is to teach; (4) Tennyson's poetry must display more human sympathy; and (5) Tennyson, if he is to establish his claim to greatness, must write a long poem — a sustained work on a single theme. *The Princess* indicates a response to all these ideas.

The subject of woman's education and of her place in the

scheme of the universe was eminently congenial to Tennyson. He had been concerned with feminine characters in his previous poetry and seems to have entertained an immoderate idea of the sanctity of woman.[81] The originality of the framework and the story of *The Princess* is undeniable. Nevertheless, the extent to which the author was indebted to his age in the selection and treatment of his topic must not be underestimated.

It is just possible that he owed the genesis of *The Princess* to the review of *Poems, Chiefly Lyrical* in the *Westminster Review* of January 1831. The critic, probably Fox, after quoting "The Burial of Love" had said:

Had we space we should discuss this topic. It is of incalculable importance to society. Upon what love is, depends what woman is, and upon what woman is, depends what the world is, both in the present and in the future. There is not a greater moral necessity in England than that of a reformation in female education. The boy is a son; the youth is a lover; and the man who thinks lightly of the elevation of character and the extension of happiness which woman's influence is capable of producing, and ought to be directed to the production of, in society, is neither the wisest of philosophers nor the best of patriots. How long will it be before we shall have read to better purpose the eloquent lessons, and the yet more eloquent history, of that gifted and glorious being, Mary Wollstonecraft?

The idea for a poem suggested by this paragraph may have lodged in the mind of the poet who had been told by the same critic that he "should have distinct and worthy objects before him, and consecrate himself to their promotion," should "excite in a good cause the sustained enthusiasm that is sure to conquer." There is reason to suspect the influence of this reviewer, for Tennyson seems to have commenced the poem in the eighteen thirties. A preliminary version of part I of *The Princess*, entitled "The New University," is extant in a mutilated notebook which Sir Charles Tennyson described in the *Cornhill Magazine,* and which he has since permitted me to examine. In the same notebook there is a variant draft of the first thirty lines of "The Gardener's Daughter," which was begun at Cambridge and probably reached a nearly final state by the middle of 1833. Recalling Hallam Tennyson's statement that the poet talked over the plan of *The Princess* with his wife-to-be in 1839, Sir Charles concludes that "Tennyson began work on *The Princess* certainly not later than 1839 — eight years before publication — and it may be several years earlier." [82]

As the *Westminster* indicated, the opening salvo in the campaign for the legal, social, and educational emancipation of women had been fired by Mary Wollstonecraft in her *Vindication of the Rights of Woman*, first published in 1792. As early as 1810, Sydney Smith in the *Edinburgh Review* had advocated the betterment of women's education.[83] From the very year of its foundation, the *Westminster* had supported the women's cause; and while under Fox's direction, the *Monthly Repository* had been outspoken in a feminist crusade.[84] In an article "On the Condition of Women in England," April 1833, William Bridges Adams declared in italics, *"Women must be regarded and treated as the equals of men, in order to work the improvement of man himself."* [85] By 1844 the number of books and articles on the position of women was steadily increasing.

It has been suggested by both Lounsbury and S. E. Dawson that Tennyson, in his choice of a theme for *The Princess,* was in advance of his age and did not reflect a contemporary interest.[86] Dawson says, "It was only after many years that . . . [the surface thought of England] became conscious of anything being wrong in the position of women." But in March 1844 the *Athenaeum* opened a review of Mrs. Hugo Reid's *A Plea for Woman* with these words: "It is no unimportant sign of the times and of the tendencies of opinion, when books multiply on one particular subject. We have counted on 'our library table,' within a short period, not less than sixteen works having reference, in some direct form, to the present condition of woman — her 'mission,' her 'influence,' her power to 'regenerate society,' her rights, claims, duties, vocation, education, and so forth." The *Athenaeum* gave Mrs. Reid's *Plea* two detailed and sympathetic notices.[87] The second was devoted entirely to her chapter on the education of women. Although the opening of the women's colleges at Oxford and Cambridge and the suffragette movement may have been years in the future, Tennyson was not ahead of his age. He read the signs of the times, laid aside the Arthuriad which he was ready to write, and in the spring of 1845 took up in earnest the idea that had been in his mind for years.[88]

It appears, then, that Tennyson must have conceived of himself as fulfilling in *The Princess* one of the urgent demands of his critics. He was grappling with a major problem of the age and reflecting the various opinions of his contemporaries on women. There could be no question but that *The Princess* was concerned with modern life and was forged "in the crucible of the era." [89] The story began and ended in a modern setting, but this time the introduction and conclusion were no mere excuses for an excursion into fantasy: the fanciful element had a direct bearing on the question raised by present-day characters in the introduction. By digressing into his favorite age of chivalry, the poet was not escaping from the actual world but was bringing home to that world what was of immediate concern to it. The land of make-believe to which he turned afforded scope for poetical expression. He could idealize real life and at the same time achieve a practical end.[90] Here seemed to be the opportunity for combining the real and the ideal as the medieval artists had done. Perhaps the mock-heroic treatment owed something to Leigh Hunt, who had said of the "Morte d'Arthur" in the *Church of England Quarterly Review* in 1842, "It treats the modes and feelings of one generation in the style of another, always a fatal thing, unless it be reconciled with something of self-banter in the course of the poem itself, or the mixture of light with grave. . . . The impossibility of a thorough earnestness must, somehow or other, be self-acknowledged."

Having used the old-world trappings to beguile the fancy and as a camouflage for didacticism, the poet could finally unfold the message of his tale. In *The Princess* he assumed the role of teacher concerning the highest relationships of life. In painting the proper function of woman and man, of wife and husband, and in showing the place of children as a cohesive and refining force in human existence, he was dealing with subjects both immediate and timeless in their significance. Through these same subjects he could touch the deepest wellsprings of human sympathy and emotions.

The Princess, moreover, distinctly appears to be Tennyson's answer to the pressure of the reviewers for a poem of sufficient length and complexity to give conclusive proof of his powers.[91] Concerning his decision to publish in 1842, he is quoted as saying, "I felt certain of one point then: . . . if I meant to make any mark at all, it must be by shortness, for the men before me had been so diffuse, and most of the big things except 'King Arthur' had been done." [92] Yet in 1847 he greeted the public with a poem in seven sections, composed of over three thousand lines of blank verse. The conclusion that Tennyson accepted the gauntlet of the critics seems inescapable.

Since the poet appears to have taken every measure to accomplish all that the reviewers expected of him, it is not surprising to find it recorded by Mrs. Browning that his hope for the success of *The Princess* "grew to the height of his ambition." [93]

ADVANCING REPUTATION:
THE PRINCESS

THE RECEPTION OF THE PRINCESS

For some time before the appearance of *The Princess,*
gossip about Tennyson's new poem was current in literary circles.[1]
To the poet's annoyance a rumor of its impending publication
leaked into an Edinburgh newspaper several months before he
had determined to trust it to the public.[2] By the summer of 1847,
if not earlier in that year, *The Princess* was already in print, and
Tennyson was correcting proofs. But as he had done in the past,
he wavered when he approached the final step; and he wrote to
Moxon, "I have not at all settled whether I shall publish them
[the proofs] now or in the Autumn." [3] The autumn came and
went, and still the poet postponed the decision. Finally, realizing
the necessity for action if the Christmas trade was not to be missed,
he informed the publisher in an undated letter from Mablethorpe, "I am putting the last touches to the 'Princess.' I trust
there will still be time when I come up to get the book out by
Christmas." [4] Moxon did his best. On December 14 he inserted
advertisements in the newspapers that *The Princess* would be
ready "in a few days." The poem was published on Saturday,
December 25.[5] By the narrowest margin it had earned the clas-
sification of a "Christmas book"; but through its author's indecision, it had lost the gift sales that it might have had. With the
long Christmas week end, the book could have sold little until
the following week.

Meanwhile, the anticipation of a literary event of some proportions titillated the reading public. A number of the reviews bear
witness to the eagerness with which the poem had been awaited.[6]
Tennyson's adherents confidently believed that it would be of
a great and noble nature, the fulfillment of the poetic destiny
toward which he had been progressing for seventeen years. *The*

Princess was not precisely what they had expected. Many were taken by surprise, and not a few were disappointed.[7] Nevertheless, the poem was not greeted by the press with "almost universal disparagement," as Lounsbury maintains and reiterates with fulminations against the "crass lack of appreciation" of the early reviews and the "inanity" and "twaddle" that passed for criticism.[8]

The critical response to *The Princess* was extensive and almost immediate. By the end of January twelve daily or weekly journals had noticed it.

First in the field was the *Athenaeum* on January 1, 1848, with an article by the dramatic poet, J. Westland Marston,[9] who rendered an adverse judgment upon the poem as a whole. His opening sentence set the keynote of the review: "There is so much to admire in this volume that we cannot wish it unwritten, — but so much also to censure that, while we could recognize the whole if tendered as a pledge of genius, we cannot accept it as a due consummation of that faculty." In spite of the admission that the poem contained "pictorial beauty and a delicate apprehension of motive and feeling to which our current poetry can furnish few parallels," the critic's final verdict was, "Lecture rooms and chivalric lists, modern pedantry and ancient romance, are antagonisms which no art can reconcile. With the power which Mr. Tennyson has here evinced for the familiar and the ideal regarded separately, it is much to be deplored that by their unskilful combination he has produced simply — the grotesque."

Four days later, on January 5, the *Guardian*,[10] a conservative weekly launched in 1846 with Gladstone among its founders, honored *The Princess* with the first and longest review in the literary section. "Exquisite, indeed; and destined surely never to be forgotten" were the first words of this appreciative notice. Although the lighter and burlesque part of the poem made the greatest appeal to the reviewer, who confessed to a feeling that there was a general falling off in interest and power after page 112, he called Tennyson "*a poet*" and wrote that to the "ominous supposition" that poetry was becoming extinct "the name of Tennyson, and the poem which lies before us, is a sufficient answer. Its fresh glowing descriptions — its entirely novel imagery

— its strength of language, classic diction, and graphic power —
instinct as it nevertheless is, in parts, with sentiments which
clearly mark the poet's age and country; these excellencies in
Mr. Tennyson's new work make one feel that poetry belongs to
all times alike; is the universal language of mankind."

On January 8 a critic in the *Sun*,[11] the evening daily that
had previously noticed the *Poems* of 1842, eulogized Tennyson
throughout three and a half columns. The publication of *The
Princess*, he said, proved that the poet had not been idle. Jeer
as the author of *The New Timon* might, Tennyson's new work
would delight posterity as well as the present generation; and,
added to his previous poems, it amply justified the pension
granted by Peel. The new poem was not a satire on women but
"a nobler eulogium upon the sex than any yet written even by
Alfred Tennyson himself. The main purpose of 'the medley' is
to demonstrate the harmonious diversities of the scheme of Prov-
idence, to reveal the natural concord produced by the very dis-
similarities of the two sexes, and to prove that as each of them
has its particular duties and capacities, so should these duties be
fulfilled, and those capacities cultivated by each exclusively." Of
the passage in which the Princess kisses the wounded Prince, the
reviewer said, "This . . . would alone be sufficient to stamp the
volume with the signet of true poetry. It is delicate, glowing,
natural, eloquent, and impassioned. It is worthy of Tennyson."

Also on January 8, three weeklies — the *Spectator*, the *Examiner*, and *Howitt's Journal* — printed reviews of *The Princess*.
The *Spectator*, one of the few periodicals to view the poem with
derision, said, "Mr. Tennyson has here engrafted the weaknesses
and affectations of the Cockney school upon the worst peculiarities of his own style; he has chosen a subject which is narrow,
uninteresting, unnatural, and absurd, not to say offensive . . .
while . . . the merest mechanics of great verse-making are frequently disregarded."

The *Examiner* and *Howitt's Journal*, however, compensated
for the *Spectator*'s abuse. The critic in the *Examiner*, presumably
John Forster, asked and answered in the affirmative the question
whether the new poem evinced an advance in Tennyson's

powers. "Thought, feeling, and expression," he maintained, "are balanced with happier and more finished results. . . . We will not say that the poem is not irregular, even clumsy, in its structure; but it is built of gold." The reviewer for *Howitt's Journal,* probably William Howitt,[12] asserted that Tennyson was "one of the few who have succeeded in a fresh generation to the purely poetic power" of the "great poetic brotherhood" of the earlier part of the century. Some readers might not enjoy the new volume so much as his former ones because it contained only one long poem in blank verse. "Some therefore, will miss the usual variety, others still more the rich musical cadences of his lyrics." Nevertheless, "the poem is one of the most original and beautiful that Tennyson has yet produced" and is evidence that he is a "poet of progress," who takes a "deep interest" in the affairs of the day. "He studies the spirit of the time, and he works in it." He handles the problem of women's rights with "perfect instinct, true to nature and common sense," and "gives . . . the true philosophy of the question, clear, simple, strong, and irrefragible [*sic*]."

The *Atlas,* on January 15, came to much the same conclusion as the *Athenaeum*: "There are charming passages in this poem — passages which Mr. Tennyson has rarely excelled; but, as a whole, we must repeat that the *Princess* is unequal and incongruous." A week later the *Britannia,*[13] a conservative weekly, delivered a brusque opinion of the poem in a column of short notices in smaller type than the proper reviews. "This is the weakest of all Mr. Tennyson's productions," the writer said. "Such an abominable collection of far-fetched prettiness was surely never heaped together before." But on the same day the *Morning Post,* which had given Tennyson such unqualified applause in 1842, rallied to his support, declaring, "In spite of the artful depreciations which a weekly contemporary,[14] of small claims and great pretensions to literature has cast upon him, we must pronounce Alfred Tennyson to be a poet, and even no ordinary poet." In this critic's opinion, "a great philosophical thesis is discussed . . . and satisfactorily settled" as the poem proceeds. "The merits of the work," he said, "are chiefly these: — A sonorous march of words, of which not one is superfluous, for the style is concise and pithy to an extraordinary degree; a great fervour of thought, and an energy which, in the descriptions, rings again upon the ear; and now and then such an originality of conception and boldness of illustration as we might search long in the pages of the greatest poets before we should find anything to surpass."

During the month of January the provincial newspapers also began to take notice of *The Princess*. On January 6 the *Dumfries-shire and Galloway Herald* reprinted the greater part of the review from the *Athenaeum*. Two days later the *Manchester Examiner* filled nearly two columns with remarks on Tennyson and quotations from his new poem. The reviewer became eloquent over the beauty and power of "Locksley Hall," "The Lotos-Eaters," "The Vision of Sin," "Morte d'Arthur," and several others among the poems of 1842. And as impressed as he was with "Morte d'Arthur," he asserted that it was "pitched, indeed, in a lower key, and altogether in a lighter strain" than *The Princess*. Another favorable review appeared in the *Sheffield Times* on January 29.[15] The critic thought that the lyric, "Come down, O maid, from yonder mountain height," was "perfect, and such as no other writer of the present day could approach." He did not doubt that *The Princess*, medley though it was, would "be highly prized by all lovers of the Beautiful in poetry."

To sum up the criticism of the first month, it appears that *The Princess* was not received by the early reviewers without appreciation. The *Spectator* and the *Britannia* were disparaging. The *Athenaeum* and the *Atlas*, while perceiving merit in the poem, found its general effect unsatisfactory. But a majority of the first reviews were distinctly favorable.[16] At the distance of a hundred years, it is difficult to assess the relative effect of each of these reviews upon public judgment; but it does not seem that the papers which were hostile to the new work were necessarily those with the most influence, as Lounsbury maintains.[17] His criterion of circulation is a point to be taken into consideration, but with some people the word of one critic took precedence over that of another. Mrs. Browning, for instance, attached the most weight to the articles in the *Examiner*, with those in the *Atlas* a close second, while William Allingham, writing to Ralph Waldo Emerson in December 1847, classed the *Athenaeum* as the "most influential" journal in literary matters.[18] From the point of view of circulation alone, the *Athenaeum* probably reached the largest number of readers,[19] and the *Dumfries-shire and Galloway Herald* extended the knowledge of Marston's opinions on *The Princess*. Yet by the same token, in 1845 the *Examiner* had a circulation of 6,000 and the *Sun* 4,000 to the *Spectator's* 3,500. The circulation of the *Morning Post* was below 3,000, but it was read "exclusively by the upper classes." [20] While the influence of the provincial papers did not reach far beyond the local community, the notices published in them are indicative of Tennyson's widening fame.

Lounsbury believes that, besides general disapproval, the early criticism was characterized by a "complete misunderstanding of the nature and intention of the poem." [21] But again he seems to be mistaken. The reviewers who objected to the incongruousness of *The Princess* showed their realization that the poem grew out of the situation described in the Prologue.[22] Seven of eleven notices pointed out the moral of the poem; [23] and the *Sun*, the *Examiner*, and the *Morning Post* expatiated upon the poet's teachings.

Succeeding statements in Lounsbury's version of the reception of *The Princess* also require scrutiny. The failure, he says, of the first reviewers to understand the purpose of the work was rectified by later critics. "The general approbation the poem met soon showed itself in the changed tone of the critical press," and there was a steady progression of more favorable printed criticism, culminating in Aubrey de Vere's review in the *Edinburgh,* October 1849, and Charles Kingsley's in *Fraser's Magazine,* September 1850. "It is very noticeable in the case of this publication [*The Princess*]," Lounsbury says, "that the longer the reviews of it were delayed, the more cordial and appreciative they were." [24] This is an oversimplified, if not an entirely inaccurate, representation of the criticism of *The Princess*. To be more exact, some of the highest praise that the poem received was printed in the early weeks after its publication. Within six weeks, more than twice as many approving reviews as derogatory ones had been printed.[25] Furthermore, the current of approbation did not flow in a steadily rising stream. Censure and commendation continued to be mingled during the months that followed; and in August *Tait's Edinburgh Magazine,* a former partisan of Tennyson's, spoke out sharply against the poem. Actually, some of the most disparaging criticism that the poet had encountered since 1833 appeared in *Blackwood's* and the *Christian Remembrancer,* April 1849.

Four appreciative articles were published in the monthly journals for February 1848. That hardy perennial, the *Gentlemen's Magazine,* observed, in the first article of the issue, that it could ill afford to overlook any production of Tennyson's, whose name "is so justly distinguished, and so united in our minds with the idea of poetical excellence." The reviewer voiced some objections to the poem but assured the reader, "There is no imperfection that is injurious to the effect of the whole." Besides the "loveliest scenery," the work was said to contain "much also of deeper thought and higher sentiment and reflective wisdom . . . embodied in simple and emphatic words, adorned with imagery, and moulded in the finest harmony of metre." The *Metropolitan* declared in italics that it was not among those who were disappointed with *The Princess.* Although largely content to reproduce the story with extensive extracts, the reviewer asserted at the end of his quotations, "We have read the poem through three times attentively, each time with increased pleasure and admiration, and will only add our wish that each succeeding year be ushered in with as sweet a poet gift." The critic in *Lowe's Edinburgh Magazine,* who discussed *Poems,* 1842, as well as *The Princess,* remarked at some length upon Tennyson's "powerful interest in, and insight into, the character of the present age" and upon the value of his political philosophy. After telling the story of *The Princess* in detail by means of long extracts, the writer of the article affirmed his "conviction, that the prospects of the future, as they are discoverable in their causes, working in the multiform present, are the groundwork and motive of the entire work." He cautioned his readers not to be misled in their judgment of the poem by surface beauties and seeming trivialities but to search deeply for the "occult meanings." [26] The *Christian Reformer,* a Unitarian organ,[27] in the briefest notice of the four magazines, was very amicable toward Tennyson and called *The Princess* the "most welcome and most worthy of the Christmas books."

The *Quarterly Review* for March, in an article previously ascribed to Sara Coleridge but tentatively identified by Mr. M. F. Brightfield as by Lockhart,[28] adopted a careful and judicious air with regard to *The Princess.* The first part of the critique was devoted to a history of Tennyson's career and to assessing certain elements in his poetry.[29] The critic advanced a number of strictures against the new work but attempted to sum up its beauties as well. Its "characteristic merits," he decided, were "that it unites abundance of lovely imagery with dramatic power." While the poem must be a disappointment to those who "expected to see his [Tennyson's] poetry condense into the philosophic or expand into the epic style . . . it is such a work as none but a man of genius would have wrought, and worth far more than most philosophies and religions in verse with which the world has been edified."

In April the *Eclectic Review,* one of the most important vehicles of Dissenting opinion,[30] quoted extensively from *The Princess,* saying that it is "characterized by much fine poetry; but that it is also (and this is his [Tennyson's] prevailing fault) distinguished by want of unity of design and by inequality of construction." The distinctive feature of this review, however, was its reference to *The Princess* as a "sign of the times." In this respect, the reviewer said, "the work before us offers much for reflection. . . . here we have one of our most delightful poets, though commencing half in *badinage,* warming as he dwells upon *her* [Mary Wollstonecraft's] cherished subject, 'the rights of women,' and pleading those rights with a force and an eloquence which the world has scarcely witnessed before."

Also in April *Sharpe's London Magazine* [31] took a temperate view of the poem: "Like every poem bearing the stamp of originality, 'The Princess' has been violently abused, and as violently praised. . . . Truth, as usual, lies between the two extremes. The full measure of Mr. Tennyson's fame has yet to be made up; but

'The Princess' is not the less a charming and most imaginative poem."

In the *North British Review* for May, Coventry Patmore [32] displayed his admiration for Tennyson in a tedious attempt to read an allegory of science and the modern intellect into *The Princess*. But on May 22 the *Dublin Evening Herald* asserted that, while Tennyson was gradually emancipating himself from his original flaws of style, *The Princess*, as a whole, lacked "rounded symmetry of form." "So much of grave and gay, of serious and sarcastic, of mystic and natural, of philosophic and childish, of paradox and puzzle, enter into the development of the plot," the reviewer wrote, "that . . . the grand effect is missed of; the 'medley' becomes a labyrinth, and we are glad to escape at last with the conviction that many of the windings led nowhere, and that we have made very slight progress at the expense of much (certainly delightful) wandering."

A detailed critique of the poem in the High Church *English Review* [33] for June was enthusiastic. "Pictorial beauty, sweet fancy, aristocratic grace, true poetic feeling, and most apt and happy language," said the critic, "are the main characteristics of this very charming poem, and are amply sufficient to secure its earthly immortality." Faults there were; but "with all its drawbacks, 'the Princess' is one of the most charming poems, take it for all in all, in our own or any language, and should be recognized as such."

This article in the *English Review* was notable in another respect. Most of the previous reviewers, though aware of the didactic element in *The Princess*, had attempted to evaluate it chiefly by artistic standards and had ignored Tennyson's effort to charge the poem with that quality which previously had been thought lacking in his poetry. The *English Review* placed the moral aspect of criticism before any other test. It first sought out "that distinctive purpose which is to be found in most works of the day that exhibit any claim to superiority, and which is certainly not absent from Tennyson's 'Princess.' " "We look accordingly," the reviewer declared, "in a new poem from such a man as Tennyson, for something more instructive than 'the Corsair,' more philosophical than 'the Lay of the Last Minstrel;' we look for the revelation or exposition of some one important truth; and we have found it." After setting forth the argument of *The Princess* and discussing the various attitudes toward women expressed in the poem, the critic passed on to purely literary considerations.

But the sunshine of the *English Review* did not protect the poem from unseasonable blasts in August. The critic in the *Literary Gazette,* probably Jerdan again, assured his readers that the delay in noticing *The Princess* had been occasioned by indecision over what to say. "Who will question," he cried, "the true poetry of this production, or who deny the imperfections, (mostly of affectation, though some of tastelessness) which obscure it?" Although he proposed to put forth the poem's defects and beauties impartially, leaving the final judgment to the reader, he weighted the scales with considerable animosity. The reviewer for *Tait's Edinburgh Magazine* made no pretense about his dissatisfaction. He confessed to an omission in not having reviewed *The Princess* sooner, but defended himself with the comment, "If we forgot Alfred Tennyson, it was only when he had forgot himself." The poem was nothing more than "prattle," and he would not have believed the work by Tennyson if the title page of a reputable publisher had not declared it to be so. This reviewer was almost alone in ascribing to Tennyson the chief object of satirizing "learned ladies, who want to be legislators, and the equals of man at the polling-booth and in the legislative chambers." He felt that the poet was opposing an "invincible" force which ought to grow in power amid general rejoicing, "for it gauges the rising of Christian civilization."

An article in *The Times,* October 12, 1848, possibly by Manley Hopkins,[34] father of the poet Gerard, was a milestone in Tennyson's literary career and is symptomatic of his growing importance. By discussing his earlier poems as well as *The Princess, The Times* served notice to its thirty thousand readers [35] that Tennyson was a poet who could not be ignored. The opening lines may have amused some but can hardly have pleased the object of their levity:

Stand forth, Alfred Tennyson. Rise from thy sofa; lay aside thy cigar;

come and give account of thy misdoings against the majesty of poetry. Dost thou plead guilty to three volumes of musical mysticism of which thou art indicted; or, dost thou cry "not guilty," set up a justification, and throw thyself upon the country? Well, be it so. Thou shalt be tried by thy peers.

The critic immediately dropped the mock judicial air, however, and showed understanding and appreciation of the poet's work. Tennyson was described as a descendant in poetical tradition of Shelley and Keats, but one whose poetry was not a mere combination of their attributes. Indeed, Tennyson was already the leader of his own school, "and Browning and Miss Barrett have sat at his lecture." He and his followers were distinguished from the preceding generation of poets in that "they look forwards, not back. . . . Tennyson chooses to float on and with the age. He wishes to move with the mass of his fellow-beings. . . . He finds the present good, and the future likely to be better." Traits of his poetry were said to be a "suggestiveness," a "sensuous appeal to mind through euphonious metres and rhythm," and a "prodigality of images and pictures." His imagery sometimes became overcrowded in its profusion; and half-formed allusions were too often hurriedly left behind to cloud the reader's perception. Passing on to individual poems, the critic pronounced "The Two Voices" Tennyson's "best poem; . . . he supports himself long on the wing, and comes home well and truly to his ultimate destination. . . . There is real poetry in *Œnone*, and sweet wild music in the *Lady of Shalott*." Surrendering himself completely to the melody and word-painting of the latter poem, the reviewer wrote, "It is pure, sensuous poetry. We forbear to ask too closely what hidden meanings dwell in its misty dreaminess. We would not for the world break our toy to discover its concealed music." [36] He concluded regretfully that *The Princess* did not fulfill the expectation raised by the previous poems. "The faults remain unchanged, the affected singularities of style are more numerous than before. Pity that where feeling and fancy and the poetic temperament are so strongly manifested, an author's care for his fame should be too slight to use those gifts with discretion — to set his jewels in consistent workmanship."

This survey in *The Times* of Tennyson's poetry as a whole was followed in April 1849 by two articles of a similar nature in *Blackwood's* and the *Christian Remembrancer.* Prior to the spring of 1849, there had been several indications of Tennyson's literary standing. On January 8, 1848, two weeks after the publication of *The Princess,* the *Sun* asserted that the fame won by *Poems, 1842,*

is pretty well known by this time among the homesteads of England, among the green pasturages of Ireland, by the tarns of Scotland, and, if actual experience can be believed, in the backwoods of Canada and the United States. A volume of Tennyson looks like any one of your old classics — well thumbed and reverently dog's-eared. His melodies are loved, not merely by sentimental young ladies; they are the intellectual food of strong men and learned. . . . People of all ages, of both sexes, and of the most extreme opinions, are numbered amongst those who have imbibed a natural and unaffected relish for our poet.

In March 1848, after Alfred Dixon Toovey had accused Tennyson of childishness and absurdity in his *Biographical and Critical Notices of the British Poets of the Present Century,*[37] the *Weekly Chronicle,* a Whig paper with an excellent reputation for its criticism, thought a quotation from these remarks sufficient to prove to its readers "what a dunce Mr. Toovey must be." [38] The *Quarterly Review,* in the same month, spoke of Tennyson's *"popularity"* and analyzed with some perspicacity the elements that had contributed to it: his songs "arrest the attention of those who cannot go far in a pure poetic atmosphere; his ballads and idylls delight numbers who wish but to find in any poem they take in hand a moral lesson or a tale of the heart, in an ornate and compendious form; his gayer movement and lighter touch please many who would be scared by the grave impetuosity of Shelley." But in addition to these grounds for popular acclaim, Tennyson had an "imagination which the true lovers of poetry can alone fully feel, and a command of diction finer and deeper than is needed for any but their satisfaction." With *The Times* finally feeling called upon to notice Tennyson, what was the considered verdict of *Blackwood's* and the *Christian Remembrancer?*

The author of the article in *Blackwood's* was William Henry

Smith, a minor poet, philosopher, and writer, who was a copious contributor to this journal.[39] He was a friend of Mill, Maurice, and Sterling and had assisted the latter two with the *Athenaeum* during their brief editorship. According to Smith, "Poetry of the very highest order, coupled with much affectation, much defective writing, many wilful blunders, renders Alfred Tennyson a very worthy and a very difficult subject for the critic. The extreme diversity and unequal merit of his compositions, make it a very perplexing business to form any general estimate of his writings." The critic believed that the poet had begun his authorship under the influence of "*a bad school of taste. . . .* Above this influence he often rises, but he has never quite liberated himself from it." And now Smith began to speak out in terms which Lounsbury would have us believe the critics had long since abandoned, constrained by fear of what the public would tolerate.[40] It was a pity that "Claribel," a "mere monotonous chant," had been allowed to remain the opening piece of the first volume of *Poems.* "And why were these two absurd songs *To the Owl* still preserved?" The "Ode to Memory" "craves to be extinguished" and "ought in charity to be forgotten. An utter failure throughout. . . . we do not think there is a single redeeming line in the whole of it." He called "A Song" ("A spirit haunts the year's last hours") "an odious piece of pedantry"; "The Poet" and "The Poet's Mind," "fulsome, self-adulatory nonsense." Furthermore, "They must be far gone in dilettantism who can make an especial favourite of such a caprice as . . . ["The Lady of Shalott"] — with its intolerable vagueness, and its irritating repetition, every verse ending with the 'Lady of Sha*lott*,' which must always rhyme with 'Came*lot*.'" The refrains in "The Sisters," "Oriana," and "Mariana" were a "species of odious iteration." Like Christopher North seventeen years earlier, Smith turned in the latter part of his review to the poems that he admired. "The Lotos-Eaters" was an "especial favourite" from which he quoted liberally. A companion to it, in a "noble strain," was "Ulysses," most of which he extracted. He also approved of "St. Simeon," "Locksley Hall," and "Lady Clara Vere de Vere." "The Talking Oak" and "The Day-Dream" were "both admirable." "Will Waterproof" and

"Walking to the Mail" he selected as good examples of Tennyson's powers in the comic strain.

When Smith reached *The Princess*, he commented only upon its beauties, quoting "no passages from this poem, such as we might deem faulty, or vapid, or in any way transgressing the rules of good taste." He added, however, "It does not follow that it would have been impossible to do so." The poem in his estimation was not of so high an order as might be aspired to, but he doubted if Tennyson would ever do anything higher. Even so, he thought that Tennyson had added his name "to that list of English poets, who have succeeded in establishing a permanent reputation on a few brief performances — a list which includes such names as Gray, and Collins, and Coleridge."

The critic for the *Christian Remembrancer*, identified by Tennyson as "Mr. Chretien," no doubt Charles Peter Chretien,[41] although not so harsh as Smith on individual poems, was less charitable in his general estimate. *The Princess* exhibited no metamorphosis in the poet's methods. He still wandered "through the enchanted ground," sleeping "in every cool grot and pleasant arbour," rejoicing "in dreams." His outstanding quality was his excellent diction. "Verily, Mr. Tennyson is a sweet singer as a poet need wish to be. But a poet should wish to be something more." No warrior in a good cause, "He is rather the minstrel, lingering, and trifling, and harping, at the castle gate." He had a remarkable "skill in introducing a multitude of details into his picture without breaking its repose," Chretien observed, but such a "microscopic delineation is, to a great extent, artificial; and all artificial beauty slides easily into defect." As a result of this method of detached description, the poet generally represented nature as calm; neither could he portray human passion skillfully. Because of his delight in the static, he went frequently to the past and the classical for inspiration as a source of illustration. He cast a soft, delicate light over everything he painted, whether the effect was appropriate or not. In some respects his concern with his age and particularly with modern science was happy, but in a sense it was evidence of the extent to which he was circumscribed by the present. Aware of "his privilege to aspire to the rank of a prophet," he delighted in a "kind of vague anticipation. . . . He looks forward to a higher state of society, in which some general good shall result from the conflicts of base and noble, of true and false, of knowledge and opinion. The poet is to have no small share in the work. But how he is to forward it, appears not. . . . He is not far enough above the common mind to see into futurity."

Sorrowfully, Chretien was compelled to register complete disillusionment: "It is not then as a poet of our common humanity that Mr. Tennyson can hope for lasting fame. . . . He has raised no structure of mighty verse on the platform of philosophy. . . . His poems are not pregnant with sweet wisdom, or studded with the sententiousness of a refined morality. . . . No one could call him a Christian poet. . . . We do not say that his poems are never touched even by a reflected beam of the sun of religion. . . . But this does not amount to much." After such a condemnation there could be but one conclusion: "Mr. Tennyson is not a great poet. We can scarcely any longer hope that he will achieve greatness. Into that highest circle of the sons of song, who are wise beyond their generation, and belong only accidentally to the age in which they live, and compete for no honours which are not wider than their own time and country, he cannot ask to enter." As to his eminence, however, there could be no doubt. Beyond question, "he is the poet of the day; nor has any rival yet appeared who seems likely to dethrone him. . . . He is far enough above mediocrity for the full vindication of his dignity. He may sit in his place for many years. We will pay him due homage, with one reservation. If he is king, it is not in a generation of giants."

While Smith in *Blackwood's* had foreseen an enduring, if small, reputation for Tennyson, Chretien thought it purely ephemeral, gloomily predicting that his fame would have evaporated in a hundred years. Both men had practically lost faith in Tennyson's ability to fulfill the promise which had been seen in him. Both represent an independence of judgment which ignored public opinion and attempted to look beyond the poet's popularity.

With Aubrey de Vere's article in 1849 and Charles Kingsley's in 1850, the critical pendulum swung back to laudation of *The*

Princess. But both these young men were friends and personal admirers of Tennyson, and it is surely erroneous to attribute their panegyrics to the pressure of popular approval. De Vere, himself a poet, had engaged in many discussions of poetic theory with the future laureate and had listened to lines from *The Princess* during its earliest stage of composition. His review in the *Edinburgh,* October 1849, bears much the same relation to *The Princess* that Spedding's had to the *Poems* of 1842.[42] Knowing the poet's intention, he made the strongest case possible for the purpose and execution of the poem; and Tennyson rewarded him for his efforts with a letter of appreciation.[43]

According to De Vere, *The Princess,* in being a medley, resembled the age — an age whose society blended tradition and innovation, whose politics displayed the struggle of opposing principles of government, whose cities boasted "a Gothic church close to a Byzantine fane or an Italian basilica." In structure the poem corresponded to the plan set forth in the Prologue. While a fantasy in appearance, like *A Midsummer-Night's Dream* and *The Tempest,* its chief concern was the contemplation of human life:

> The abundant grace and descriptive beauty which meet the superficial eye, constitute but its external charm. Studying his work with that attention which the labour of a true poet should always command, we soon discover that . . . it is eminently human in sentiment, and that the human gradually rises higher and higher into the moral. The poem plays with the arbitrary and the theoretical; but it plays with them only to make them their own confutors. Such is the lore we learn from human life. Our follies are our most effectual instructors. . . .
>
> The deep and rich humanity with which this poem, notwithstanding its fanciful plot, is replete, can hardly be illustrated by quotations.

De Vere was conscious of some slight faults, but they amounted to no more than details; and he passed on to enumerate a succession of Tennyson's excellencies, most of which *The Princess* illustrated. In the first place, Tennyson's "vein of tenderness and pathos" has a "peculiar sweetness." Secondly, the "descriptive power exhibited throughout the whole of 'the Princess' is of the highest order." Thirdly, in his poetry as a whole, the "versatility of his imagination" is impressive. Lastly, as his own individuality has become more pronounced in his later poems, their power has proportionately increased. In addition to these points, De Vere asserted, "The moral range of Mr. Tennyson's poetry, too, is as wide as the imaginative. . . . he is . . . happy in the delineation of those human affections which depend not on instinct or imagination alone, but which, growing out of the heart, are modified by circumstance and association, and constitute the varied texture of social existence." Finally, he found the poet's "intellectual region" no "less ample" than his moral range. "Many of his poems are the embodiment of deep philosophical speculations on the problem of life."

Kingsley's article in *Fraser's Magazine* for September 1850 [44] appeared after the publication of the third edition of *The Princess,* in which a good many textual changes had been made and the intercalary songs had been added. Among other things, Kingsley discussed the question of women's education, mentioned the poem's moral, and pointed out the purpose of the newly added songs. But it is of special interest to note the emphasis which he put upon the portrayal of modern life in *The Princess*:

> Tennyson shows himself more than ever the poet of the day. In it more than ever the old is interpenetrated with the new — the domestic and scientific with the ideal and sentimental. He dares, in every page, to make use of modern words and notions, from which the mingled clumsiness and archaism of his compeers shrinks, as unpoetical. Though, as we just said, his stage is an ideal fairy-land, yet he has reached the ideal by the only true method, — by bringing the Middle age forward to the Present one, and not by ignoring the Present to fall back on a cold and galvanized Mediævalism; and thus, he makes his "Medley" a mirror of the nineteenth century, possessed of its own new art and science, its own new temptations and aspirations, and yet grounded on, and continually striving to reproduce, the forms and experiences of all past time. The idea, too, of *The Princess* is an essentially modern one.

Gerald Massey's series of five papers entitled "Tennyson's Princess" in the *Christian Socialist,* during the autumn of 1851, is the high-water mark of eulogy of the poem. The following two sentences from the September 27 article exemplify his attitude: "The 'Princess' has all the lyrical beauty of Tennyson's former poems, it is as gorgeous in imagery, as sparkling in quaint and playful fancies, while the diapason of its rhythm ranges from the faeriest flutings of elf-land music up to the grand movements of a conqueror's regal march. And above all, it is essentially a song of Progress, timed to the beating pulses of the living Present."

A glance back at the critical fortunes of *The Princess* during a period of almost four years recalls sharp dissent over its merits; but the approval exhibited within the first few weeks after the poem's appearance prevailed. If all the reviews that evidenced any appreciable amount of adverse criticism be grouped with those that clearly saw no virtue in the poem, the favorable articles still outnumber the unfavorable ones.[45] Moreover, several of the critiques entered on the debit side gave the poem considerable credit in certain respects.

This is not to say, however, that the critics were at last satisfied with Tennyson. More than half of those who alluded to the matter did not think that he had advanced. Forster alone declared specifically that he had.[46] De Vere remarked that in his later works Tennyson had increased in power, but he did not explicitly mention *The Princess*.[47] Kingsley only said that "perhaps" the poet rose higher in *The Princess* than in any of his previous poems.[48] Patmore thought the poem Tennyson's "greatest work" but said that, though the poet had gone a long way toward redeeming his reputation, he had not yet done his best.[49] Marston voiced a more representative opinion: "We find in these pages little which denotes advance. . . . No wholesome severity has discarded former puerilities. . . . The only new attribute . . . is a certain facility of incident." [50] Chretien found "his faults and his beauties still the same; an alteration in degree, but not in kind; an improvement, if any, which was not a development." [51] *The Times* even detected a retrogression. The *Spectator* bluntly averred, "*The Princess* will not increase the reputation of Alfred Tennyson, but rather diminish it"; the *Atlas* agreed that the poem would not advance the author's fame. *Sharpe's London Magazine* amusingly expressed the feeling of many: "Listening for the diapason of the oracle, the votaries have assembled round their sacred oak of Dodona, and have heard but the wind musically murmuring among its leaves."

However much some of the reviewers liked *The Princess*, they reiterated a now familiar complaint. Once more, instead of prophesying, Tennyson was merely singing. He had disregarded their advice and had betrayed their trust. Some of the most appreciative critics of *The Princess* were the most vehement in denouncing him for shirking his duty and in calling upon him again to assume his social responsibility. Forster, compelled to admit that *The Princess* was not "great," exclaimed,

> What the poem contains is greater than the poem itself. Why should Mr Tennyson have thrown all this into a *medley*? He had something serious to say — why graft it on burlesque? . . . Eminently, in the manliness of his thoughts, in the largeness of his view, and in his power of clothing the familiar in our human passions and affections "with golden exhalations of the dawn," he is worthy to be the poet of our time. *Why does he not assume his mission?* Why does he discredit it with trifling and with puerilities unworthy of him? . . . In the *Princess* we have more decisive evidence of his powers for a sustained and solid exercise of poetry than has heretofore been given. But it is yet only an omen for the future. Its glorious promise has yet to be fulfilled.[52]

The *Sun* charged the poet thus: "Let Mr. Tennyson reflect that, having 'the gift of poesy,' a strange responsibility devolves upon him; and that his heart being stirred so profoundly with 'the divine *afflatus*,' he has a glorious mission to fulfil — for, to employ his own truthful language . . . he is among those '*Poets whose thoughts enrich the blood of the world.*'" The *Gentleman's Magazine* looked forward to

> creations of a higher kind, where Fancy, instead of reigning alone and supreme in her own enchanting dominion, is content to submit herself to a still greater power, and be a ministering and willing handmaid, happy to adorn and beautify the temple of *living* truth, where are assembled the affections, passions, interests, and actions, in all their changeful and conflicting progress through the social system of the *present* world, which poetry has but to enter, and she may make her last and latest domain the richest she has ever possessed.

Hope was the note struck by other reviewers. The *Atlas* told Tennyson that he had chosen to "misapply his powers" and hoped that he would redeem himself in the future. The *Eclectic* hoped for a poem no less beautiful but more "systematic." *Sharpe's London Magazine* said, "We hope some day to welcome from his pen a work . . . with yet higher reach than he has attempted." *The Times* expressed a "hearty wish that Tennyson may be even now working at his forge to produce a great and permanent work. To disuse his talent is a crime in the possessor of it, and a wrong to the community."

In the light of the criticism of *The Princess,* what then can be said of Tennyson's reputation prior to the publication of *In Memoriam?* In January 1848 it had been asserted that his poems were treasured throughout the United Kingdom and that their fame had spread to the hinterland of the American continent. [53] By 1850 *Poems,* now issued in one volume, had reached the sixth edition and *The Princess* a third.[54] The poet's popularity had become an accepted fact: and in April 1849 the *Christian Remembrancer,* no worshiper at the shrine, declared that he was at the top of the poetical heap. Not only was he supreme in public favor, but he was without a rival. His eminence had become great enough to preclude a serious challenger. Admiration of Tennyson was no longer considered *avant-garde* but was said by the *Westminster Review* in July 1849 to be "strictly orthodox." [55] Still, nearly all critics refused him the title of a great poet. Friend as well as enemy denied it to him; and when Aubrey de Vere attempted to make that claim for him in the *Edinburgh Review,* October 1849, he found it, as Spedding had in 1843, deleted from his copy by the editor. As much as De Vere and others might dilate upon Tennyson's reflection of the age, his high purpose, his human sympathy, and his intellectual and philosophical stature, there was an extensive feeling among the reviewers that he had refused to undertake his appointed task. He had woven a beautiful fabric, but he had abused his commission to fashion a work that could stand beside *Paradise Lost* and Shakespeare's plays. The critics' reaction tended to be like that of a dissatisfied shopper — "It's very nice, but not exactly what I had in mind."

THE EFFECT OF THE REVIEWERS ON *THE PRINCESS*

The final text of *The Princess* appears to have owed a great deal, both to its benefit and to its detriment, to the criticism printed in periodicals before the publication of the third edition.

But once again, it is first necessary to determine Tennyson's knowledge of the reviews in order to establish the extent of their influence.

His son says in the *Memoir* that Aubrey de Vere's article in the *Edinburgh Review* "interested" him.[56] An excerpt from a letter by the poet to William J. Rolfe, printed in Rolfe's single-volume edition of Tennyson's works, shows that he read the review in the *Quarterly*; and a letter to De Vere makes it certain that he saw the critique in the *Christian Remembrancer*.[57]

On April 15, 1848, Mrs. Browning wrote from Florence to Mary Russell Mitford, "You speak of Tennyson's vexation about the reception of the 'Princess.'"[58] There can scarcely be any doubt that the vexation referred to was at the critical reception of *The Princess* rather than over the reaction of the general public or of individual readers whose opinions he might have learned of. The poem seems to have sold well, so that there could have been little reason for annoyance on that score.[59] He was not likely to hear much adverse comment in the circle of admirers among whom he moved. FitzGerald, of course, was the exception; but he wrote on May 5, 1848, that he was "considered a great heretic for abusing" *The Princess*.[60] And Tennyson had prepared himself for FitzGerald's judgment by writing to him soon after publication, "My book is out and I hate it, and so no doubt will you."[61] If the poet was vexed by the reviews at a date early enough for Mrs. Browning to have received Miss Mitford's letter, which had traveled from England to Italy before April 15, the inference is justifiable that he was aware of the notices of *The Princess* in the *Athenaeum,* the *Atlas,* and the *Spectator*; and he may have been stung as well by the remarks in the concluding paragraph of Forster's article in the *Examiner*. In addition, there is the suggestion in an undated letter to De Vere (probably early in 1850) that the poet distinctly wished to see reviews of *The Princess*; for he wrote to his friend, "The review in the *Westminster* was not one of 'The Princess' but of two or three of the old Poems."[62]

A word at the outset concerning the successive editions of *The Princess* is required to make the study of the changes in the text intelligible.[63] As has been previously mentioned, *The Princess* originally appeared on December 25, 1847. The second edition probably came out in January or February 1848. Certainly it had been issued by the end of April. There were a few slight alterations in this edition, and the dedication to Henry Lushington was added. In the third edition, published at the end of January or during the first two weeks of February 1850, the text had undergone extensive revision, and the six rhymed songs, now so familiar, had been inserted between the seven sections of the poem. The chief additions in the fourth edition of late March or early April 1851 were the "weird seizures" of the Prince; and in the fifth edition, published in February 1853, there was a further expansion of the Prologue. With this edition, the poem very nearly reached its final form, though a number of minor changes were made later. It is apparent that the second edition was brought out too early for the poet to have altered the text appreciably and before he could have seen more than the earliest notices. Accordingly, it is largely in the third edition that one must seek for the effects of the reviews. The fourth and fifth editions must also be taken into account; but there is no need to go beyond them.

A tabulation of the passages in *The Princess* singled out by the reviewers for stricture reveals that thirty-five were thus censured. Of these thirty-five, eight, or slightly less than a fourth, were altered in the third edition. A number of the adverse comments on these passages were captious or scarcely valid,[64] and the poet made it abundantly evident that he would not be browbeaten into unnecessary emendations. At the same time, while the percentage of revised readings is not high, the words, phrases, or lines which he did change prove that he could profit from the critics' censure to a significant degree.

The *Quarterly* seems to have been responsible for the omission of the lines,

> we tweezer'd out
> What slender blossom lived on lip or cheek
> Of manhood,
>
> (1st ed., p. 21, lines 9–11)

from the third edition; for the Tory journal had said, "A hero, 'blue-eyed and fair of face, with lengths of yellow ringlet like a girl,' who when he has 'tweezered out the slender blossom of manhood that lives on his lip and cheek,' passes well for a tall young lady, can hardly grow in the course of a few months into a fitting mate for a magnificent Princess." While Tennyson retained the lines describing the Prince as blue-eyed, fair of face, and yellow-ringleted, he was able to diminish the impression of the Prince's lack of manliness by deleting the reference to the slender blossom of manhood upon his lip and cheek.

The *Guardian* thought that the following lines were an example of Tennyson's tendency not to be "always simply classical" in his diction or perfectly lucid in expression:

> she demanded who we were,
> And why we came? I *minted* nothing false,
> But, *your example pilot*, told her all.
> *Up went the hush'd amaze of hand and eye.*
>
> (1st ed., p. 53, lines 5–8) [65]

In the third edition the last two lines remained the same, but "minted nothing false" was changed to "fabled nothing fair." The *Guardian* again questioned the poet's diction when he wrote of the arch at the outskirts of the women's preserves as "Inscribed *too dark for legible* . . ." (1st ed., p. 21, line 17). *Sharpe's London Magazine*, emphatically denouncing the same line, said, "It is pure tyranny to put a sentence or two to the torture, in order to show his power, and throw upon the world such maimed and truncated objects as 'too dark for legible.' " The offending phrase disappeared from the third edition, and a much more explicit and functional passage was substituted:

> . . . an arch,
> Whereon a woman-statue rose with wings
> From four wing'd horses dark against the stars;
> And some inscription ran along the front,
> But deep in shadow.
>
> (3d ed., p. 23, lines 12–16)

As a result of strictures in the *Quarterly*, Tennyson also clarified the lines depicting the embrace of the Prince and Princess:

>   She turn'd; she paused;
>   She stoop'd; and with *a great shock of the heart*
>   *Our mouths met: out of langour leapt a cry,*
>   Crown'd Passion from the brinks of death, and up
>   Along the shuddering senses struck the soul,
>   And closed on fire with Ida's at the lips.
>
>   (1st ed., p. 149, lines 12–17) [66]

"The *shock* of this meeting," said the *Quarterly* reviewer, "is communicated to the nerves of the reader, and not pleasantly. The last three lines are as obscure as the others are inharmonious." The revised reading of the third edition ran,

>   She turn'd; she paused;
>   She stoop'd; and out of langour leapt a cry;
>   Leapt fiery Passion from the brinks of death;
>   My spirit closed with Ida's at the lips.
>
>   (2d ed., p. 159, lines 12–15)

The remaining four passages that appear to have been modified in response to criticism were censured on metrical grounds.[67] The *English Review* considered the line,

>   Among us, all out of breath, as pursued,
>
>   (1st ed., p. 83, line 13)

indefensible and suggested the insertion of an "if" before "pursued" to make it scan correctly. Tennyson disregarded this specific advice, but he reworded the line to make it regular iambic pentameter:

>   Among us, out of breath, as one pursued.
>
>   (3d ed., p. 90, line 3)

The *Spectator* printed the following three passages as prose, saying that they "may be broken up into lines, but they defy anyone to make verses of them":

>   *She spake*
>   With kindled eyes: we rode a little higher
>   To cross the flood by a narrow bridge, and came
>   On flowery levels underneath the crag,
>   Full of all beauty.
>
>   (1st ed., p. 63, lines 2–6)

> Empanoplied and plumed
> We enter'd in, and waited, fifty there
> To fifty, till the terrible trumpet blared
> At the barrier.
>
> > (1st ed., p. 117, lines 8–11)

> With stroke on stroke the horse and horseman, came
> As comes a pillar of electric cloud,
> Flaying off the roofs and sucking up the drains,
> And shadowing down the champain till it strikes
> On a wood, and takes, and breaks, and cracks, and splits,
> And twists the grain with such a roar that the Earth
> Reels, and the herdsmen cry.
>
> > (1st ed., p. 119, lines 6–12)

Patmore, in the *North British Review,* joined the *Spectator* with regard to the last passage, writing, "We think that nothing can justify such lines as these." In the first instance, Tennyson expunged extra syllables by rewriting part of the second and almost the entire third line:

> > > She spake
> With kindled eyes: we rode a league beyond,
> And, o'er a bridge of pinewood crossing, came
> On flowery levels underneath the crag,
> Full of all beauty.
>
> > (3d ed., p. 68, lines 4–8)

A slight alteration effected the same result in the second passage, making the third line much more pleasing to the ear:

> Empanoplied and plumed
> We enter'd in, and waited, fifty there
> Opposed to fifty, till the trumpet blared
> At the barrier.
>
> > (3d ed., p. 126, lines 5–8)

In the last of the three criticized passages not all the deviations from the regular pattern of blank verse were erased, since the poet was manifestly attempting to produce a special effect; but he corrected the chief flaw which resulted from the possibility of scanning line three,

> Flaying off the roofs, and sucking up the drains,

as an alexandrine. Although there was a trochaic substitution in the first foot, by deleting "off," he reduced the possible number of feet in the line:

> Flaying the roofs, and sucking up the drains.
>
> (3d ed., p. 128, line 6)

He also excised an extra syllable in the next to the last line by omitting "the":

> And twists the grain with such a roar that Earth
> Reels, and the herdsmen cry.
>
> (3d ed., p. 128, lines 9–10)

In addition to these remarks upon the metrical aberrations of specific lines, many of the critics deplored the liberties which Tennyson had taken with his blank verse or regretted that as a whole the versification of *The Princess* was not more polished. A few of the periodicals, such as the *Gentleman's Magazine* and the *Examiner*, were pleased with the meter; and *Sharpe's London Magazine* said that, although the blank verse of *The Princess* lacked the finish of some of the shorter poems, Tennyson had prevented it "from degenerating into the chopped-up prose of Byron." But the majority of the critics were of the opposite opinion. Marston asserted in the *Athenaeum*, "False or deficient quantities occur with a frequency which suggests that they have been deliberately adopted"; and he reminded Tennyson that "correct monotony is less displeasing than awkward and unmusical license." The *Spectator* was caustic over the poet's disregard of "the merest mechanics of great verse-making." The *English Review* objected to the occasional freedom of rhythm which Tennyson allowed himself, and the *Quarterly* wished that the poem had been "rendered smoother and richer throughout." Even Patmore, with his personal admiration of the poet, held that Tennyson had attempted effects with meter which it was incapable of producing and pronounced that "artifice pushed beyond its limits, looks like a want of art." [68]

This dissatisfaction with the versification of *The Princess* seems to have resulted in a thoroughgoing revision of its metrical structure in an effort to achieve more evenness and regularity of movement. According to Pyre, Tennyson made a total of sixty-nine alterations in the poem "for the express purpose apparently of removing extra-syllables." [69] To be sure, a number of extra-syllabic lines remain in the final text, but they do not minimize the pains that the poet took to overcome metrical deficiencies and to strengthen his verse.

The real or supposed incongruity of the poem, however — the "fearless intermixture" of past and present and of grave and gay, as the *Quarterly* called it — absorbed the reviewers' principal attention. The scheme and structure of the poem were not without defenders,[70] but the opposition skirmished briskly. Marston in the *Athenaeum* declared,

> The grand error of the story is the incoherency of its characteristics. Its different parts refuse to amalgamate. They are derived from standards foreign to each other. The familiar and the conventional impair the earnestness of the ideal: — and what might else have been appreciated as genial satire loses its force from its juxtaposition to tragic emotion. Nor are these opposite elements used as contrasts to each other. It is sought to identify them; but in the attempt to fuse both, each parts with its distinctiveness.

He had no objection to Tennyson's having introduced into his poem "the associations and feelings of modern life," but the manners of the present had been dwelt upon without reflecting its passions; and "even had the feelings as well as the habits of these times been expounded in the tale, its subsequent transition to formal dignity and old heroics would have destroyed all mental congruity." The critic for the *Atlas* advanced much the same argument:

> The ideal and the literal are constantly intermixed. . . . The poet does himself injustice by assuming a suit of motley, which turns his high mission into burlesque. Grave truths are here set down side by side with pitiful conceits and sinister jests; exquisite scraps of fancy are put forth in a masquerade of quaint modes and dry humours; the age of chivalry and steam are made to dance together; chronology and costume are set at defiance; and the moral which is finally evolved loses half of its earnestness and beauty by being overlaid with satirical whim and banter.

As has already been seen, Forster too had strong feelings on this last point: the poet "had something serious to say — why graft it on burlesque?" [71] Conversely, the *Guardian*, no less aware of the disparity in tone between the earlier and later sections of the book, was sorry that frivolity had been abandoned for seriousness. Why not make it all burlesque? The *Quarterly* and the *Eclectic* also were disturbed by the conflicting aspects of the medley. In the estimation of the *Quarterly*, the resultant incongruity was the major defect in the poem. The mingling "of modes and phrases of all ages, past and present," was deplorable enough. But the poem suffered from an even worse effect: "The low key at which it is pitched indisposes the mind for the higher strains to which the piece changes." The reviewer in the *Eclectic* thought the work "*bizarre*, indeed grotesque" with its strange jumble of "grave matter of fact and wild fancies, solemn disquisitions, and sportive ridicule."

In censuring *The Princess* because of the clashing features of its plot, the reviewers were not unaware of the poet's attempt in the Prologue to reconcile the inconsistencies. Marston granted that "the author has anticipated our exceptions. . . . But this consciousness of an eccentric plan can scarcely excuse it. We fancy that the Prologue is in reality an apologetic supplement." [72] The *Eclectic* agreed with this interpretation and was inclined to believe that Tennyson, having seen his mistake, would avoid it in the future. The *Spectator* expressed Marston's opinion more pointedly: "The origin explains, but does not excuse the poem." The *Atlas* felt that possibly by his introduction Tennyson had put himself beyond stricture, but was no less disappointed with the poet's product.

As is to be expected, the third edition discloses the poet's pains to counteract these basic objections. Lounsbury himself, who sweepingly denies the influence of the reviewers in the alterations of the poems republished in 1842, concedes that much of the rewording of *The Princess*, particularly in the Prologue and Conclusion, was done in an endeavor to placate unfavorable criticism. [73] But we must go beyond such a general admission of fact in order not only to see the nature and extent of the poet's emendations but also to evaluate their effect upon the final structure of the poem.

The extensive revision of the Prologue was manifestly intended to make a more convincing explanation of the oddities of the story and to overcome its incongruity of tone. The first significant modification occurs in the account of the group storytelling in which the youths had engaged at the university during the Christmas vacation. Lilia knew of the game but wondered what kind of tales men really told among themselves, and Walter then elucidated as follows (the readings of the first and third editions are given in parallel columns):

And Walter nodded at me; "He began,	And Walter nodded at me; "He began,
The rest would follow; so we tost the ball:	The rest would follow, each in turn; and so
What kind of tales? why, such as served to kill	We forged a sevenfold story. Kind? what kind?
Time by the fire in winter."	Chimeras, crotchets, Christmas solecisms,
(1st ed., p. 10, lines 14–17)	Seven-headed monsters only made to kill
	Time by the fire in winter."
	(3d ed., p. 11, lines 5–10)

The "sevenfold story" with each narrator following in turn, of which *The Princess* will be a counterpart, gives the impression of a much more formal and orderly performance than "so we tost the ball." The "chimeras, crotchets," and "Christmas solecisms" prepare the reader for the anachronisms that are likely to result in *The Princess,* which may itself become a "seven-headed monster."

The emphasis that the poet intended to place on this point and his sensitiveness on the matter are evident from the notes he left on the poem, for he tells us, "The 'Tale from mouth to mouth' was a game which I have more than once played when I was at Trinity College, Cambridge, with my brother undergraduates. Of course, if he 'that inherited the tale' had not attended very carefully to his predecessors, there were contradictions; and if the story were historical, occasional anachronisms." [74] In the

first edition Tennyson had partially vitiated such a defense by
making the poet in the story warn his associates to be especially
alert to avoid inconsistencies:

> To which I said,
> "Take care then that my tale be follow'd out
> By all the lieges in my royal vein . . ."
>
> (1st ed., p. 12, lines 1–3)

But in the third and following editions he dropped this admoni-
tion by the poet, who simply says,

> "Then follow me, the Prince,"
> I answer'd, "each be hero in his turn!"
>
> (3d ed., p. 12, lines 13–14)

Thus Tennyson rid himself of a claim to a unity of treatment
throughout, and at the same time he added another explanatory
touch concerning the genesis of the poem. If it was made clear
that a different undergraduate assumed the role of Prince and
narrator in each section, it would not be so difficult for readers
to account for the conflicting elements of the poem, for under
such conditions inconsistencies might very well creep in.

The emendations in the remarks of the maiden aunt, who urges
the poet to commence his tale, also helped the unity of the poem:

And "tell one" cried the solemn
maiden aunt.
"Why not a summer's as a winter's tale?
A tale for summer, as befits the
time;
And something it should be to
suit the place.
Grave, moral, solemn, like the
mouldering walls
About us."

(1st ed., p. 11, lines 2–7)

"Why not now?" the maiden
Aunt.
"Why not a summer's as a winter's
tale?
A tale for summer, as befits the
time,
And something it should be to
suit the place,
Heroic, for a hero lies beneath,
Grave, solemn!"

(3d ed., p. 11, lines 12–17;
my italics)

. . . till the maiden aunt
(A little sense of wrong had
touch'd her face
With colour) turn'd to me: "Well
— as you will —

. . . till the maiden aunt
(A little sense of wrong had
touch'd her face
With colour) turn'd to me with
"As you will;

Just as you will," she said; "be, *Heroic* if you will, or what you
  if you will,   will,
Yourself your hero."   Or be yourself your hero if you
  (1st ed., p. 11, lines 11–15)   will."
                  (3d ed., p. 12, lines 5–9;
                  my italics)

The reiteration of the initial word "Heroic" in the revised edition
performs a double function. On the one hand, it serves notice that
the tone of the poem is to be pitched from the beginning in a
high key. On the other, particularly as a result of the allusion
to Sir Ralph, the hero who "lies beneath," it prepares us for the
chivalric features of the narrative that occur in parts V and VI.
It is difficult not to believe that, when Tennyson made these
changes, he had in mind the statement in the *Quarterly* that the
early part of the poem was pitched too low and Marston's comment that the "subsequent transition to formal dignity and old
heroics" destroyed "all mental congruity."

The Interlude introduced between parts IV and V in the third
and later editions continued more specifically the preparation
begun in the Prologue for tilt and tournament and for the noble
sentiments of the last three sections:

> So Lilia sang: we thought her half-possess'd,
> She struck such warbling fury through the words;
> And, after feigning pique at what she call'd
> The raillery, or grotesque, or false sublime —
> Like one who wishes at a dance to change
> The music — clapt her hands and cried for war,
> Or some grand fight to kill and make an end:
> And he that next inherited the tale
> Half turning to the broken statue, said,
> "Sir Ralph has got your colours: if I prove
> Your knight and fight your battle, what for me?"
> It chanced, her empty glove upon the tomb
> Lay by her like a model of her hand.
> She took it and she flung it. "Fight," she said,
> "And make us all we would be, great and good."
> He knightlike in his cap instead of casque,
> A cap of Tyrol borrow'd from the hall,
> Arranged the favour and assumed the Prince.
>   (3d ed., p. 100, line 10 to p. 101, line 9) [75]

The poet's efforts here are transparent. By means of the Interlude, he sharply marked the shift from levity to sobriety. He inserted a reason for the change in mood and distinctly warned the reader that the story was about to veer to a new tack. He as much as said to Marston that there was no intention of making the ridiculous and the sublime coalesce; and, through calling attention to the opposing aspects of the poem, he attempted to produce the contrast which had been thought lacking in the original version. Furthermore, the distinct break between the two halves of the poem lessened the impression that the moral element was grafted on to the burlesque; and thus the "familiar and conventional" might less "impair the earnestness of the ideal." [76]

Two lines added in the fourth edition at the beginning of part VI also remind the reader of the deepening note to be expected in the last two sections of the poem, so that the transition may not seem so abrupt:

> For so it seem'd, or so they said to me,
> That all things grew more tragic and more strange.
> (4th ed., p. 136, lines 6–7)

A number of the alterations and additions in the Conclusion of the third edition expanded the excuse for the structure of *The Princess* and reflected the criticism it had received. There was a slight attempt in the second edition to decrease the original impression that the poet had not been sure of his intentions when he began to write. In the first edition the Conclusion read:

> Here closed our compound story which at first
> Had only meant to banter little maids
> With mock-heroics and with parody:
> But slipt in some strange way, crost with burlesque,
> From mock to earnest, even into tones
> Of tragic, and with less and less of jest.
> (1st ed., p. 161, lines 1–6)

The second edition ran:

> Here closed our compound story which at first
> Perhaps, but meant to banter little maids . . .
> (2d ed., p. 161, lines 1–2) [77]

In the third edition the suggestion of the poet's uncertainty about the true purpose of the poem was suppressed:

> So closed our tale, of which I give you all
> The random scheme as wildly as it rose:
> The words are mostly mine; for when we ceased
> There came a minute's pause, and Walter said,
> "I wish she had not yielded!" then to me,
> "What, if you drest it up poetically!"
> So pray'd the men, the women: I gave assent.
>
> (3d ed., p. 171, lines 1–6)

The idea of the poem's uneven progress had disappeared; for with the addition of the Interlude, the tale no longer "slipt in some strange way . . . / From mock to earnest," since Lilia had called for true sublime. The poet also glances at the improbabilities of the story and dissociates himself from the responsibility for them — "I give you all / The random scheme as wildly as it rose." The poem is the product of seven minds, not one; the poet is presented with the problem of embellishing and retelling a story already recounted by others. And if certain of the reviewers thought that some of the passages were extravagant and some of the images far-fetched,[78] Tennyson inserted a refutation of their strictures in the Conclusion and alluded to it in his notes. "In defence of what some have called the too poetical passages," he says, "it should be recollected that the poet of the party was requested to 'dress the tale up poetically,' and he was full of the 'gallant and heroic chronicle.' "[79]

Confronted with dressing up the tale, the fictitious poet, in a passage added in the third edition, is made to expand upon the difficulties of resolving the opposing forces of the story:

>   I gave assent:
> Yet how to bind the scatter'd scheme of seven
> Together in one sheaf? What style could suit?
> The men required that I should give throughout
> The sort of mock-heroic gigantesque,
> With which we banter'd little Lilia first:
> The women — and perhaps they felt their power,
> For something in the ballads which they sang,
> Or in their silent influence as they sat,

Had ever seem'd to wrestle with burlesque,
And drove us, last, to quite a solemn close —
They hated banter, wish'd for something real,
A gallant fight, a noble princess — why
Not make her true-heroic, true-sublime?
Or all, they said, as earnest as the close?
Which yet with such a framework scarce could be.
Then rose a little feud betwixt the two,
Betwixt the mockers and the realists:
And I, betwixt them both, to please them both,
And yet to give the story as it rose,
I moved as in a strange diagonal,
And maybe neither pleased myself nor them.

                    (3d ed., p. 171, line 7 to p. 172, line 13)

The maids desire seriousness throughout, as had the *Atlas* and
the *Examiner*. The men, like the *Guardian*, want a frolic at the
girls' expense; and Tennyson admitted the impossibility, within
the structure adopted for the poem, of entirely satisfying both
camps. While there is little reason to believe with the *Athenaeum*
and the *Eclectic* that originally the Conclusion was an "apologetic
supplement," it came close to being one in the third edition.
Tennyson's complacent admission that he was seeking to please
opposing factions of opinion reveals *The Princess* for what it is —
not the "herald-melody" of the higher education of women, but
an attempt at a compromise that would be offensive to neither
point of view.[80] In the last line the self-depreciatory move to
disarm hostile criticism is reprehensible.

Another unfortunate afterthought was the introduction, in the
fourth edition in 1851, of the "weird seizures" of the Prince. Dawson, who says that the poet "must have had some definite object
in inserting them," is puzzled over what that object could have
been.[81] The reason is not far to seek. Hallam Tennyson observes
in the *Memoir* that the Prince's "too emotional temperament was
intended from an artistic point of view to emphasize his comparative want of power." But the key to the additions lies in the
next sentence: " 'Moreover,' my father writes, 'the words "dream-
shadow," "were and were not" doubtless refer to the anachronisms and improbabilities of the story.' "[82] Apparently Tennyson
had continued to brood over the improbabilities of his story and

had cast about for a further means of appeasing his censors, until he hit upon the idea of the "weird seizures." Although the suggestion for their trancelike aspect may have been partly autobiographical,[83] they possibly owe something to the comment in the *Quarterly*, which we know Tennyson read, that a story like *The Princess* required an element of the supernatural.

Even such apologists for Tennyson as Lounsbury and Dawson consider the addition of the "weird seizures" needless and regrettable.[84] As Dawson points out, the physical blight with which the poet afflicted his hero is offensive and inartistic. More than that, the hereditary character of the Prince's disease and its medical diagnosis by the court-Galen make the Prince's assurance that he is cured by the Princess's regeneration difficult to accept. The Prince's seizure at the conclusion of part IV and the dreamlike nature of the joust detract from the vividness of the action. Also, after the Prince has fallen unconscious under Arac's blows, the statements concerning his mental condition at the beginning of part VI and again in part VII are confusing.[85] By attempting to make the outlines less distinct, Tennyson blurred his picture; and with the "weird seizures" of the Prince, he merely added a truly grotesque and disconcerting feature to an already overburdened structure.

A final expansion of the text designed to aid in explaining the poem occurred in the fifth edition. The poet in the Prologue actually reads from the chronicle about the deeds of the medieval Amazon:

> "O miracle of women," said the book,
> "O noble heart who, being strait-besieged
> By this wild king to force her to his wish,
> Nor bent, nor broke, nor shunn'd a soldier's death,
> But now when all was lost or seem'd as lost —
> Her stature more than mortal in the burst
> Of sunrise, her arm lifted, eyes on fire —
> Brake with a blast of trumpets from the gate,
> And falling on them like a thunderbolt,
> She trampled some beneath her horses' heels
> And some were whelm'd with missiles of the wall,
> And some were push'd with lances from the rock,

And part were drown'd within the whirling brook:
O miracle of noble womanhood!"

                                   (5th ed., p. 3, lines 6–19)

Previously, the chronicle had only been described, and the poet
had carried it about with his finger marking his place. Now,
through having a passage read, Tennyson set forth a noble proto-
type for his Princess. Moreover, he set the stage more thoroughly
for Lilia's demand that the story be resolved by a fight and for
the subsequent clash of pseudo-medieval knights.

   Having studied Tennyson's measures to combat incongruity
and to escape anachronisms through the fifth edition, we must
redirect our attention to the third, in order to consider another
series of emendations, this time largely felicitous, which apparently resulted from one of Aubrey de Vere's remarks in the *Edinburgh Review*. Tennyson wrote to De Vere soon after the third
edition had been published, "You will find that I have in some
measure adopted your suggestions, not entirely." In another letter, which cannot have been written very long after the first, he
said,

   I assure you I experienced a very lively gratification in finding that
my recent alterations had met your approval and not your's only but
your mother's and sister's. I am not quite satisfied with it, and I think
that one or two of the ballads might be improved or others substituted
but I have done with it at present. . . .
   I have not the *Edinburgh* with me, and so cannot give you the exact
passage in the critique; but I know there is mention made therein of
"The Princess" coming out among the dying and the dead. Now I
certainly did not mean to kill anyone, and therefore I put this new line
into the king's mouth,
                I trust that there is no one hurt to death,
and in the old tourneys it really did happen now and then that there
was only a certain amount of bruises and bangs and no death.[86]

In the new version Gama, addressing Ida among the wounded,
says,

                              see how you stand
         Stiff as Lot's wife, and all the good knights maim'd,
         I trust that there is no one hurt to death,
         For your wild whim.

                        (3d ed., p. 142, line 16 to p. 143., line 1)

But further than this single example, what suggestions of De Vere's had Tennyson adopted? He seems to have ignored several points that his friend felt to be weaknesses in the poem,[87] but one stricture appears to have been responsible for a number of very important emendations that strengthen and unify the character of the Princess. De Vere had written that there was an occasional failure to distinguish between the real and the assumed character of the Princess, such as the instance when she discourses brilliantly at High Table, to the admiration of her colleagues. He had put his finger upon a very pertinent point, and Tennyson's searching reëxamination of the entire characterization of his heroine, touched off by this comment, resulted in some valuable changes. A certain amount of dissatisfaction with Ida's temperament expressed by both the *Gentleman's Magazine* and the *Quarterly* may have increased Tennyson's concern.[88] Also, the *Quarterly* had charged that the high tone and awful dignity of the Princess's victory chant, "Our enemies have fallen," was out of keeping with the preceding parts of the poem; [89] and it seems highly probable that this reproof lay behind some of the attempts to increase the stature of the heroine and to make her solemn song plausible.

In the Prologue in the third edition we find Walter Vivian calling for a great Princess:

> "Take Lilia, then, for heroine" clamour'd he,
> "And make her some great Princess, six feet high,
> Grand, epic, homicidal; and be you
> The Prince to win her!"
>
> (3d ed., p. 12, lines 10–13)

The poet agrees, commands each of his male companions to follow in turn as storyteller, and declares,

> Heroic seems our Princess as required.
>
> (3d ed., p. 12, line 15)

Here Tennyson set forth the true nature of his Princess. The *Sun* had felt it necessary to inform its readers that the purpose of *The Princess* was not to satirize women, and seven months later *Tait's Edinburgh Magazine* had perversely declared that the main object of the poem was to combat the desires of women for political equality with men. The poet seems to have been trying in his revised edition to make it clear from the first that he was not belittling his heroine. He realized that the greater her proportions when erring, the finer her character would be when purged by humility. In the original version it might have been possible for a reader to conceive of Princess Ida as a foolish, willful, headstrong girl, made ludicrous by gentle satire, illogically put on a pedestal and almost deified in the later sections of the poem. This was an element of incongruity which the author methodically set about to eradicate.

The actual story, then, begins with a heroic Princess as determined in the Prologue. We get our first specific information about her from the lips of her father, King Gama, who relates her doings to the Prince and his companions. Compare the readings of the first and third editions:

I would you had her, Prince, with
   all my heart,
With my full heart: but there
   were widows here,
Two widows, Lady Psyche, Lady
   Blanche;
They fed her theories, in and out
   of place
Maintaining that with equal hus
   bandry
The woman were an equal to the
   man.
They harp'd on this; with this
   our banquets rang;
Our dances broke and buzz'd in
   knots of talk;
Nothing but this: my very ears
   were hot
To hear them. Last, my daughter
   begged a boon
A certain summer-place which I
   have
Hard by your father's frontier:
   I said no,

I would you had her, Prince, with
   all my heart,
With my full heart: but there
   were widows here,
Two widows, Lady Psyche, Lady
   Blanche;
They fed her theories, in and out
   of place
Maintaining that with equal hus
   bandry
The woman were an equal to the
   man.
They harp'd on this; with this
   our banquets rang;
Our dances broke and buzz'd in
   knots of talk;
Nothing but this: my very ears
   were hot
To hear them: knowledge, so my
   daughter held,
Was all in all; they had but been,
   she thought,
As children; they must lose the
   child, assume

Yet being an easy man, gave it; and there,
All wild to found an University
For maidens, on the spur she fled; and more
We know not.

> (1st ed., p. 18, line 8 to p. 19, line 3)

The woman: then, Sir, awful odes she wrote,
About the losing of the child, — and rhymes
And dismal lyrics prophesying change,
Beyond all reason: these the women sang;
And they that knew such things — I sought but peace;
No critic I — would call them masterpieces:
They master'd me. At last she begged a boon
A certain summer-place which I have
Hard by your father's frontier: I said no,
Yet being an easy man, gave it; and there,
All wild to found an University
For maidens, on the spur she fled; and more
We know not.

> (3d ed., p. 19, line 12 to p. 20, line 16)

In the first edition it might be supposed that the Princess is merely the dupe and tool of Lady Blanche and Lady Psyche. In the third she has assimilated their instruction and makes her own pronouncements concerning the needs of women. She becomes a dynamic figure, assuming leadership. The additions commence the process of making her intellectually heroic, and the "awful odes" specifically indicate her poetic propensity, which is later to be demonstrated. Mine host at the inn adds further testimony to the grandeur of the Princess in two lines inserted in the third edition:

> She once had past that way; he heard her speak;
> She look'd as grand as doomsday and as grave.
>
> (3d ed., p. 22, lines 9–10)

A subtle distinction in the aims of the Princess is introduced in her admonitions to the new pupils. In the first edition she had said,

> We give you welcome: not without redound
> Of fame and profit unto yourselves ye come.
>
> (1st ed., p. 25, lines 13–14)

In the third edition (p. 28, line 14) "use" and "glory" were substituted for "fame" and "profit." The first reading had suggested that vanity and worldly ambition were at the back of the Princess's desire for a female university. Now her objects are immeasurably higher. She is motivated by a desire for service to humanity and a hope for a lasting name based on sure foundations of worth.

The passage that De Vere had cited in the *Edinburgh* and that had started this chain of revisions was altered to produce a similar effect. Originally, at dinner in the Hall the Prince had kept his eyes

> Intent upon the Princess, where she sat
> Among her grave Professors, scattering gems
> Of Art and Science.
>
> (1st ed., p. 45, lines 8–10)

De Vere had commented, "In the college hall . . . we would have been better pleased to hear of her 'grave professors' having scattered 'gems of art and science,' than of the Princess herself having riveted admiring eyes by her skill in so idle a pastime." In the third edition the passage became:

> Intent on her, who rapt in glorious dreams,
> The second-sight of some Astraean age,
> Sat compass'd with professors; they, the while,
> Discuss'd a doubt and tost it to and fro.
> A clamour thicken'd, mixt with inmost terms
> Of art and science.
>
> (3d ed., p. 48, lines 13–18)

The Princess, imbued with visions of progress for womankind, is shown to rise above the petty vanity and the desire for intellectual display that infect the lesser minds of her female dons. Her pride is obliterated and her greatness of nature further stressed by the alteration of the following lines, where more directness of expression is achieved as well:

My princess, O my princess! true
   she errs;
For being, and wise in knowing
   what she is,
Three times more noble than
   three score of men.
      (1st ed., p. 51, lines 16–18)

My princess, O my princess! true
   she errs;
But in her own grand way: being
Three times more noble than
   three score of men.
      (3d ed., p. 57, lines 1–3)

Another addition in the Princess's comments after the singing of "Tears, idle tears" and "O Swallow, swallow" enhances her majesty and seems to have been deliberately inserted to fore-shadow her later stately victory ode:

> . . . but great is song
> Used to great ends: ourselves have often tried
> Valkyrian hymns, or into rhythm have dash'd
> The passion of the prophetess; for song
> Is duer unto freedom, force and growth
> Of spirit than to junketing and love.
>   (3d ed., p. 77, line 16 to p. 78, line 1)

Two extensive and most consequential omissions in Ida's speech to Lady Blanche near the end of part VI complete the poet's work of bringing the Princess's character into harmony. When Lady Blanche reproves the Princess for admitting the Prince, Florian, Cyril, and Violet's cousin to the women's university to be nursed, Ida answered in the first edition,

> What! in our time of glory when the cause
> Now stands up, first, a trophied pillar — now
> So clipt, so stinted in our triumph — barred
> Even from our free heart-thanks, and every way
> Thwarted and vext, and lastly catechised
> By our own creature! one that made our laws!
> Our great she-Solon! her that built the nest
> To hatch the cuckoo! whom we called our friend!
> But we will crush the lie that glances at us
> As cloaking in the larger charities
> Some baby predilection: all amazed!
> We must amaze this legislator more.
> Fling our doors wide!
>   (1st ed., p. 137, line 17 to p. 138, line 11)

It was a false stroke to indicate that Ida's decision to throw open her female sanctuary to all the wounded knights was caused by anger and spite toward Lady Blanche. De Vere's reproach that Ida's true nature was not always consistently preserved was certainly applicable here, since the action of granting succor to all should spring from rising pity and a growing human sympathy. By deleting Ida's recrimination of Lady Blanche, the poet produced a more natural emotional development and preserved the dignity of her character.

The excision of the Princess's irate dismissal of Lady Blanche and of her bitter remarks to the Prince's father was even more necessary to the preservation of her dignity. The Princess had cried,

> Go, help the half-brain'd dwarf, Society,
> To find low motives unto noble deeds,
> To fix all doubt upon the darker side;
> Go, fitter thou for narrowest neighbourhoods,
> Old talker, haunt where gossip breeds and seethes
> And festers in provincial sloth: and you,
> That think we sought to practice on a life
> Risk'd for our own and trusted to our hands,
> What say you, Sir? you hear us: deem ye not
> 'Tis all too like that even now we scheme,
> In one broad death confounding friend and foe,
> To drug them all? revolve it: you are man,
> And therefore no doubt wise.
>
> (1st ed., p. 138, line 19 to p. 139, line 11)

As much as Tennyson himself might like to rail at society and the gossip-ridden provincial villages he knew so well, to make Ida do so was ill conceived. Just at the time when nature was beginning the work of softening and transforming her into a pure Victorian maiden, "meek" and "mild," it was both unfortunate and out of character to portray her as a virago with an alarming penchant for invective and sarcasm.

The rhymed intercalary songs are the last, and by no means the least, feature that the final text of *The Princess* owes to the reviewers. There can be no question that because of criticism the songs were added to emphasize the part played by the child.

Tennyson says in his notes, "The child is the link thro' the parts as shown in the songs which are the best interpreters of the poem. Before the first edition came out, I deliberated with myself whether I should put songs between separate divisions of the poem; again I thought that the poem would explain itself, but the public did not see the drift." [90]

Other considerations springing from the reviews may have contributed to the poet's decision to insert the songs. Upon one thing the critics had been in almost unanimous agreement: with the exception of the querulous Jerdan, they had rhapsodized over the original lyrics in blank verse, repeatedly quoting and admiring them.[91] Tennyson could have no misgivings as to how an additional set of lyrics, a form in which he was an undoubted master, would be received. *Howitt's Journal* had said that since *The Princess* was a single poem in blank verse, some would "miss the usual variety, others still more the rich musical cadences of his lyrics." It had regretted, moreover, that the parts sung by characters within the story had not been put into a lighter meter contrasting with the regular verse of the poem as a whole. The *Morning Post,* too, had thought that the songs should deviate in meter from the rest of the poem, and it cited the practice of Moore, Byron, and Scott to substantiate "this reasonable theory." The poet must have realized that supplementary lyrics would add considerably to the attractiveness of his work. Those who missed the lyrical vein prominent in his former volumes and those who called for variety in meter could scarcely fail to be pleased. Since the songs would aid the unity of the poem, they offered one more opportunity to combat the impression of incongruity.

Upon close examination, then, the remarkable extent to which *The Princess* is indebted to contemporary criticism becomes apparent. The importance of current literary theories in the original conception of the poem has already been seen. No less influential were the opinions of the reviewers in determining its final form. If Tennyson was led to expect too much from the poem, the critics' dissatisfaction drove him to make it in many respects a more acceptable production. His attention to a number of details singled out in specific passages, his polishing of the meter, most of his attempts in the Prologue, the Interlude, and the Conclusion to diminish incongruity and to bring the separate elements of the poem into balance, his ennobling and unifying of the character of the Princess, and his introduction of the songs between the sections, all were salutary. Yet along with these virtues he inserted some deplorable effects in the Conclusion and the hopelessly confusing "weird seizures" of the Prince. In 1844 Carlyle described Tennyson as a man "carrying a bit of Chaos about him . . . which he is manufacturing into Cosmos." [92] But in spite of ability, diligence, and the suggestions of the reviewers, the poet never entirely succeeded in eliminating chaotic features from *The Princess.*

Chapter Five

THE PINNACLE OF SUCCESS:
IN MEMORIAM

THE RECEPTION OF *IN MEMORIAM*

In Memoriam, that monument to the religious question-
ings of the nineteenth century as well as to the memory of Arthur
Henry Hallam, was published by Moxon on June 1, 1850.[1] The
product of seventeen years of rumination engendered by the sudden death of Tennyson's college friend in Vienna on September 15, 1833, the elegy came before the reading public unheralded
by publisher's advertisements and without its author's name on
the title page.

There was little doubt, however, as to the identity of the pen
from which the unusual work emanated. On Wednesday, May 29,
Mudie's Select Library advertised in the London daily papers
that fifty copies of Tennyson's new poem would be available on
Saturday, the day of publication. And on that day the fifty copies
were announced as in circulation.[2] The *Sun* in August complained that the opportunity of revealing the author's name from
internal evidence had been cut off by the rumors linking the
poem with Tennyson "even prior to the day of its publication."
The first periodicals to notice the book, the *Spectator* and the
Examiner, unhesitatingly informed their readers on June 8
that Tennyson was the writer and Hallam the person to whom
the poem was addressed. A week later the *Atlas* pretended to be
vexed that speculations and learned disquisitions had thus been
anticipated by the "outspokenness of our periodical critics, who
blurt out the secret before the volume is a week old. . . . the
whole truth even now stands revealed to the world. There is no
mystery about it." Only the *Literary Gazette* distinguished itself
by welcoming on June 15 "a female hand" to "the Muses' ban-

quet," after it had already listed *In Memoriam* as by Tennyson in its column of new books on June 1.[3]

The reception of *In Memoriam* by the periodicals during the year of its publication was in general extremely laudatory.[4] The weekly journals printed in London, as usual the first to notice a new work, responded with no fewer than nine reviews during the month of June. The *Leader,* the newly established republican paper captained by George Henry Lewes and Thornton Hunt,[5] and the faithful *Examiner* were fervid in their commendation. Lewes, who wrote the encomium in the *Leader,* called Tennyson the "greatest living poet" and judged *In Memoriam* superior to "Lycidas." "The comparison," he said, "is not here of genius, but of feeling. Tennyson sings a deeper sorrow, utters a more truthful passion, and singing truly, gains the predominance of passion over mere sentiment." He concluded with a prophetic opinion of the poem, "We shall be surprised if it does not become the solace and delight of every house where poetry is loved. A true and hopeful spirit breathes from its pages. . . . All who have sorrowed will listen with delight to the chastened strains here poured forth *In Memoriam.*" The *Examiner,* in an article presumably by Forster, was no less eulogistic. *In Memoriam* was not unworthy of comparison to Milton's "Lycidas," Petrarch's and Shakespeare's sonnets, and Dante's "Purgatorio" and "Paradiso." Tennyson's poem, the writer said,

is a pathetic tale of real human sorrow, suggested rather than told. It exhibits the influence of a sudden and appalling shock, and lasting bereavement, in the formation of character and opinion. It is the record of a healthy and vigorous mind working its way, through suffering, up to settled equipoise and hopeful resignation. The effect of the poem, as a whole, is to soften yet to strengthen the heart; while every separate part is instinct with intense beauty, and with varied and profound reflections on individual man, on society, and on their mutual relations. It is perhaps the author's greatest achievement. A passion, deep-felt throughout it, has informed his ever subtle thoughts and delicate imagery with a massive grandeur and a substantial interest.

The *Guardian,* which had approved of *The Princess,* was as appreciative of *In Memoriam.* Although it was not so enthusiastic as the *Leader* and the *Examiner,* it declared, "Judged even by the standard of Shakespeare and Spenser, Mr. Tennyson will not be found wanting." [6]

Even the weeklies that had handled *The Princess* severely had overcome their aversion for Tennyson to a remarkable degree. The *Spectator* quoted approvingly sections LXXXIX ("Witch-elms that counterchange the floor") and CVI ("Ring out, wild bells") [7] and said, "The volume is pervaded by a religious feeling, and an ardent aspiration for the advancement of society. . . . These two sentiments impart elevation, faith, and resignation; so that memory, thought, and a chastened tenderness, generally predominate over deep grief." The *Spectator* found fewer of the eccentricities of style against which it had been protesting for twenty years and felt that the scheme of the poem was "favourable to those pictures of common landscape and daily life, redeemed from triviality by genial feeling and a perception of the lurking beautiful, which are the author's distinguishing characteristic." If the reviewer in the *Literary Gazette*, possibly Jerdan, whose long editorship was just coming to an end,[8] mistook the identity of the author, he had only the warmest praise for the poem. The *Atlas* had been completely won over, though the critic doubted that the poem would "find as large a circle of readers as other emanations of Tennyson's muse." The series of poems which make up the whole work "are entirely worthy of the poet," he said. "They overflow with plaintive beauty. They are the touching heart-utterances of a genuine and noble sorrow. There is a homeliness and simplicity about them which bear ample testimony to their truth. There is nothing ornate or elaborate in them; they are thoughtful, chastened, and subdued." The *Britannia*, which had looked upon *The Princess* as despicable, conceded that in the new poem, amidst some repetition of the poet's old faults, there were beauties "which take their place at once and for ever in the poetry of England." The *Athenaeum*, in another review by J. Westland Marston,[9] firmly endorsed the volume:

> It belongs to those deepest forms of poetic expression which grow out of the heart and stand distinguished from those which have their origin in the imagination. . . . In its moral scope the book will endear itself to all who suffer, both by its vivid appreciation of their grief and by

its transmutation of that grief into patience and hope. No worthier or more affecting tribute could be rendered to the dead than one which, like this, converts the influence of their memory into solace for the living.

Reviewing Tennyson for the first time, the Unitarian *Inquirer* [10] alone found more to blame than to praise; but its attitude cannot be called hostile. It was "grateful for the purity and elegance that breathe throughout the volume" and desisted from quoting examples of the "mellow fruit" shining out amid the "weeds" in order not to overthrow "our critical objections to the poem as a whole." The objections of this sectarian journal, whose reviews were devoted almost entirely to religious works,[11] could not have had much effect upon the literary world in the face of the approval of the *Athenaeum*, the *Examiner*, the *Spectator*, and the *Atlas*, not to mention the other weeklies.

It was somewhat curious that Forster in the *Examiner*, sharing the view of the critic for the *Atlas*, should think that *In Memoriam* would not "become immediately popular." Henry Taylor privately expressed the same opinion. On July 1, 1850, he wrote to Miss Isabella Fenwick, "Have you read Tennyson's 'In Memoriam'? It is a wonderful little volume. Few — very few — words of such power have come out of the depths of this country's poetic heart. They might do much, one would think, to lay the dust in its highways and silence its market towns. But it will not be felt for a while, I suppose; and just now people are talking of the division of last Friday." [12]

But Lewes' forecast was the correct one, and the prophets of gloom had reckoned without the people and without the praise of the press. Besides the notices in the London weeklies, favorable reviews and excerpts from *In Memoriam* were printed by various newspapers throughout the United Kingdom during the month of June.[13] In July additional complimentary articles appeared. Encomiums of the poem flowered in the periodicals for August. The *North British Review*, in the first elaborate critique of *In Memoriam*, sounded the note that succeeding critics echoed: "There are certain great epochs in the history of poetry. The publication of 'Paradise Lost' was one of these. The next, which was at all similar in importance, was the appearance of the 'Excursion.' . . . Our immediate impression upon the perusal of 'In Memoriam' was that it claimed a place in the very highest rank, and that it was the first poem of historical importance which has appeared since the 'Excursion.' " Franklin Lushington, one of the family to whom Tennyson was so closely bound by ties of affection and marriage, proclaimed in *Tait's Edinburgh Magazine* that *In Memoriam* was "the finest poem the world has seen for very many years." [14] "Its title," he said, "has already become a household word among us. Its deep feeling, its wide sympathies, its exquisite pictures, its true religion, will soon be not less so. The sooner the better." Patmore, writing in the *Palladium,* a newly established Edinburgh magazine, was practically breathless with adulation.[15] Tennyson's new work contained "the best religious poetry that has ever been written in our language — if we except a very few of the lovely and too seldom appreciated effusions of George Herbert." After quoting section CIII ("On that last night"), Patmore remarked, "In our opinion, there is nothing nearly equal to the above, in splendour of language and imagination, depth and classicality of thought and feeling, perfection of form, and completeness in every way, in the whole scope of modern English poetry." [16] *Sharpe's London Journal* exclaimed,

All the qualifications which have rendered him [Tennyson] so acceptable to the critical readers and discreet lovers of poetry, are here displayed in their matured excellence: — the graceful diction and exquisite harmony of versification; the subtle flights of thought and fancy; the delicate sense of beauty and keen appreciation of the beautiful; the power of condensation, and of presenting the commonest objects in a new and unexpected light; — these and many more characteristics of his genius are observable in the pages of *"In Memoriam."*

Hogg's Instructor found "high merit" in the poem's "general tone of lofty spiritualism. . . . The thoughts awakened by reflections on life and death — on the reality life and the reality death — give to this work that vitality which outlives mere beauty of description and mere pathos of sentiment." The *Court Journal* cried, "Never yet did fairer wreath deck the tomb where lies the loved and lost; chisel never yet fashioned monumental marble more graceful, more expressive of the homage paid by the living to the dead, than in this tribute of a sorrowing heart to the memory of one so beloved."

At the end of August, two of the London daily newspapers added their voices to these paeans. The *Sun* called *In Memoriam* a "masterpiece of poetic composition" and asserted, "Of the exquisite simplicity of the whole effusion we cannot speak in terms of too earnest admiration." The ever-loyal *Morning Post* maintained, "Only a poet would have conceived the idea; and Wordsworth himself, in his happiest moments, would not have produced a more touching or beautiful composition." Concerning the sections which make up the poem, the *Post* remarked, "It is not merely the intensity of feeling which they manifest nor the musical power and simplicity of the language which gives so great a charm and so absorbing an interest to these stanzas; it is the harmony and depth of thought, illustrated and adorned with the riches of a fertile fancy and a well-stored intellect, which form their chief excellence and repay with the disclosure of new beauties every fresh perusal."

By the beginning of September *In Memoriam* had reached a second edition and probably a third.[17] Sir Charles Tennyson says that there were 5,000 copies in the first edition;[18] and it is likely that a larger number was printed for the second and third editions. The book was selling at a phenomenal rate, setting at naught all predictions to the contrary.

Three articles in the magazines and reviews for September, which appeared about the first of the month, continued the flood of panegyric. For the *Eclectic Review* the chief importance of the poem lay in "the revealment of greatness in the spirit of the artist." And "the second great value of the book" was said to be its "expression of a cycle of experience common to thoughtful humanity." Charles Kingsley in *Fraser's Magazine* thought *In Memoriam* "the noblest English Christian poem which several centuries have seen." The *English Review,* while mercilessly exposing Tennyson's lack of faith (to which I shall return presently), described the poem as "an heirloom bequeathed to our nation, and to be treasured by it, as long as the English tongue endures."

The October number of the *Westminster Review* devoted nine-teen pages to an article which was in no sense critical and can only be described as a fulsome eulogy of both author and work.

In the criticism of *In Memoriam* during the first four months after its publication, the reviewers had a good deal to say concerning the poem's technical or literary qualities — its unity, diction, meter, and monotony. They generally agreed that the sometimes almost unconnected sections of the work did not destroy its total effect. *Hogg's Instructor* felt that though the poem was "thus made up of a series of detached parts, yet is the unity of the whole unbroken, because there is ever a recurrence to one and the same melancholy event." The *Morning Post* said, "Not only is the unity of design and of subject apparent throughout, but the thoughts follow each other in a natural sequence, the continuity of which renders it necessary to contemplate the work as a whole in order fully to appreciate its beauties." The *Eclectic* declared, "An organic unity informs the whole; unity of feeling and of interest." And Lushington in *Tait's* asserted that the poem was "perfect and unique as a whole, to a degree and in a style very rarely reached."

The diction, always one of the focal points of attack on Tennyson, met with more approval than censure. Some critics, such as those in the *Inquirer*, the *Britannia*, and the *Court Journal*, repeated the old charges of quaint and obscure phraseology. Marston and Lushington, in the *Athenaeum* and *Tait's*, respectively, were more directly concerned with the poet's problem of expressing succinctly metaphysical conceptions and objected that the language did not always represent with sufficient clarity abstract ideas. More representative of the prevailing opinion was that of the *Eclectic*: "As regards words merely, Tennyson is undeniably one of the greatest of *Expressers*. His is the master's facility. His are the 'aptest words to things.' In expert 'fitting' of the one to the other, his present practice far exceeds even his original gift. Unerring is his speech, as opulent. It is ever *adequate* to the thought. The balance of the two brings about lucidness, unex-ampled, in thought so large, feeling so deep, poetry so subtle."

The stanza in which the poem was written provoked extensive

comment, but the weight of critical opinion was strongly in its favor.[19] The *Leader* remarked, "How exquisitely adapted the music of the poem is to its burden; the stanza chosen, with its mingling rhymes, and its slow, yet not imposing march, seems to us the very perfection of stanza for the purpose." The *Eclectic* called the stanza a "happy one"; *Sharpe's London Journal* said that it was "most happily selected"; and Kingsley in *Fraser's* pronounced it "exquisitely chosen." The *North British Review* went so far as to say, "This seems to us to be one of the most perfect rhymed measures for continuous verse ever invented." [20]

There were, however, a few dissenting voices. The *Inquirer,* for instance, complained, "The measure is of too obvious facility, and, in a less masterly hand, might break into the very false gallop of verses. Even in spite of the division into short canzonets or sonnets, which breaks the continuity of the air, there is a poverty and sameness in it which produces weariness and fatigue, so that there is danger of losing the full appreciation of the burden for want of greater variety and strength in the verse." The *Christian Reformer,* also wishing for more variety, regretted that Tennyson had confined himself to one meter. The *Sun* thought the stanza "at the first somewhat unpalatable from its monotony," yet confessed in the end to being overcome by its "irresistible fascination." The *Westminster,* charmed by the rhyme scheme of the stanzas, maintained that "the sweetness of the notes, the earnest truth of the thought, the comprehensiveness of the love, relieve them of all monotony."

The question of the monotony of the poem was also raised by other reviewers. The *Spectator* felt that there was "inevitably something of sameness in the work" and that the subject was "unequal to its long expansion." The *Atlas* believed that the sections were "too mournfully monotonous," and even Forster in the *Examiner* conceded an "unavoidable monotony." But this point of view did not go unchallenged. *Hogg's Instructor* said that, although the poem might appear to be monotonous, "to many this very monotony will be its chief beauty." And the *English Review* asserted, "It might be presumed, that such a work, extending to pages 210, upon the same simple theme, would be monotonous: but this is scarcely the case. At least, if there be any monotony here, the monotony of sorrow, it is so eminently beautiful, that we could not wish it other than it is."

Among the general features of the poem, the portrayal of English landscape and of domestic scenes and affections elicited unanimous approbation.[21] But probably the most interesting aspect of the criticism of *In Memoriam* is the attitude of the reviewers toward its religious doctrine. A vast majority·commended this element of the work and, with a somewhat human tendency to read more into the meaning than the poet had actually expressed, found the theology sound and the faith inspiring. Kingsley rejoiced as follows: "Blessed it is to find the most cunning poet of our day able to combine the complicated rhythm and melody of modern times with the old truths which gave heart to the martyrs at the stake, to see in the science and history of the nineteenth century new and living fulfilments of the words which we learnt at our mothers' knee!" [22] Patmore maintained that the reader was exalted by the strains in which "sorrow is gradually shown to be the teacher of a pure, or rather the only pure philosophy" and "secular knowledge is humbled before loving faith." [23] The *Guardian* and the *Spectator* said that the volume was "full of religious feeling." The *Morning Post,* in a notice of *Fraser's Magazine* for September, spoke of "the pure Christianity" of *In Memoriam.* The *North British Review* asserted that the poem uttered primary Christian truths, which the age, having lost, was in the process of recovering; and *Tait's* mentioned the volume's "true religion." For the *Sun* the "philosophy" of the poem was "ever pure and lofty." The *Westminster* thought the poem was thoroughly devout, and the *Prospective Review* cherished the poet's declaration for faith over knowledge.

In this overwhelming tide of laudation, only three instances of protest have come to light. The *Britannia* noticed "an almost total absence of those higher consolations which religion should suggest." "We miss," the reviewer said, "those hues of cheerfulness and manly resignation with which Christianity invests the outpourings of her stricken children." Yet he was moved to comment on section cvi ("Ring out, wild bells"), "It is suggestive, healthy, full of generous aspirations, poetical, sympathetic, Christian." The *Court Journal* feared that Tennyson did "not always seek his consolation at the one sufficing source," but hoped that the passages which compelled such a remark had been misconstrued. The critic for the High Church *English Review* alone examined in detail Tennyson's theological position.[24] Although some of his views were extreme, he anticipated by some eighty-six years Mr. T. S. Eliot's dictum that *In Memoriam* is more conspicuous for the doubt than for the faith which it expresses.[25] In the first place, he took the poet to task for not capitalizing in the proem the pronouns referring to the Divinity. Concerning the lines,

> O thou that after toil and storm
>   Mayest seem to have reach'd a purer air,
>   Whose faith has centre everywhere,
> Nor cares to mix itself in form,
>
> Leave thou thy sister when she prays,
>   Her early Heaven, her happy views;
>   Nor thou with shadow'd hint confuse
> A life that leads melodious days,
>
> (XXXIII, 1–8)

he charged, "It is most falsely, and, we may add, offensively assumed, that the unbeliever in Christianity can possess a faith of his own, quite as real and as stable as that of the believer!" He suspected Tennyson of being *"an exclusive worshipper of the beautiful."* The lines,

> There lives more faith in honest doubt
> Believe me, than in half the creeds,
>
> (XCVI, 11–12)

he pronounced "infinitely mischievous." The stanza,

> Tho' truths in manhood darkly join,
>   Deep-seated in our mystic frame,
>   We yield all blessing to the name
> Of Him that made them current coin,
>
> (XXXVI, 1–4)

he declared to be "simply and purely blasphemy." He viewed with distrust Tennyson's apparent acceptance of the principles of evolution and concluded, "We remain undecided as to Mr. Tennyson's faith, though we opine, that, strictly speaking, *he has none,* whether negative or affirmative, and advise him, for his soul's good, to try to get one!"

But in spite of this attack upon the poet's theology, the critic preserved an adulatory respect for his work. For the first time in the contemporary criticism of Tennyson, aesthetic qualities outweighed moral values. Tennyson, he said, "*teaches* us nothing; he needs teaching himself; he is rather an exponent of this age's wants, than one who can in any measure undertake to satisfy them. And yet, with all this, we repeat, he is a great poet; and great he for ever will remain."

It was now generally agreed that Tennyson was not only the leading poet of the day but a poet of commanding genius. The *Leader* had already proclaimed him the "greatest living poet." The *Eclectic* had found his "greatness" revealed by *In Memoriam.* The *Standard of Freedom,* noticing *Fraser's* for September, called him "that great poet." [26] As one reviewer put it, he had become "the rage," [27] and the *Globe* said on September 4, 1850, "For one genuine reader of Wordsworth there are thousands who relish Tennyson."

At last Tennyson was thought to have fulfilled his promise and to have accepted the mission that had been envisaged for him. *Sharpe's London Journal* had felt it necessary to lament "the apparent absence of any direct or intelligible aim" in his previous poetry and had been unable to "discover in it that genuine sympathy . . . with . . . human progress generally found in the highest order of poetry." "But the present volume," the critic said, "abounds with noble aspirations and generous sentiments which reflect equal glory on the philanthropist and the poet, and which prove to us that we have not been wrong in classing Alfred Tennyson among the great and moving spirits of the age." The *Eclectic* also testified to the poet's achievement. *Poems,* 1842, and *The Princess* had shown that Tennyson's nature was "eminently elevated, pure . . . sympathizing, genuine, refined," but also that it was "a reserved and fastidious one." His skill and artistry had

made him seem "removed and distant. Rarely was a direct sentiment or sympathy, the central influence of a poem." With *In
Memoriam,* however, "All wants are now amply compensated by
one continuous revealment of our poet in his spiritual individuality; one exclusive outlet of personal feeling and sympathies.
Their expression is enlarged into relevance with universal humanity." [28] The poem contains "the poetic solution of every-day
problems of thought." In addition, "More than once, a penetrating poet's glance is turned on this age itself. A calmly attuned
voice is raised in testimony to 'The mighty hopes that make us
men:' a voice of large trust, of deep-seated faith, of long prophecy;
singing of that 'crowning race,' the 'flower and fruit' of that, in
us the seed."

Thus *In Memoriam* was believed to embody all the qualities
which the age expected of poetry. The poem awakened chords
of universal human sympathy. It played upon and ministered to
emotions experienced by all men at one time or another. It was
eminently of the day and concerned itself with the solution of
current problems; it was complete with prophecy and the doctrine of progress; it inculcated the moral of faith and hope derived from the catharsis of suffering. Tennyson had finally produced an elevated, sustained, and unified poem of a philosophical
nature and had convinced most of his contemporaries that he was
a vigorous and profound thinker.

It was the consensus of the reviewers that *In Memoriam* was
the great work which had been awaited from Tennyson's pen.
The poem was neither an epic nor a drama, as had been prescribed, but it was a work to stand beside *Paradise Lost* and *The
Excursion,* beside the "Purgatorio" and "Paradiso" of Dante, and
the sonnets of Petrarch and Shakespeare. Of the periodicals that
made the comparison, only the *Inquirer,* admittedly reactionary
in matters of literary taste, thought *In Memoriam* inferior to
"Lycidas." [29]

A work of such eminence was naturally thought to be of timeless significance. Through his mastery of poetic technique, Tennyson was said to have embalmed his "great thoughts" and "elevated
feeling" "for the ages." *In Memoriam* contained "joys, in which

our children and our children's children will participate as largely as ourselves." The thoughts of the poet "who revolves the problems of free-will and fate, and gives utterance to his feelings of awe and hope . . . [are] not 'such perishable stuff as dreams are made of,' but they 'wander through eternity.'" And to the memory of Arthur Hallam, the poem was "a monument 'more lasting than brass,'" "a memorial more lasting than bronze." [30]

THE LAUREATESHIP

Wordsworth had died on April 23, 1850; and, while the praise of *In Memoriam* was steadily mounting, the office of poet laureate, left vacant by his death, remained unfilled. The discussion prevalent in literary circles about an appropriate successor was echoed in the press. Although Chorley assiduously advanced Mrs. Browning's claims in the *Athenaeum*, the most likely candidates were conceded to be Tennyson and Leigh Hunt.[31] The Queen had acted promptly in offering the post on May 8 to Samuel Rogers, the literary veteran, famous as a host and connoisseur as well as a poet. But Rogers, then eighty-seven, declined the honor because of his age,[32] and the laureateship went unoccupied until the autumn.

On September 7, 1850, the Prime Minister wrote to the Queen: "Lord John Russell has had the honour of receiving at Taymouth a letter from the Prince. He agrees that the office of Poet Laureate ought to be filled up. There are three or four authors of nearly equal merit, such as Henry Taylor, Sheridan Knowles, Professor Wilson, and Mr Tennyson, who are qualified for the office." [33] On October 3 Russell wrote to Rogers, "H. M. is inclined to bestow it on Mr Tennyson, but I should wish, before the offer is made, to know something of his character, as well as of his literary merits." [34] The old poet having vouched for Tennyson's respectability, Russell informed Prince Albert on October 21, "Mr Tennyson is a fit person to be Poet Laureate"; [35] and on November 5 Sir Charles Phipps, Keeper of the Privy Purse, wrote to Tennyson for the Queen, offering him the post "as a mark of Her Majesty's appreciation of your literary distinction." [36] Tennyson, after a day's hesitation, accepted; and the appointment was officially made on November 19, 1850.[37] It seems to have been received with general satisfaction by the public, though Chorley, who admitted there was no question of Tennyson's merit, grumbled about the "multiplication of . . . benefices to a single subject." [38] The *Leader* reported the appointment with pleasure, saying that "the name of ALFRED TENNYSON is so beloved that any good fortune befalling him will delight the public." [39] Hunt, like a good loser, wrote in his new periodical, *Leigh Hunt's Journal,*

> If the Office in future is really to be bestowed on the highest degree of poetical merit, and on that only (as being a solitary office, it unquestionably ought to be, though such has not hitherto been the case), then Mr. Alfred Tennyson is entitled to it above any other man in the kingdom; since of all living poets he is the most gifted with the sovereign poetical faculty, Imagination. May he live to wear his laurel to a green old age; singing congratulations to good Queen Victoria and human advancement, long after the writer of these words shall have ceased to hear him with mortal ears.[40]

Wordsworth had raised the dignity of the laureateship to a new level in public esteem; and if the Queen's intention was to preserve this high standing, Tennyson was the obvious, and actually the only, choice. *In Memoriam* had elevated him to an unassailable pinnacle. His appointment as poet laureate was the accolade for twenty years of poetic endeavor.

FURTHER APPRAISAL OF *IN MEMORIAM*

The year 1850 was one of previously unparalleled success for Tennyson. Not only had he finally won practically unanimous critical acclaim and the laureate's bays as well, but he had also escaped from financial difficulty. Mrs. Browning wrote to Miss Mitford that she understood his returns from Moxon were five hundred pounds; [41] and in addition to this, he had his stipends from the government.

The succeeding year, 1851, opened auspiciously, with a fourth edition of *In Memoriam* appearing in January.[42] An article on *The Remains in Verse and Prose of Arthur Henry Hallam* in the *North British Review* for February quoted a number of stanzas from *In Memoriam* and devoted almost as much space to Tennyson as to Hallam. Between January 18 and March 1 the *Sheffield and Rotherham Independent* printed a long adulatory article in four installments on *In Memoriam*. In June the *Wesleyan-Methodist Magazine* added its voice to the chorus of praise, saying that the poem exemplified "the refining, elevating, spiritualising, and chastening influence which Christianity has exercised upon modern poetry, — furnishing it with nobler ethics; inspiring, but not to disappoint, 'immortal longings;' and infusing the spirit of heaven-ward faith and charity."

During August and September three essays on "Tennyson and His Poetry" by Gerald Massey were published in the *Christian Socialist*.

Tennyson [he said] is the greatest, the sweetest, and the perfectest of our living singers. There is wondrous witchery in his verse. He is born a singer, and he has perfected his art, till it is the most natural of things. . . . He has . . . pruned the young luxuriance of his style, and now his poetry is unequalled, — save by that of Keats, — in choiceness and nicety of epithet, while at the same time, as in "Dora," and parts of "In Memoriam," he equals Wordsworth, in his simple grandeur and absence of ornateness, without ever dwindling into (what I venture to call) the latter's childishness and triviality.

Massey also brought out a number of other aspects of Tennyson's poetry that he considered exemplary. The author, he asserted, was "a great democratic poet . . . democratic in his universal sympathies, democratic in his treatment of things lowly, and in his frequent utterance of stern and democratic truths." He wrote with a cheerful voice of "Progress." He was a "true teacher" and had "a lofty sense of the poet's mission." He was a "poet-seer." He looked upon poetry, not as a "glittering foil," but as a "two-edged sword . . . to lop off the accursed cancer that is eating into the bosom of our motherland, and to pierce to the heart of wrong . . . throughout the world." And if some people complained of his obscurities, then the answer was, "Read him, again and again, and if so be you do not understand him, then there is manifest danger that you are not quick of comprehension." In these articles Tennyson was seen once more as fulfilling all the qualities which the Victorian critics looked for in poetry.

With this sort of unrestrained appreciation in the air, *In Memoriam* reached the fifth edition, "5,000 strong," during November 1851. Henry Taylor wrote in a letter of that month to Sir Edmund Head that "except Wordsworth for some ten years of his life," Tennyson "is the only really popular poet since Byron." [43]

The success of *In Memoriam* was too much for *The Times*; and at last "The Thunderer" was stirred to set the record straight on November 28, 1851, with a critique of three and a half columns entitled "The Poetry of Sorrow." The reviewer, possibly Manley Hopkins,[44] began by upbraiding the critics for failing to be severe enough upon young authors to purge them of their more obvious faults and blemishes. Pompously he remarked, "Few people, intellectually or morally, are benefited by having their own way. A true critic is a physician of the mind, and his treatment strengthens the constitution of an author." "Perhaps of modern poets," he continued, "Mr. Tennyson has met with fewest obstacles on the high-road to reputation. Mr. Tennyson . . . has grown into the most resolute mannerist in England, except Mr. Carlyle. His faults of taste and language are stereotyped, and he now writes his affectations in capitals." Although the critic was charitable enough to say, "English literature possesses no work which, in compass and unity, can be justly compared with *In Memoriam*," he felt there were two major defects in the poem — "the enormous exaggeration of the grief" and "the tone of . . . amatory tenderness." In connection with the first point, he maintained that Hallam is portrayed as having such extraordinary virtues that the reader cannot sympathize with him. As an example of the second, he quoted the following lines:

> So, dearest, now thy brows are cold,
>   I see thee what thou art, and know
>   Thy likeness to the wise below,
> Thy kindred with the great of old.
>
> But there is more than I can see,
>   And what I see I leave unsaid,
>   Nor speak it, knowing Death has made
> His darkness beautiful with thee.
>
> (LXXIV, 5–12)

"Very sweet and plaintive these verses are," he commented; "but who would not give them a feminine application?" [45]

A third fault in *In Memoriam,* and in Tennyson's poetry as a whole, was obscurity. To his own misfortune, the reviewer illustrated his objection. Here was a specimen which was difficult "not from excess, but want of meaning":

> Oh, if indeed that eye foresee
>   Or see (in Him is no before)
>   In more of life true life no more
> And Love the indifference to be,
>
> So might I find, ere yet the morn
>   Breaks hither over Indian seas,
>   *That Shadow waiting with the keys,*
>   *To cloak me from my proper scorn.*
>
> (XXVI, 9–16) [46]

"That a Shadow should hold keys at all," he said, "is a noticeable circumstance; but that it should wait with a cloak ready to be thrown over a gentleman in difficulties, is absolutely amazing." Another stanza that soared beyond the critic's comprehension was:

> That each, who seems a separate whole,
>   Should *move his rounds and fusing all*
>   *The skirts of self again, should fall,*
>   *Remerging in the general Soul.*
>
> (XLVII, 1–4)

"We have applied every known test, without detecting the smallest trace of sense," he remarked, "and are confident that the 'blind clerk' at the General Post-office would abandon the effort when he came to *fusing the skirts of self.*" Tennyson's allusions often puzzled the critic as well. For example, he was unable to fathom what was meant when Hallam's face was described thus:

> And over those ethereal eyes
>   *The bar of Michael Angelo.*
>
> (LXXXVII, 37–40)

In addition, the critic observed, "Mr. Tennyson frequently allows his amplitude of coloured and stately phrases to seduce him into line after line of grand sounding dactyls and spondees out of which it is extremely hard to draw any message of wisdom or utterance of common sense." He cited instances of this tendency and passed on to give others of "grammatical inaccuracy" that became a "frequent source of mist and doubtfulness in language."

Near the end of the article, the reviewer, trying to make amends for some of his adverse comment, turned "with very sincere pleasure to notice some of the finer and purer qualities of this book and its author." Obsequiously he declared, "We wish Mr. Tennyson to number us with his friends." But he could only muster praise for Tennyson's "mastery of diction" and his "unbroken music of . . . rhythm"; and his final comment was, "Small as this book is, it may be abridged with profit."

The opinion of *The Times,* however, does not seem to have altered the taste for Tennyson, and the paper drew upon itself the telling satire of an article in *Tait's* and the methodical rejoinders of Frederick W. Robertson in a lecture delivered at the Mechanics' Institution at Brighton and published within the year of its delivery.[47]

THE EFFECT OF THE REVIEWERS ON
IN MEMORIAM

The influence of the reviewers upon *In Memoriam* is not demonstrably great. Perhaps it is foolhardy to speculate upon their effect on the composition of such a subjective poem. Certainly, the "earliest jottings, begun in 1833," were inspired by a soul-rending grief over Hallam's death and were written to relieve the poet's emotions. He says in his notes concerning the sections of the poem, "I did not write them with any view of weaving them into a whole, or for publication, until I found that I had written so many." [48] Where the wounded spirit crying in the dark leaves off and the conscious artist takes control, it is impossible to tell; and the manuscript of the poem, now in the Trinity College library, is under permanent interdiction imposed by the the second Lord Tennyson. Nevertheless, at some juncture, the shift in the writer's point of view occurred, and in the light of Tennyson's sensitivity it is difficult not to suspect that the decision to proceed with the "Elegies" and to try to weave them into a unified whole may have owed something to the reviewers, though undoubtedly the encouragement and prodding of friends were also prominent factors. From the very beginning the reviewers had emphasized the need for speculative poetry and had applauded some of his attempts at it. The *Westminster Review*, in 1831, had praised the metaphysics of "Supposed Confessions of a Second-rate Sensitive Mind." Mill had said, in 1835, that a poet must develop the philosophical side of his nature as much as the poetical, and North had complained that Tennyson's poetry was lacking in thought. "The Two Voices" was hailed by a number of the reviewers of *Poems*, 1842, as the most important poem in the volumes; and *The Times*, in 1848, said that it was his best piece. The *Christian Remembrancer*, in 1849, registered disillusionment because Tennyson had written no great poem with philosophy as its basis. To proceed with the "Elegies" — to unify and add to them — manifestly offered an opportunity to produce a long philosophical work and to include in it other qualities which the critics desired. Tennyson afterwards remarked to Knowles of *In Memoriam*, "It's too hopeful, this poem, more than I am myself"; [49] and one can scarcely avoid the impression that, faint as sometimes the hope is, the poet was led to express more than he felt because he thought it ought to be said. I do not mean to suggest that he calculatingly sat down to produce a "best seller," but apparently his thinking and his ultimate construction of the work were affected, often perhaps unconsciously, by the reiterated demands of the critics.[50] Mr. P. F. Baum writes, "The poem's greatest handicap of disunity springs from Tennyson's deliberate extension of his professed subject, the consolation which came to him from his hard won belief in personal immortality, to include an assured prophecy of a golden age upon earth." [51] Prophecy of the future of the human race based on a faith in progress was what the reviewers had called for, and they had extravagantly commended the poet for his efforts in this direction. If the remarkable correspondence of *In Memoriam* to their dictates resulted from nothing more than that Tennyson was completely a product of his age, it must be granted that the contemporary literary criticism was a part of the intellectual climate in which the poem developed.

Two passages are worthy of mention as embodying other ideas which the reviewers had expressed. In the first, the beauty of a purposeless universe is compared to that which

> lurks
> In some wild Poet, when he works
> Without a conscience or an aim.
>
> (xxxiv, 6–8)

In the second, the poet gives tongue to the need for human association and sympathy:

> I will not shut me from my kind,
> And, lest I stiffen into stone,
> I will not eat my heart alone,
> Nor feed with sighs a passing wind.
>
> • • • • •
>
> I'll rather take what fruit may be
> Of sorrow under human skies.
>
> (cviii, 1–4, 13–14)

A third passage betrays the poet's attempt to anticipate certain strictures that might be raised against his production and perhaps an uneasiness over what the critics might think of a poem concerning private emotions instead of public inspiration and action:

> I sing to him that rests below,
> And, since the grasses round me wave,
> I take the grasses of the grave,
> And make them pipes whereon to blow.
>
> The traveller hears me now and then,
> And sometimes harshly will he speak:
> "This fellow would make weakness weak,
> And melt the waxen hearts of men."
>
> Another answers, "Let him be,
> He loves to make parade of pain,
> That with his piping he may gain
> That praise that comes to constancy."
>
> A third is wroth: "Is this the hour
> For private sorrow's barren song,
> When more and more the people throng
> The chairs and thrones of civil power?

> A time to sicken and to swoon,
>   When Science reaches forth her arms
>   To feel from world to world, and charms
> Her secret from the latest moon?"
>
> Behold, ye speak an idle thing:
>   Ye never knew the sacred dust:
>   I do but sing because I must
> And pipe but as the linnets sing.
>
> (XXI, 1–24)

There were few alterations in the published text of *In Memoriam* in response to adverse criticism. As the author told Aubrey de Vere, what he had written, he had written;[52] and he stood by it with commendable constancy. Of the twenty-five passages that were censured, he made only minor changes in three, all of which had been singled out by *The Times*.[53] "The Thunderer" had said that the "disproportion of phrase" in *In Memoriam* occasionally bordered "on blasphemy" and had asked,

> Can the writer satisfy his own conscience with respect to these verses?
>   "But, brooding on the dear one dead,
>   "And all he said of things divine,
>   "*(And dear as sacramental wine*
>   "*To dying lips is all he said.)*"
>
> [XXXVII, 17–20]

For our part, we should consider no confession of regret too strong for the hardihood that indicted them.

Tennyson did not remove the offending comparison, but he modified it to read,

> (And dear to me as sacred wine
> To dying lips is all he said.)

By the alteration he emphasized the purely personal application intended. No longer could a careless reader accuse him of asserting that Hallam's words were as efficacious to a human soul as consecrated wine.

In the same article *The Times* remarked of the lines,

> A happy lover who has come
>   To look on her that loves him well;
>   Who *lights* and rings the gateway bell,
> And *learns her* gone, and far from home,
>
> (VIII, 1–4)

"Here it is evident that '*lights*' and '*learns*' are used with extreme incorrectness. The construction requires us to suppose that the lover arrives in a dark evening with a lantern, and gropes about the brick wall until he finds the bell." To guard against such an unintelligent interpretation, the poet inserted an apostrophe before "lights."

In the third instance Tennyson changed "cloak" to "shroud" in the lines already mentioned about the Shadow with the keys, making them,

> That Shadow waiting with the keys
> To shroud me from my proper scorn.
>
> (XXVI, 15–16)

Through this emendation he intensified the suggestion of death, which the critic in *The Times* had obtusely failed to perceive.

Despite the lack of conclusive evidence, it appears highly probable that the reviewers were responsible for certain elements of *In Memoriam*; and while the strictures on individual passages brought about few revisions in the text, the three examples of the influence of *The Times* show that Tennyson remained attentive to published criticism.

Chapter Six

CONCLUSION

With the publication of *In Memoriam* and the appointment as poet laureate, Tennyson had achieved an eminence from which death alone would dislodge him. The struggle was behind him, and the forty-one remaining years of his life were almost a prolonged and glowing Indian summer. Its serenity was not completely unbroken. All his later works were not received by the press with unanimous applause; and amid the prevailing chorus of adulation, there were occasional strident notes of disapproval. But from 1851 onward his place as the chief poet of the age was secure. Not only was his popularity phenomenal, but his title to greatness was generally accepted. And even in our own day, when his reputation has suffered seriously from the reaction to all things Victorian, the iconoclastic Mr. Eliot has called him "a great poet." [1]

The study of Tennyson's career from 1827 through 1851 reveals that he was not so much abused by the reviewers as has been supposed, but that they exerted a continuous pressure upon him to teach more than to delight, to be speculative and analytical rather than poetical. The picture of him as a poet who slowly made his own way to popular acclaim in spite of persistent opposition from the press is exaggerated. Although he was roughly handled in some of the reviews of *Poems, 1833*, he did not again meet with anything like the virulent sarcasm in the *Quarterly*. From a very early date he was recognized as a true poet, and especially during the years from 1842 to 1850 he was given much high praise. The greater part of the adverse criticism he received resulted not so much from what he had done as from what he had failed to do.

In the reviewing of Tennyson from 1827 to 1851, his friends and acquaintances had a part that is not to be disregarded, but that can easily be overestimated. Arthur Hallam's review in the *Englishman's Magazine* may have done almost as much to retard

Tennyson's reputation as to advance it, for Hallam's eulogy stirred North's bile and helped to bring forth Croker's scorn. In 1842 the *Christian Remembrancer* cited this article as indicating that Tennyson was writing according to an erroneous theory of poetry, and in 1848 the *Quarterly* quoted it to show that he was originally a poet of sensation and closely linked with Keats and Shelley. The efforts of Sterling, Milnes, and Spedding after the publication of *Poems,* 1842, however, were of considerable value in protecting Tennyson from further attack; and the latter's systematic argument for Tennyson's powers in the *Edinburgh Review* was of great importance, as was Aubrey de Vere's defense of *The Princess* in the same periodical in 1849. Although Coventry Patmore's laborious allegorical interpretation of *The Princess* may have convinced a few people of Tennyson's high seriousness, it brought ridicule upon itself from other journals. Franklin Lushington's article in *Tait's Edinburgh Magazine,* Patmore's in the *Palladium,* and Charles Kingsley's in *Fraser's Magazine* increased the reverberating eulogy of *In Memoriam.* But in all the notice of Tennyson by his partisans, their favorable attitude was equaled or exceeded by reviews emanating from unbiased sources. Thus, while criticism colored by personal feeling appears to have figured in the growth of Tennyson's reputation, his contemporary fame was by no means the result of puffery by his friends.

The various ways that the reviewers affected Tennyson have already been shown in detail, and he, indeed, seems to have altered several hundred lines of his poetry as a result of adverse criticism; but in the matter of correcting specifically censured passages (in which he never blindly accepted the critics' verdict, as the Brownings supposed), his monitors in the press had a greatly diminished influence after the period of silence.

Upon his poetic theory and practice the reviewers seem to have had a far-reaching effect. Late in life he told Knowles that from boyhood he had always felt the "passion of the past." "It is the distance," he said, "that charms me in the landscape, the picture and the past, and not the immediate to-day in which I move." [2] But the critics had frowned upon this element in his work; and in spite of this undying feeling within him, after his first two poetical ventures he continually attempted to make his poetry reflect the "immediate to-day," which did not appeal to him, and to prophesy of the future, which did not beckon him. He began his career by writing poetry with little trace of the era of its genesis, but by 1845 he was telling Aubrey de Vere that "a poem should reflect the time and place." [3] By his own admission, originally he took more delight in the beautiful than in the good. Yet in *In Memoriam* he cast a derogatory light upon the beauty created by a poet without a conscience or an aim. With the critics harping on the necessity for didacticism, his poetry eventually became infused with moral and religious teaching to such an extent that he was almost thought of as "a writer of philosophical treatises." [4]

When Tennyson attempted the things that the reviewers demanded, he did so not with a shallow desire for popularity and financial success but because he allowed himself to become convinced that the qualities for which they called were necessary to great poetry. Because of this conviction, he made a concentrated effort to achieve those qualities, even though some of them were actually foreign to his temperament.

As Elizabeth Browning wrote in a letter to Browning concerning the proper relationship between an author and his critics, "Suggestions from without may . . . be accepted with discrimination sometimes, to the benefit of the acceptor"; [5] and Tennyson is not to be censured for attention to the reviewers per se: it is a question of his discrimination, which seems to have supported him in some instances and to have played him false in others. Much of the rewriting and emending to which the critics incited him in *Poems, Chiefly Lyrical, Poems, 1833,* and *The Princess* was commendable. He probably profited as well from chastening some of the excessive sensuousness of his early poetry. Yet his assiduous correcting led him to introduce some unhappy afterthoughts, such as the "scritches" of the jay and the "weird seizures" of the Prince. The compulsion to prophesy may have induced him to impair the unity of *In Memoriam.* Most of all, the critics seem to have injured the lasting value of a portion of his work by encouraging him to incorporate in it so much that is now of only historical interest and by turning the splendid singer into an often platitudinous preacher and teacher. By producing the type of poetry which the critics required, Tennyson won the hearts and minds of his contemporaries, both great and small; but by catering to the tastes of one age, he jeopardized his reputation with the next. From the excessive depreciation it has suffered in the present century, his name is beginning to revive, and the fine poetry that he did write cannot fail to secure permanent approval; yet, seeking in his work to unite the transient with the abiding, he may have produced much with only an ephemeral appeal.

LIST OF REVIEWS

BIBLIOGRAPHY

NOTES

INDEX

LIST OF
REVIEWS OF TENNYSON'S POETRY
IN BRITISH PERIODICALS, 1827-1851

This list has been compiled from published and unpublished bibliographies and studies of Tennyson, from some of the recent books on individual periodicals of the nineteenth century, and from a search of the files of more than two hundred quarterly reviews, magazines, and newspapers. It contains a number of items which have never before been available in one place and, in addition, fifty-two previously unrecorded articles on Tennyson. References for the identification of the authorship of anonymous reviews are given in the notes to the text.

1827

Literary Chronicle and Weekly Review, May 19, p. 308. Brief notice of *Poems by Two Brothers.*

Gentleman's Magazine, June, XCVII, Part I, 609. Brief notice of *Poems by Two Brothers.*

1829

Athenaeum, July 22, p. 456. Short review of "Timbuctoo."

1830

Atlas, June 27, V, 411. Short review of *Poems, Chiefly Lyrical.* Robert Bell(?).

Spectator, August 21, III, 637–639. Review of *Poems, Chiefly Lyrical.*

Felix Farley's Bristol Journal, September 25, p. [4]. Notice of *Poems, Chiefly Lyrical.*

1831

Westminster Review, January, XIV, 210–224. Review of *Poems, Chiefly Lyrical.* William Johnson Fox (?).

Tatler, February 24, February 26, II, 593–594, 601–602. Review of *Poems, Chiefly Lyrical.* Leigh Hunt.

New Monthly Magazine, March, XXXIII, 111–112. Review of *Poems, Chiefly Lyrical.*

Englishman's Magazine, August, I, 616–628. "On Some of the Characteristics of Modern Poetry, and on the Lyrical Poems of Alfred Tennyson." Arthur Henry Hallam.

1832

Blackwood's Edinburgh Magazine, May, XXXI, 721–741. Review of *Poems, Chiefly Lyrical.* John Wilson ("Christopher North").

Athenaeum, December 1, pp. 770–772. Review of *Poems,* 1833.
Literary Gazette, December 8, pp. 772–774. Review of *Poems,* 1833. William Jerdan (?).
Spectator, December 15, V, 1190–1191. Review of *Poems,* 1833.
Atlas, December 16, VII, 842. Review of *Poems,* 1833. Robert Bell (?).

1833

Metropolitan, January, VI, 9 (Notices of New Works). Brief notice of *Poems,* 1833.
Monthly Repository, January, N.S., VII, 30–41. Review of *Poems, Chiefly Lyrical* and *Poems,* 1833. William Johnson Fox.
New Monthly Magazine, January, XXXVII, 69–74. Review of *Poems,* 1833. Edward Bulwer (?).
Tait's Edinburgh Magazine, January, II, 540. Brief notice of *Poems,* 1833.
True Sun, January 19, p. [3]. Review of *Poems,* 1833. John Forster (?).
Quarterly Review, April, XLIX, 81–96. Review of *Poems,* 1833. John Wilson Croker.

1835

London Review, July, I, 402–424. Review of *Poems, Chiefly Lyrical* and *Poems,* 1833. John Stuart Mill.

1842

Examiner, May 28, pp. 340–341. Review of *Poems,* 1842. John Forster.
Sun, May 28, p. [4]. Short review of *Poems,* 1842.
Spectator, June 4, XV, 544. Review of *Poems,* 1842.
Atlas, June 25, XVII, 410–411. Short review (under heading "New Editions") of *Poems,* 1842.
Christian Remembrancer, July, IV, 42–58. Review of *Poems,* 1842. Francis Garden (?).
Monthly Review, July, N.S., II, 369–375. Review of *Poems,* 1842.
Tait's Edinburgh Magazine, August, N.S., IX, 502–508. Review of *Poems,* 1842.
Athenaeum, August 6, pp. 700–702. Review of *Poems,* 1842. Henry Fothergill Chorley.
Morning Post, August 9, p. 6. Review of *Poems,* 1842.
Weekly Dispatch, August 21, p. 406. Short review of *Poems,* 1842.
Quarterly Review, September, LXX, 385–416. Review of *Poems,* 1842. John Sterling.
Cambridge University Magazine, October, II, 629–639. Review of *Poems,* 1842.
Christian Teacher, October, N.S., IV, 414–423. Review of *Poems,* 1842. Signed J. J.
Church of England Quarterly Review, October, XII, 361–376. "The Modern School of Poetry." Review of *Poems,* 1842. Leigh Hunt.

Westminster Review, October, XXXVIII, 371–390. Review of *Poems,* 1842. Signed R. M. M. (Richard Monckton Milnes).

Literary Gazette, November 19, pp. 788–789. Review of *Poems,* 1842. William Jerdan (?).

London University Magazine, December, I, 286–314. Review of *Poems,* 1842. Signed W. A. C. (possibly William Arthur Case).

1843

Edinburgh Review, April, LXXVII, 373–391. Review of *Poems,* 1842. James Spedding.

1844

Foreign and Colonial Quarterly Review, January, III, 202–215. "Modern Poets — Tennyson, Marston, and Browning."

1845

Chambers's Edinburgh Journal, July 12, N.S., IV, 25–29. "The Poetry of Alfred Tennyson."

British Quarterly Review, August, II, 46–71. Review of *Poems,* 1842.

Dumfries-shire and Galloway Herald and Register, October 16, pp. [1] and [4]; October 23, pp. [1] and [4]. "Alfred Tennyson." George Gilfillan.

1847

Tait's Edinburgh Magazine, April, N.S., XIV, 229–234. "Alfred Tennyson." Signed George Gilfillan.

Hogg's Weekly Instructor, December 25, VI, 281–284. "Alfred Tennyson."

1848

Athenaeum, January 1, pp. 6–8. Review of *The Princess.* J. Westland Marston.

Guardian, January 5, pp. 13–14. Review of *The Princess.*

Dumfries-shire and Galloway Herald and Register, January 6, p. [4]. Reprint of the major part of the review of *The Princess* in the *Athenaeum.*

Examiner, January 8, pp. 20–21. Review of *The Princess.* John Forster.

Howitt's Journal, January 8, III, 28–29. Review of *The Princess.* William Howitt (?).

Manchester Examiner, January 8, p. 3. Review of *The Princess.*

Spectator, January 8, XXI, 41–42. Review of *The Princess.*

Sun, January 8, p. [3]. Review of *The Princess.*

Atlas, January 15, XXIII, 42–43. Review of *The Princess.*

Howitt's Journal, January 15, III, 39–42. "The Poet's Mission" (a detailed allegorical interpretation of "The Lady of Shalott"). Signed Henry Sutton.

Britannia, January 22, p. 61. Brief notice of *The Princess.*

Morning Post, January 22, p. 3. Review of *The Princess.*

Sheffield Times, January 29, p. 2. Review of *The Princess.*

Christian Reformer, or Unitarian Magazine and Review, February, N.S., IV, 111–113. Short review of *The Princess.* Signed C.

Gentleman's Magazine, February, N.S., XXIX, 115–131. Review of *The Princess.*

Lowe's Edinburgh Magazine, February, N.S., III, 245–258. Review of *Poems, 1842,* and *The Princess.*

Metropolitan Magazine, February, LI, 220–229. Review of *The Princess.* Signed M.

Dumfries and Galloway Standard and Advertiser, February 16, p. [2]. Reprint of considerable portion of the review of *The Princess* in *Lowe's Edinburgh Magazine.*

Quarterly Review, March, LXXXII, 427–453. Review of *The Princess.* John Gibson Lockhart (?).

Eclectic Review, April, 4th Ser., XXIII, 415–423. Review of *The Princess.*

Sharpe's London Magazine, April, VI, 139–141. Review of *The Princess.*

North British Review, May, IX, 43–72. Review of *The Princess.* Coventry Patmore.

Dublin Evening Herald, May 22, p. [2]. Review of *The Princess.*

English Review, June, IX, 286–297. Review of *The Princess.*

Tait's Edinburgh Magazine, August, N.S., XV, 554–555. Review of *The Princess.*

Literary Gazette, August 12, pp. 530–532. Review of *The Princess.* William Jerdan (?).

The Times, October 12, p. 3. Review of *Poems, 1842,* and *The Princess.* Manley Hopkins (?).

1849

Blackwood's Edinburgh Magazine, April, LXV, 453–467. Review of *Poems, 1842,* and *The Princess.* William Henry Smith.

Christian Remembrancer, April, XVII, 381–401. Review of *The Princess* (including remarks on some of the pieces in *Poems, 1842*). Charles Peter Chretien.

Westminster Review, July, LI, 265–290. Review of *Poems, 1842.* Signed Is. Is.

Edinburgh Review, October, XC, 388–433. Review of *Poems, 1842,* and *The Princess, The Poetical Works of Shelley,* ed. Mary Shelley, and *The Life, Letters, and Literary Remains, of John Keats,* ed. Richard Monckton Milnes. Aubrey de Vere.

1850

Examiner, June 8, pp. 356–357. Review of *In Memoriam.* John Forster.

Spectator, June 8, XXIII, 546. Review of *In Memoriam.*

Scotsman, June 12, p. [3]. Short notice of *In Memoriam* made up largely of quotations from the reviews in the *Examiner* and the *Spectator.*

Dumfries-shire and Galloway Herald and Register, June 13, p. [2]. Condensation of the review of *In Memoriam* in the *Spectator.*

Athenaeum, June 15, pp. 629–630. Review of *In Memoriam.* J. Westland Marston.

Atlas, June 15, XXV, 379. Review of *In Memoriam.*

Literary Gazette, June 15, p. 407. Brief notice of *In Memoriam.* William Jerdan (?).

Caledonian Mercury, June 17, p. [3]. Review of *In Memoriam.*

Greenock Advertiser, June 18, p. [4]. Condensation of the review of *In Memoriam* in the *Spectator.*

Dumfries and Galloway Standard and Advertiser, June 19, p. [3]. Brief notice of *In Memoriam.*

Inquirer, June 22, IX, 389–390. Review of *In Memoriam.*

Leader, June 22, I, 303–304. Review of *In Memoriam.* George Henry Lewes.

Guardian, June 26, p. 477. Review of *In Memoriam.*

Perthshire Advertiser, June 27, p. [4]. Short notice of *In Memoriam* made up largely of quotations from the reviews in the *Examiner* and the *Spectator.*

Britannia, June 29, p. 410. Review of *In Memoriam.*

Manchester Examiner and Times, June 29, Supplement, p. 3. Review of *In Memoriam.*

Christian Reformer, July, N.S., VI, 439–441. Short review of *In Memoriam.* Signed C.

Gentleman's Magazine, July, N.S., XXXIV, 59–60. Brief notice of *In Memoriam* (in "Notes and Correspondence of the Month").

Westminster and Foreign Quarterly Review, July, LIII, 572. Brief notice of *In Memoriam.* Signed H.

Dumfries and Galloway Standard and Advertiser, July 3, p. [1]. Short notice of *In Memoriam* made up largely of quotations from the reviews in the *Examiner* and *Spectator.*

Critic, July 15, N.S., IX, 355–356. Review of *In Memoriam.*

Ayr Observer, July 16, p. [2]. Review of *In Memoriam.*

British Quarterly Review, August, XII, 291–292. Review of *In Memoriam.*

Dublin University Magazine, August, XXXVI, 209–224. "Latter-Day Poets." Review of *In Memoriam,* Aubrey de Vere's *Greece,* Alfred Lee's *Empire of Music,* and Henry Taylor's *Virgin Widow.*

Hogg's Instructor, August, N.S., V, 365–368. Review of *In Memoriam.*

North British Review, August, XIII, 532–555. Review of *In Memoriam.*

Palladium, August, I, 94–100. Review of *In Memoriam.* Coventry Patmore.

Sharpe's London Journal, August, XII, 119–121. Review of *In Memoriam.*

Tait's Edinburgh Magazine, August, N.S., XVII, 499–505. Review of *In Memoriam.* Franklin Lushington.

Court Journal, August 10, p. 505. Short review of *In Memoriam.*

Edinburgh News and Literary Chronicle, August 24, p. 8; September 14, p. 8. Extended critique of Tennyson's poetry as a whole (including *In Memoriam*). Signed G. C.

Sun, August 29, p. [3]. Review of *In Memoriam.*

Morning Post, August 31, p. 2. Review of *In Memoriam.*

Eclectic Review, September, 4th Ser., XXVIII, 330–341. Review of *In Memoriam.*

English Review, September, XIV, 65–92. "New Poetry. — Tennyson, Browning, and Taylor."

Fraser's Magazine, September, XLII, 245–255. Review of *Poems,* 1842, *The Princess,* and *In Memoriam.* Charles Kingsley.

Morning Herald, September 5, p. 6. Short review of *In Memoriam.*

Prospective Review, October, VI, 306–331. Review of *In Memoriam.*

Westminster and Foreign Quarterly Review, October, LIV, 85–103. Review of *In Memoriam.* Signed Is. Is.

1851

Literary Gazette, January 18, p. 52. Brief notice of *In Memoriam.*

Sheffield and Rotherham Independent, January 18, p. 6; January 25, p. 6; February 1, p. 6; March 1, p. 6. Extended review and commentary on *In Memoriam.* Signed W.

North British Review, February, XIV, 486–514. Review of *The Remains in Verse and Prose of Arthur Henry Hallam.*

People's and Howitt's Journal, May, IV, 185–186. List of topic headings for each section of *In Memoriam.*

Wesleyan-Methodist Magazine, June, 4th Ser., VII, Part I, 587–588. Review of *In Memoriam.*

Christian Socialist, August 30, September 6, September 20, II, 140–142, 155–157, 187–190. "Tennyson and His Poetry." Signed Gerald Massey.

Christian Socialist, September 27, October 4, October 11, October 18, November 1, II, 204–207, 220–222, 236–238, 246–247, 284–286. "Tennyson's 'Princess.' " Signed Gerald Massey.

The Times, November 28, p. 8. "The Poetry of Sorrow." Review of *In Memoriam.* Manley Hopkins (?).

BIBLIOGRAPHY

Adams, William Bridges. "On the Condition of Women in England," *Monthly Repository*, April 1833, N.S., VII, 217–231.

Alford, Henry. *Life, Journals, and Letters of Henry Alford*, ed. Frances Alford. London, Oxford, and Cambridge, 1873.

Allingham, William. *William Allingham: A Diary*, ed. Helen Allingham and D. Radford. London, 1907.

—— *Letters to William Allingham*, ed. Helen Allingham and E. Baumer Williams. London, New York, Bombay, and Calcutta, 1911.

Baum, Paull F. *Tennyson Sixty Years After*. Chapel Hill, 1948.

Beattie, William. *Life and Letters of Thomas Campbell*. 3 vols. London, 1849.

Benson, Arthur C. *Alfred Tennyson*. London, 1904.

Benson, Dorothea M., Lady Charnwood. *An Autograph Collection and the Making of It*. New York, 1930.

Bibliographies of Twelve Victorian Authors, compiled by Theodore G. Ehrsam, Robert H. Deily, and Robert M. Smith. New York, 1936.

The Book of Gems, the Poets and Artists of Great Britain, ed. Samuel Carter Hall. 3 vols. London, 1836–1838.

Bourne, H. R. Fox. *English Newspapers: Chapters in the History of Journalism*. 2 vols. London, 1887.

Bowden, Marjorie. *Tennyson in France*. Manchester, 1930.

Bradley, A. C. *A Commentary on Tennyson's In Memoriam*. 3d ed. London, 1929.

Brightfield, Myron F. *John Wilson Croker*. Berkeley, California, 1940.

—— "Lockhart's *Quarterly* Contributors," *PMLA*, LIX (1944), 491–512.

Bristed, Charles Astor. "English Poetry and Poets of the Present Day," *Knickerbocker Magazine*, June 1845, XXV, 534–540.

Brookfield, Arthur M. "Some Letters from Arthur Hallam," *Fortnightly Review*, LXXX (1903), 170–179.

Brookfield, Charles and Frances. *Mrs. Brookfield and Her Circle*. 2 vols. 3d ed. London, 1906.

Brookfield, Frances M. *The Cambridge "Apostles."* London, 1906.

Browning, Elizabeth Barrett. *The Letters of Elizabeth Barrett Browning*, ed. Frederic G. Kenyon. 2 vols. London, 1897.

—— *Letters of Elizabeth Barrett Browning Addressed to Richard Hengist Horne*, ed. S. R. Townshend Mayer. 2 vols. London, 1877.

Browning, Robert. *Robert Browning and Alfred Domett*, ed. Frederic G. Kenyon. London, 1906.

────── *The Letters of Robert Browning and Elizabeth Barrett Barrett, 1845–1846* [ed. Robert Barrett Browning]. 2 vols. London, 1899.

Burton, Katherine. "Hallam's Review of Tennyson," *Modern Language Notes*, XLV (1930), 224–225.

The Cambridge Bibliography of English Literature, ed. F. W. Bateson. 4 vols. Cambridge, England, 1940.

Carlyle, Thomas. *The Correspondence of Thomas Carlyle and Ralph Waldo Emerson, 1834–1872*, ed. Charles Eliot Norton. 2 vols. London, 1883.

────── *Letters of Thomas Carlyle to John Stuart Mill, John Sterling, and Robert Browning*, ed. Alexander Carlyle. London, 1923.

A Catalogue of Books Published in the United Kingdom During the Year 1850. London, Sampson Low, 1851.

A Catalogue of Books Published in the United Kingdom During the Year 1851. London, Sampson Low, 1852.

A Catalogue of Books Published in the United Kingdom During the Year 1853. London, Sampson Low, 1854.

"The Centenary of 'The Quarterly Review,'" *Quarterly Review*, CCX (1909), 731–784.

Champneys, Basil. *Memoirs and Correspondence of Coventry Patmore*. 2 vols. London, 1900.

Church, Alfred J. *The Laureate's Country*. London, 1891.

Clayden, P. W. *Rogers and His Contemporaries*. 2 vols. London, 1889.

Coleridge, Samuel Taylor. *Specimens of the Table Talk of the Late Samuel Taylor Coleridge* [ed. Henry N. Coleridge]. 2 vols. London, 1835.

Collins, John Churton. *Illustrations of Tennyson*. London, 1891.

Curwen, Henry. *A History of Booksellers, the Old and the New*. London, 1873.

Dawson, S. E. *A Study; with Critical and Explanatory Notes, of . . . The Princess*. 2d ed. Montreal, 1884.

Dickens, Charles. *The Speeches of Charles Dickens*, ed. Richard Herne Shepherd. London, 1937 (Rosemary Library).

Dictionary of National Biography, ed. Leslie Stephen and Sidney Lee. 22 vols. Reissue. London, 1908–1909.

Dixon, W. MacNeile. *A Primer of Tennyson*. London, 1896.

Donne, William Bodham. *William Bodham Donne and His Friends*, ed. Catharine B. Johnson. London, 1905.

Eidson, John O. *Tennyson in America*. Athens, Georgia, 1943.

Eliot, T. S. *Essays Ancient and Modern*. London, 1936.

Elwin, Malcolm. *Victorian Wallflowers*. London, 1934.

The English Catalogue of Books Issued in the United Kingdom, 1801–1836, ed. Robert A. Peddie and Quintin Waddington. London, 1914.

Everett, Edwin M. *The Party of Humanity: The Fortnightly Review and Its Contributors, 1865–1874.* Chapel Hill, 1939.

Fausset, Hugh I'Anson. *Tennyson: A Modern Portrait.* London, 1923.

FitzGerald, Edward. *Letters and Literary Remains of Edward FitzGerald,* ed. William Aldis Wright. 3 vols. London, 1889.

———*Letters of Edward FitzGerald,* ed. William Aldis Wright. 2 vols. London and New York, 1894.

———*Some New Letters of Edward FitzGerald,* ed. F. R. Barton. London, 1923.

Ford, George H. *Keats and the Victorians: A Study of His Influence and Rise to Fame, 1821–1895.* New Haven, 1944.

Fox, Caroline. *Memories of Old Friends,* ed. Horace N. Pym. London, 1882.

Fox, William Johnson. "Living Poets; and Their Services to the Cause of Political Freedom and Human Progress. — No. 3. Alfred Tennyson," in *Lectures Addressed Chiefly to the Working Classes* (I, 248–265). London, 1845.

Garnett, Richard C. *The Life of W. J. Fox, Public Teacher and Social Reformer, 1786–1864.* London and New York, 1910.

Gilfillan, George. *A Second Gallery of Literary Portraits.* Edinburgh and London, 1850.

Gordon, Mary. *Christopher North: A Memoir of John Wilson.* 2 vols. Edinburgh, 1862.

Graham, Walter. *English Literary Periodicals.* New York, 1930.

———"Some Infamous Tory Reviews," *Studies in Philology,* XXII (1925), 500–517.

Granniss, Ruth S. *A Descriptive Catalogue of the First Editions in Book Form of the Writings of Percy Bysshe Shelley.* New York, 1923.

Green, Joyce. "Tennyson's Development during the 'Ten Years' Silence' (1832–1842)," *PMLA,* LXVI (1951), 662–697.

Grierson, Herbert J. C., and J. C. Smith. *A Critical History of English Poetry.* London, 1944; 2d and revised ed., London, 1947.

———"The Tennysons," in *The Cambridge History of English Literature,* ed. A. W. Ward and A. R. Waller (XIII, 23–48). Cambridge, England, 1916.

Gwynn, Stephen. *Tennyson: A Critical Study.* London, 1899.

Haight, Gordon S. "Tennyson's Merlin," *Studies in Philology,* XLIV (1947), 549–566.

Hall, Samuel Carter. *A Book of Memories of Great Men and Women of the Age.* London, 1871.

———*Retrospect of a Long Life; from 1815 to 1883.* 2 vols. London, 1883.

Hallam, Arthur Henry. *The Writings of Arthur Hallam,* ed. T. H. Vail Motter. New York and London, 1943.

Hindle, Wilfred H. *The Morning Post, 1772–1937*. London, 1937.

The History of The Times: II. The Tradition Established, 1841–1884. London, 1939.

Horton, Robert F. *Alfred Tennyson: A Saintly Life*. London, 1900.

House, Humphry. "The Hopkinses," *Times Literary Supplement*, November 4, 1949, p. 715.

Howitt, Mary. *Mary Howitt: An Autobiography*, ed. Margaret Howitt. 2 vols. London, 1889.

Howitt, William. *Homes and Haunts of the Most Eminent British Poets*. 2 vols. London, 1847.

Hunt, Leigh. *The Autobiography of Leigh Hunt*. 3 vols. London, 1850.

—— *The Correspondence of Leigh Hunt*, ed. Thornton Hunt. 2 vols. London, 1862.

Jennings, Henry J. *Lord Tennyson: A Biographical Sketch*. New ed. London, 1892.

Jerdan, William. *The Autobiography of William Jerdan*. 4 vols. London, 1852–1853.

Kingsley, Charles. *The Life and Works of Charles Kingsley*, ed. Frances Kingsley. 19 vols. London, 1901–1903.

Kitchel, Anna T. *George Lewes and George Eliot*. New York, 1933.

Knowles, James. "Aspects of Tennyson, II," *Nineteenth Century*, January 1893, XXXIII, 164–188.

Lake, John. *Criticism and Taste: A Satire*. London, 1834.

Lang, Andrew. *Alfred Tennyson*. Edinburgh and London, 1901.

—— *The Life and Letters of John Gibson Lockhart*. 2 vols. London and New York, 1897.

Laws and Transactions of the Union Society. Cambridge, England, 1832.

Literary Anecdotes of the Nineteenth Century, ed. W. Robertson Nicoll and Thomas J. Wise. 2 vols. London, 1895.

Lounsbury, Thomas R. *The Life and Times of Alfred Tennyson*. New Haven, 1915.

Lucas, F. L. *Eight Victorian Poets*. Cambridge, England, 1930.

Lyall, Alfred. *Tennyson*. London, 1902.

Macaulay, Thomas Babington. "Mr Robert Montgomery's Poems and the Modern Practice of Puffing," *Edinburgh Review*, April 1830, LI, 193–210.

McLachlan, Herbert. *The Unitarian Movement in the Religious Life of England*. London, 1934.

Marchand, Leslie A. *The Athenaeum: A Mirror of Victorian Culture*. Chapel Hill, 1941.

Martin, Theodore. *Memoir of William Edmondstoune Aytoun*. Edinburgh and London, 1867.

Martineau, Harriet. *Autobiography*. 3 vols. London, 1877.

Mattes, Eleanor B. *In Memoriam: The Way of the Soul*. New York, 1951.

Maurice, Frederick Denison. *The Life of Frederick Denison Maurice,* ed. Frederick Maurice. 2 vols. London, 1884 .

Merivale, Charles. *Autobiography and Letters of Charles Merivale,* ed. Judith Anne Merivale. Oxford, privately printed, 1898; also London, 1899.

Merriam, Harold G. *Edward Moxon, Publisher of Poets.* New York, 1939.

Mill, John Stuart. *Autobiography.* London, 1873.

—— *The Letters of John Stuart Mill,* ed. Hugh S. R. Elliot. London, New York, Bombay, and Calcutta, 1910.

Mineka, Francis E. *The Dissidence of Dissent: The Monthly Repository, 1806–1838.* Chapel Hill, 1944.

Mitchell, Charles. *The Newspaper Press Directory . . . for the Year 1846.* London, 1846.

—— *The Newspaper Press Directory . . . for the Year 1851.* London, 1851.

Napier, George G. *The Homes and Haunts of Alfred Lord Tennyson.* Glasgow, 1892.

Neff, Emery E. *Carlyle.* New York, 1932.

Nesbitt, George L. *Benthamite Reviewing: The First Twelve Years of the Westminster Review, 1824–1836.* New York, 1934.

"The Newspaper and Periodical Press of London," *London Journal,* I (1845), 36, 54, 70, 90, 121, 158, 168, 200, 216, 253, 254, 268, 328, 348, 397, 407, 431, 438.

A New Spirit of the Age, ed. Richard Hengist Horne. 2 vols. London, 1844.

Nicolson, Harold. *Tennyson: Aspects of His Life, Character, and Poetry.* London, 1923.

Oliphant, Margaret. *Annals of a Publishing House: William Blackwood and His Sons.* 2 vols. Edinburgh and London, 1897.

Paden, William D. "Tennyson and the Reviewers (1829–1835)," in *Studies in English* (University of Kansas Publications, Humanistic Studies, VI, No. 4, 15–39). Lawrence, Kansas, 1940.

—— *Tennyson in Egypt: A Study of the Imagery in His Earlier Work* (University of Kansas Publications, Humanistic Studies, No. 27). Lawrence, Kansas, 1942.

Patmore, Coventry. *Courage in Politics and Other Essays, 1885–1896,* ed. Frederick Page. London, 1921.

Pearce, Helen. "The Criticism of Tennyson's Poetry: A Summary with Special Emphasis upon Tennyson's Response to Criticism as a Factor in the Development of His Reputation." Ph.D. thesis, University of California, 1930.

Peyre, Henri. *Writers and Their Critics.* Ithaca, New York, 1944.

Pope-Hennessy, James. *Monckton Milnes: The Years of Promise.* London, 1950.

Praeraphaelite Diaries and Letters, ed. William Michael Rossetti. London, 1900.

Publishers' Circular, VII (1844), VIII (1845), IX (1846), X (1847), XIII (1850), XIV (1851).

Pyre, James F. A. *The Formation of Tennyson's Style.* Madison, Wisconsin, 1921.

Rawnsley, Willingham F. "Personal Recollections of Tennyson — II," *Nineteenth Century and After,* XCVII (1925), 190–196.

Records of an Eton Schoolboy, ed. Charles M. Gaskell. London, privately printed, 1883.

Redding, Cyrus. *Literary Reminiscences and Memoirs of Thomas Campbell.* 2 vols. London, 1860.

Reid, Mrs. Hugo. *A Plea for Woman.* London, 1844.

Reid, T. Wemyss. *The Life, Letters, and Friendships of Richard Monckton Milnes, First Lord Houghton.* 2 vols. 2d ed. London, 1890.

Robertson, Frederick W. *Two Lectures on the Influence of Poetry on the Working Classes.* Brighton, 1852.

Scott, Walter B. "Tennyson and His Age, 1850–1875." Ph.D. thesis, Princeton University, 1934.

Shannon, Edgar F., Jr. "The Coachman's Part in the Publication of *Poems by Two Brothers,*" *Modern Language Notes,* LXIV (1949), 107–110.

———— "Tennyson and the Reviewers, 1830–1842," *PMLA,* LVIII (1943), 181–194.

Shepherd, Richard Herne. *Tennysoniana.* London, 1866.

[Shorter, Clement.] *The Love Story of In Memoriam.* n.p., privately printed, 1916.

Smith, Sydney. "Female Education," *Edinburgh Review,* January 1810, XV, 299–315.

Spedding, James. *Reviews and Discussions, Literary, Political, and Historical, not Relating to Bacon.* London, 1879.

Stevenson, Lionel. "The 'High-born Maiden' Symbol in Tennyson," *PMLA,* LXIII (1948), 234–243.

Strout, Alan Lang. " 'Christopher North' on Tennyson," *Review of English Studies,* XIV (1938), 428–439.

Taylor, Henry. *Autobiography of Henry Taylor, 1800–1875.* 2 vols. London, 1885.

———— *Correspondence of Henry Taylor,* ed. Edward Dowden. London, 1888.

———— *Philip van Artevelde.* London, 1834.

Tennyson, Alfred. *The Devil and the Lady,* ed. Charles Tennyson. London, 1930.

—— *Poems by Two Brothers*, ed. Hallam Tennyson. London, 1893.

—— *The Poetic and Dramatic Works of Alfred Lord Tennyson*, ed. William J. Rolfe. Boston, New York, and Chicago, 1898 (Student's Cambridge Edition).

—— *Tennyson and His Friends*, ed. Hallam Tennyson. London, 1911.

—— *Unpublished Early Poems*, ed. Charles Tennyson. London, 1931.

—— *The Works of Tennyson*, ed. Hallam Tennyson. 9 vols. London, 1908 (The Eversley Edition).

Tennyson, Charles. *Alfred Tennyson*. London and New York, 1949.

—— "Tennyson Papers," *Cornhill Magazine*, CLIII (1936), 283–305, 426–449, 534–557, 672–680.

Tennyson, Hallam. *Alfred Lord Tennyson: A Memoir by His Son*. 2 vols. London and New York, 1897.

—— *Materials for a Biography of A. T.* 4 vols. n.p., privately printed, n.d.

Terhune, Alfred M. *The Life of Edward FitzGerald*. New Haven and London, 1947.

Thomas, William B. *The Story of the Spectator, 1828–1928*. London, 1928.

[Thurston, Charles T.] *The Sister's Tragedy*. London, 1834.

" 'The Times' and the Poets," *Tait's Edinburgh Magazine*, January 1852, N.S., XIX, 18–21.

Toovey, Alfred Dixon. *Biographical and Critical Notices of the British Poets of the Present Century*. London, 1848.

Trench, Richard Chenevix. *Richard Chenevix Trench: Letters and Memorials*, ed. Maria Trench. 2 vols. London, 1888.

Tuell, Anne K. *John Sterling: A Representative Victorian*. New York, 1941.

Turnbull, Arthur. *The Life and Writings of Alfred Lord Tennyson*. London and Felling-on-Tyne, 1914.

Van Dyke, Henry. *The Poetry of Tennyson*. London, 1890.

Victoria, Queen. *The Letters of Queen Victoria . . . 1837–1861*, ed. Arthur C. Benson and Viscount Esher. 3 vols. London, 1908.

Walker, Hugh. *The Literature of the Victorian Era*. London, 1921.

Walters, J. Cuming. *Tennyson: Poet, Philosopher, Idealist*. London, 1893.

Ward, Wilfred P. *Aubrey de Vere: A Memoir Based on His Unpublished Diaries and Correspondence*. London, New York, and Bombay, 1904.

Watson, Aaron. *Tennyson*. London, 1912.

Waugh, Arthur. *Alfred Lord Tennyson: A Study of His Life and Work*. London, 1892.

Weir, W. "London Newspapers," in *London*, ed. Charles Knight (V, 337–352). London, 1841–1844.

Wise, Thomas J. *A Bibliography of the Writings of Alfred, Lord Tennyson.* 2 vols. London, privately printed, 1908.

Wollstonecraft, Mary. *A Vindication of the Rights of Woman.* London, 1792.

Yarborough, Minnie C. "Cambridge Radicals and Spanish Constitutionalists," *South Atlantic Quarterly,* XXXIX (1940), 58–76.

NOTES

For complete citation of all important British reviews of Tennyson, 1827–1851, see the List of Reviews above, pp. 169–174. For dates and places of publication of books cited, see the Bibliography above, pp. 175–182.

CHAPTER I. EARLY POEMS

1. For accounts of Tennyson's literary precocity, see Hallam Tennyson, *Alfred Lord Tennyson: A Memoir by His Son*, I, 11–12, hereafter referred to as *Memoir*; and Charles Tennyson, *Alfred Tennyson*, pp. 33–45, hereafter cited as *A. T.* Alfred's verses in *Poems by Two Brothers* had been written when he was between the ages of fifteen and seventeen (see Hallam Tennyson's edition, p. vi).

Poems by Two Brothers is sometimes said to have been published in December 1826 though dated 1827 (see, for example, Harold Nicolson, *Tennyson: Aspects of His Life, Character, and Poetry*, p. 49, and John O. Eidson, *Tennyson in America*, p. 3). But Thomas R. Lounsbury (*The Life and Times of Alfred Tennyson*, pp. 41–44) is correct in asserting that the book was published in April 1827. The preface is dated March 1827, and the volume was first advertised as "just published" on the front page of the *Lincoln, Rutland, and Stamford Mercury*, Friday, April 20, 1827. For a discussion of the publishing arrangements, see William D. Paden, *Tennyson in Egypt: A Study of the Imagery in His Earlier Work*, pp. 20–21 and 118–119, n. 44. See also my "The Coachman's Part in the Publication of *Poems by Two Brothers*," *MLN*, LXIV (1949), 107–110.

The authorship of the individual poems was identified, so far as it was possible to do so from the manuscript, after the laureate's death by the second Lord Tennyson with some assistance from his uncle Frederick. The initials of the writer are given after each piece in *Poems by Two Brothers*, ed. Hallam Tennyson.

2. Lounsbury (*Life*, p. 43) says that on April 22, 1827, the *Sunday Mercury* printed an advertisement which included the statement that *Poems by Two Brothers* "contains many exquisite pieces of verse," but this can hardly be called a critical notice.

3. That Tennyson matriculated on February 20, 1828, is a matter of record, but there has been some question about when he actually began residence at the university. Paden (*Tennyson in Egypt*, pp. 17, 112–114, n. 18) argues cogently for the belief that he went up in the autumn of 1827 and was in residence for the Michaelmas term. Charles Tennyson (*A. T.*, p. 54) adds family authority by saying that Alfred "entered Trinity in October, 1827."

4. *Memoir*, I, 47–48.

5. October 22, 1829, T. Wemyss Reid, *The Life, Letters, and Friendships of Richard Monckton Milnes*, I, 72.

6. September 14, 1829, *Memoir*, I, 46.

7. See Leslie A. Marchand, *The Athenaeum: A Mirror of Victorian Culture*, pp. 6–7, 271. Charles Tennyson (*A. T.*, pp. 91–92) attributes this review to Milnes.

8. *Memoir*, I, 45.

9. The facts of publication are given in *The English Catalogue of Books Issued in the United Kingdom, 1801–1836*, p. 582. For a discussion of the inopportune timing, see William D. Paden, "Tennyson and the Reviewers (1829–1835)," pp. 20–21.

10. For Bell's beginning date as editor, see "Robert Bell," *DNB*. On July 19, 1842, Hunt wrote to Bell thanking him for reviewing *The Palfrey* and lamenting that Bell was leaving the *Atlas* (*The Correspondence of Leigh Hunt*, II, 103).

11. This notice cannot be attributed to Rintoul with any degree of probability, since it appears that he wrote very little for his paper himself, being truly an editor who supervised the work of his staff. See William Beach Thomas, *The Story of the Spectator*, pp. 25–26. Unfortunately, the *Spectator* has no records showing the authorship of articles published during the nineteenth century.

12. I have been unable to identify the writer of this review.

13. Effingham Wilson advertised the book in the *Athenaeum*, June 19, 1830, p. 384, and in the *Literary Gazette*, June 26, 1830, p. 424.

14. *Memoir*, I, 70.

15. William Johnson Fox (in his review of Browning's *Pauline*, *Monthly Repository*, April 1833, N.S., VII, 254) wrote that his interest in Tennyson was first aroused by some of his verses reprinted in this way.

16. The poems were printed on pp. 87, 131, 242.

17. Letter from Hallam to Leigh Hunt, January 11, 1831 (*Literary Anecdotes of the Nineteenth Century*, I, 24). The poet's son (*Memoir*, I, 49) says that Bowring was the author, and George L. Nesbitt (*Benthamite Reviewing: The First Twelve Years of the Westminster Review, 1824–1836*, p. 178) repeats this assertion. Alfred J. Church (*The Laureate's Country*, p. 89) identifies the article as by John Stuart Mill; and Richard Herne Shepherd (*Tennysoniana*, p. 25) speaks of this review as "written, it is believed, by Mr. John Stuart Mill." But Paden ("Tennyson and the Reviewers," p. 22, n. 24), who refutes the same contention by Henry Curwen (*A History of Booksellers*, p. 351), is correct in maintaining its impossibility; for, as he says, Mill was not a contributor to the *Westminster* during Bowring's editorship after 1828. See Mill's *Autobiography*, pp. 129–131. Of this review Frances M. Brookfield (*The Cambridge "Apostles,"* p. 141) even suggested, "It is possible that it was Hallam himself who wrote the review alluded to above."

18. Paden ("Tennyson and the Reviewers," pp. 22–27) argues convincingly for Fox's authorship.

19. On January 7, 1831 (p. [4]), the *Sheffield Courant* quoted in its literary section the discussion of "Mariana" — the poem which the critic had labeled the best in the volume.

20. *Athenaeum*, December 28, 1833, p. 893.

21. *Literary Anecdotes*, I, 24–25.

22. The editor of the magazine from January to November 1831 was Samuel Carter Hall. See his *Retrospect of a Long Life*, I, 315–317; William Beattie,

Life and Letters of Thomas Campbell, III, 72; and "Edward George Earle Lytton Bulwer-Lytton," *DNB*. It does not appear likely that Hall was the author of the review on Tennyson. See above, p. 11.

23. The review is reprinted in *The Writings of Arthur Hallam*, pp. 182–198. Lounsbury's erroneous dating of Hallam's review (1830 for 1831) has been pointed out by Katherine Burton, *MLN*, XLV (1930), 224–225. For Moxon's proprietorship, see Harold G. Merriam, *Edward Moxon, Publisher of Poets*, p. 31.

24. *Morning Post*, August 8, 1831, p. 7.

25. "There are three things which fill my heart with sighs," *The Yorkshire Literary Annual*, ed. C. F. Edgar (London, 1832), p. 127; "Me my own fate to lasting sorrow doometh," *Friendship's Offering*, ed. T. K. Hervey (London, 1832), p. 367.

26. *Athenaeum*, October 22, 1831, pp. 683–684; *Literary Gazette*, October 15, 1831, p. 664.

27. *Memoir*, I, 95.

28. *Life*, p. 238.

29. *Memoir*, I, 84. Hallam wrote, "I suppose one ought to feel very savage at being attacked, but somehow I feel much more amused." North's own verdict, while egotistical and exaggerated, had some truth in it. He wrote (in a review of Joanna Baillie, *Blackwood's*, February 1836, XXXIX, 266), "Were it not for Us, where would they [Tennyson, Trench, and Alford] be? Nowhere. Out of Cambridge and Cockneydom, how many scores of Christian creatures have ever seen either of Alfred Tennyson's Volumes? Not fourscore. In Maga many of his best compositions have been perused with delight by tens of thousands — and as sympathy is what every poet most fervently desires, how deep ought to be — and how deep must be — his gratitude to Christopher North!"

30. *Athenaeum*, May 5, 1832, p. 288; *Spectator*, May 5, 1832, V, 424.

31. *Edinburgh Observer*, May 4, 1832, p. [4].

32. *Sun*, May 1, 1832, p. [2].

33. London, 1833, p. 29.

34. *Life*, p. 206; see also pp. 205, 227.

35. "Tennyson and the Reviewers," pp. 19–20; the full discussion covers pp. 19–31. As Paden says, the eventual article in *Blackwood's* cannot be attributed to Garden's action, since North did not notice Tennyson until long after the poet had been brought into prominence by the *Westminster*. North (*Blackwood's*, April 1833, XXXIII, 670) said that the poet had sent him an inscribed copy of *Poems, Chiefly Lyrical*. Tennyson denied emphatically any such action (*Memoir*, I, 96). If the copy North thought he had received from the poet was the one possibly presented at the publisher's office by Garden, the bait was resisted for almost two years. See Paden, "Tennyson and the Reviewers," p. 28, n. 43.

36. *Memoir*, I, 70. Hallam mentioned a letter from Spedding "dated two months ago." Since Garden's letter is linked with Spedding's as "also of very old date," Garden probably wrote in August.

37. Pressmark 9785/13. D. 45.

38. James Pope-Hennessy, *Monckton Milnes: The Years of Promise*, p. 233. Campbell's sister had been governess to Milnes's aunts; and on June 2, 1830,

Campbell wrote to her (Beattie, *Life . . . of . . . Campbell*, III, 67),."I am happy to tell you, my dearest sister, that I have at last had the pleasure of seeing young Milnes under my roof. He is a charming young man."

Campbell edited the *New Monthly* from January 1821 until December 1830. See Cyrus Redding, *Literary Reminiscences and Memoirs of Thomas Campbell*, I, 158; II, 235; and Beattie, *Life . . . of . . . Campbell*, III, 72.

39. Hallam wrote in a letter to Emily Tennyson dated 1831 that Coleridge had "rejoiced over" Charles Tennyson (*Memoir*, I, 75). Since Hallam said he was sending the reviews of the two Tennysons in the *Tatler* with the letter, it was probably written in the early part of March 1831. The *Memoir* (I, 50n.) says that Hallam "visited Coleridge at Highgate and wrote about him in his poem of 'Timbuctoo,'" which, like Tennyson's, was submitted for the Chancellor's Medal in the spring of 1829. The *Memoir* (I, 177n.) also says Tennant "had been a frequenter of Coleridge's famous gatherings at Highgate." In *Specimens of the Table Talk of the Late Samuel Taylor Coleridge*, II, 164, Coleridge apparently refers to *Poems*, 1833, rather than to *Poems, Chiefly Lyrical*.

40. Paden ("Tennyson and the Reviewers," p. 31) mistakenly says that "in all the years before 1842 the enthusiasm of Tennyson's friends appeared in print only twice"; i.e., the review of "Timbuctoo" in the *Athenaeum* and Hallam's article for the *Englishman's*. For another instance in 1838, see above, p. 27.

41. *Life*, p. 207. Hallam, who thought Bowring had written the article, would certainly have known if it had been one of the Cambridge men. Monteith wrote of it to Milnes, then in Italy, without indicating any knowledge of its authorship (Reid, *Life . . . of . . . Milnes*, I, 106). Brookfield wrote to Hallam with surprised delight (letter of January 15, 1831, printed by Arthur M. Brookfield in "Some Letters from Arthur Hallam," *Fortnightly Review*, LXXX [1903], 172, and Frances M. Brookfield in *Cambridge "Apostles,"* p. 140).

42. "Tennyson and the Reviewers," p. 28.

43. See letter from Leigh Hunt to Hall (*Memoir*, I, 163–164), and the *Book of Gems*, III, 274.

44. The opening sentences of the review scarcely suggest that it came from the pen of Milnes or one of the Apostles, and the author of *The Pleasures of Hope* and *Gertrude of Wyoming* was not likely to have written a notice praising the similar qualities of Tennyson and Keats.

45. Arthur M. Brookfield, *Fortnightly Review*, LXXX, 172, and Frances M. Brookfield, *Cambridge "Apostles,"* p. 140.

46. Reid, *Life . . . of . . . Milnes*, I, 106.

47. This letter, printed after Hallam Tennyson's custom of sometimes leaving no indication of the excisions he saw fit to make in the text of letters, was published in the *Memoir*, I, 500–501. Fortunately, he had printed for his own use all the material that he might include in the life of his father. There are copies of this invaluable mine of information, entitled *Materials for a Biography of A. T.*, in the British Museum and the Bodleian. The portions of Arthur Hallam's letter to Donne which are of importance to the discussion here are to be found in the full text printed in *Materials*, IV, 453–455. My estimate of the date of the letter is based on the first sentence,

omitted in the *Memoir*, "I know not whether anyone of the faithful has yet acquainted you with the very welcome probability that Kemble and Trench will be speedily in England, the latter perhaps within a few days." Trench actually reached England early in March. On March 6 Hailam wrote to him thanking God for his safe return (*Richard Chenevix Trench: Letters and Memorials*, I, 85).

48. This letter is in the possession of Professor Richard L. Purdy, Berkeley College, Yale University, who has graciously permitted me to quote from it.

49. Letter of August 23, 1831, *Writings of . . . Hallam*, p. 182.

50. This information is contained in the unpublished portion of the letter of August 23, 1831, partially quoted in *Writings of . . . Hallam*. The letter is now in the possession of Mr. Vail Motter, who has kindly allowed me to use it.

51. See Marchand, *The Athenaeum*, pp. 97–122, and Emery E. Neff, *Carlyle*, pp. 127–132. For a contemporary account, see Thomas Babington Macaulay, "Mr Robert Montgomery's Poems and the Modern Practice of Puffing," *Edinburgh Review*, April 1830, LI, 193–210.

52. *Autobiography of Henry Taylor, 1800–1875*, I, 195–196.

53. *Life*, p. 306.

54. *Life*, p. 227.

55. "Tennyson and the Reviewers," p. 31.

56. *Autobiography and Letters of Charles Merivale*, pp. 159–161.

57. *Trench*, I, 111.

58. Charles Tennyson, *A. T.*, p. 121.

59. *English Catalogue*, p. 582.

60. See Lounsbury, *Life*, p. 285; Nicolson, *Tennyson*, pp. 111–112; and Charles Tennyson, *A. T.*, pp. 135–136.

61. On December 15, 1832, Hallam wrote to Gaskell that he had completed a review of Tennyson's *Poems* for the *Edinburgh* (*Records of an Eton Schoolboy*, p. 178), but it was not accepted.

62. For an illuminating discussion of the meaning of the term "metaphysical" as applied to Tennyson in the reviews of the 1830's, see Paden, "Tennyson and the Reviewers," pp. 32–37.

63. The *Sheffield Mercury* did not give the author's name.

64. *Northern Whig*, December 24, 1832, p. [4]; *Scotsman*, December 29, 1832, p. [4]; *Liverpool Albion*, December 31, 1832, VII, 418.

65. Bulwer (later Bulwer-Lytton) seems to have edited this issue, probably the last under his direction. See Hall, *Retrospect of a Long Life*, I, 317, and Paden, "Tennyson and the Reviewers," p. 36, n. 50. Bulwer was referred to as the editor by the *Atlas*, January 6, 1833, VIII, 9. Whether or not he was actually the author of the review, Tennyson believed that he was. See Richard Garnett, *The Life of W. J. Fox*, p. 284.

66. The *Atlas* (VIII, 9) defended itself in the following words from the charge in the *New Monthly* that Tennyson had met with entirely too much eulogy from the press: "We are glad to see this morbid affectation met by a sensible examination of Mr. TENNYSON's poetry in the *New Monthly*. Here the question of false taste is fairly met, and the critics who were bitten by the strange glossary and extravagant conceits of the young rhymer, cast in costs of judgment. The *New Monthly*, however, would not have 'bated a

jot of its utility, if, in its side-wind at the journalists, it had thought fit to make an exception. We anticipated its analysis of Mr. TENNYSON by at least a fortnight, and were entitled to be exempted from the indiscriminate censure with which it visits our contemporaries."

67. Lounsbury (*Life*, p. 288), Nicolson (*Tennyson*, pp. 111–112), and Charles Tennyson (*A. T.*, p. 135) agree on the favorable nature of this review.

68. Malcolm Elwin (*Victorian Wallflowers*, p. 181) says that Forster was appointed literary and dramatic critic for the *True Sun* in 1832; and the review of *Poems*, 1833, in the *True Sun* and Forster's critique of *Poems*, 1842, in the *Examiner* (see above, pp. 61–62) are strikingly similar in both style and method. A repetition of phraseology also offers significant evidence that the *True Sun* article was written by Forster. In the *True Sun* the reviewer said, "Out of the very overflow from which such poems [as "Eleanore"] come, we conceive Mr. Tennyson's faults to have arisen. He is too abundant in his 'lavish lights and floating shades,' and distributes them often most indiscriminately." Nine years later Forster wrote of Tennyson in the *Examiner*, "He is acquiring one of the most valuable arts a poet can master: that of selection and compression. His imagery is less profuse; his 'lavish lights and floating shades' are scattered with more discrimination."

69. See Myron F. Brightfield, *John Wilson Croker*, pp. 349–351.

70. See, for example, Nicolson (*Tennyson*, p. 111), "Tennyson's reputation sank to zero," and Charles Tennyson (*A. T.*, p. 137), "The effect of this article was disastrous. . . . The sales of Tennyson's volume were irretrievably injured." For the sale of the book by 1840, see above, p. 32.

71. *Memoir*, I, 94.

72. Merriam, *Edward Moxon*, p. 78.

73. Samuel C. Hall writes (*A Book of Memories of Great Men and Women of the Age*, p. 284), "A laudatory review was almost sure to sell an edition of a book, and an author's fame was established when he had attained the praise of . . . [the *Literary Gazette*]."

74. *Memoir*, I, 91 (for both remarks by Hallam).

75. *Memoir*, I, 94.

76. *Memoir*, I, 91.

77. *Tennyson*, p. 111.

78. The *Quarterly* appeared on April 6, 1833. See *Spectator*, VI, 316.

79. *Sun*, April 9, 1833, p. [3].

80. *Athenaeum*, April 13, 1833, p. 234.

81. "Biographical and Critical History of the Literature of the Last Fifty Years," *Athenaeum*, November 16, 1833, p. 772.

82. John Lake's *Criticism and Taste* (1834), a wretched satire in heroic couplets, espoused Tennyson's cause, not against the *Quarterly*, but in reply to Christopher North. The poem probably attracted little attention, and its publication is not listed in the *English Catalogue*; but Lake sent a copy to Tennyson, who was sufficiently alarmed over the possibility of an answering attack in *Blackwood's* to write to North disavowing "any one grain of sympathy with the ravings of this unhappy coxcomb" (*Memoir*, I, 95).

83. Nicolson, *Tennyson*, p. 111.

84. *Englishman's*, I, 621; also *Writings of . . . Hallam*, p. 191. Hallam was realistic enough to add, somewhat fatalistically, "Nevertheless . . . we be-

lieve his participation in their characteristic excellencies is sufficient to secure him a share of their unpopularity."

85. March 6 and 15, 1833; quoted from Marjorie Bowden, *Tennyson in France*, p. 8.

86. Unpublished letter, Gladstone Papers, British Museum, Add. MSS. 44, 352, fols. 88–89, dated "Trinity, Cambridge. *Saturday 8 Nov.*" Hallam said in the letter that he had been at Cambridge for three weeks.

87. Reid (*Life . . . of . . . Milnes*, I, 73–83) gives a full account of the debate; for *Adonais*, see Ruth S. Granniss, *A Descriptive Catalogue of the First Editions in Book Form of the Writings of Percy Bysshe Shelley*, pp. 72–73.

88. See *Laws and Transactions of the Union Society*.

89. *The Life of Frederick Denison Maurice*, I, 74–76. See also John Stuart Mill, *Autobiography*, pp. 129–131.

90. Marchand, *The Athenaeum*, pp. 19–20. See also Minnie C. Yarborough, "Cambridge Radicals and Spanish Constitutionalists," *South Atlantic Quarterly*, XXXIX (1940), 61–62.

91. Yarborough, *South Atlantic Quarterly*, XXXIX, 64–65.

92. *Memoir*, I, 51–55.

93. Charles Tennyson, *A. T.*, pp. 21, 59.

94. Paden, "Tennyson and the Reviewers," p. 38.

95. *Benthamite Reviewing*, p. 163.

96. "Every issue carried either an article on the Reform Bill or a running account of it under the heading 'Reporting Progress' " (Merriam, *Edward Moxon*, p. 32).

97. Dorothea May Benson, Lady Charnwood, *An Autograph Collection and the Making of It*, p. 179.

98. Nesbitt (*Benthamite Reviewing*, p. 161) and Paden ("Tennyson and the Reviewers," pp. 38–39) both point out that the vehemence of North's attacks on Tennyson's previous reviewers came largely from political considerations.

99. Merriam, *Edward Moxon*, pp. 25–26, 30–34, 38.

100. Marchand, *The Athenaeum*, pp. 28, 61ff.

101. Merriam, *Edward Moxon*, p. 26. See also Lounsbury, *Life*, pp. 295–297.

102. For the *Athenaeum*'s fight against "puffery," see Marchand, *The Athenaeum*, pp. 97–156.

103. Thomas, *Story of the Spectator*, p. 47.

104. Margaret Oliphant, *Annals of a Publishing House: William Blackwood and His Sons*, I, 514.

105. *English Newspapers*, II, 46; Hunt wrote a letter (*Correspondence*, I, 283) to the *Morning Chronicle* repudiating the rumor that he was writing for a "Conservative" paper. In a postscript to the letter he added, "Perhaps the editor of the *Examiner* and the *Atlas*, the two other papers with which I am best acquainted, will do me the favour to transfer this letter to their columns. And I should take it as a kindness in other Reform papers, which I have not the same pleasure of seeing."

106. Hall (*Retrospect of a Long Life*, I, 317) says, "He soon made his editorship a vehicle for propagating his then advanced political creed — ultra-Radical."

107. *English Literary Periodicals*, p. 291.

108. Francis E. Mineka, *The Dissidence of Dissent: The Monthly Repository, 1806–1838*, pp. 101, 247–284.

109. Mineka, p. 187. The opprobrium with which the *Monthly Repository* was regarded about 1833 by Whigs, not to mention Tories, is illustrated by the attitude of Lucy Aiken. Although Miss Aiken is described in the *DNB* as a "Whig, with a generous love of liberty," Harriet Martineau relates (*Autobiography*, I, 305) that "she felt it was an act of friendship to warn me against appearing to know of periodicals so low as, for instance, the 'Monthly Repository' and having any information to give about dissenting ministers, like Mr. Fox." The incident occurred after Miss Martineau, who was already one of Fox's most valuable contributors, had told Henry Hallam, the historian and father of Tennyson's friend Arthur, something of the policy of the magazine and of its editor.

110. See Walter Graham, "Some Infamous Tory Reviews," *SP*, XXII (1925), 511, and Paden, "Tennyson and the Reviewers," p. 39. Lounsbury presents his theory in *Life*, p. 315; see also p. 321.

111. Brightfield, *John Wilson Croker*, p. 350. Croker had reviewed Hunt's *The Story of Rimini* in the *Quarterly Review*, January 1816, XIV, 473–481, and Keats's *Endymion*, April 1818, XIX, 204–208.

112. *Fraser's Magazine*, May 1836, XIII, 625.

113. When Mill, Molesworth, and others were projecting the *London Review*, Carlyle wrote of the scheme to Mill (*Letters of Thomas Carlyle to John Stuart Mill, John Sterling, and Robert Browning*, p. 93), "For the present I can see but a little way. Have you not for instance a Radical Review already, the *Westminster*; and Radical magazines, *Tait's*, the *Repository* and so forth? What, at bottom, is the meaning of a new Work of the same sort; what newness is there to be in the doctrines of it?"

114. Bowden, *Tennyson in France*, p. 12.

115. Bowden, p. 12.

116. For several of the references to Tennyson in *Blackwood's*, I am indebted to Alan Lang Strout's valuable article, " 'Christopher North' on Tennyson," *RES*, XIV (1938), 428–439.

117. Possibly North here confused Alfred with his brother Charles.

118. This tribute has previously been unnoticed and seems to be a second instance overlooked by Paden ("Tennyson and the Reviewers," p. 31) in which the opinion of one of Tennyson's friends was expressed in print prior to 1842.

119. The *Literary Gazette* reviewed the book on the same day without mention of Tennyson.

120. *Metropolitan*, December 1837, XX, 106 (Notices of New Works).

121. The *Edinburgh* (LXII, 301) also referred to Coleridge's comment in *Table Talk* that Tennyson should restrict himself to well-known meters and said that Alford required no such discipline.

122. The poem was published anonymously, but the catalogue of the Bodleian Library gives Thurston as the author.

123. *Table Talk*, II, 164–165.

124. *Book of Gems*, III, 274. All Hall's remarks here summarized appear on this page.

125. Charles Tennyson, *A. T.*, p. 137; *Memoir*, I, 162–163. The letter appears

under a running head of 1838, but from the context of the letter itself there can be no doubt that the date is 1837.

126. Mineka, *Dissidence of Dissent*, pp. 382–383. Hunt had linked Miss Barrett with Tennyson in "Blue-Stocking Revels," a poem published in the *Monthly Repository* (July 1837, N.S., XI–I, 39).

127. Unpublished letter, Napier Papers, British Museum, Add. MSS. 34,621, fols. 70–71. There is some uncertainty about how many copies there were in the edition of *Poems*, 1833. Charles Tennyson (*A. T.*, pp. 130, 137) says there were 450 copies, but later (p. 154) mentions "eight hundred copies of the volume."

CHAPTER II. SILENCE AND WORK

Some of the material in this chapter has been published previously in my article, "Tennyson and the Reviewers, 1830–1842," *PMLA*, LVIII (1943), 181–194. Miss Joyce Green, in "Tennyson's Development during the 'Ten Years' Silence' (1832–1842)," *PMLA*, LXVI (1951), 662–697, has questioned the findings in my article and has minimized the effect of the reviewers upon Tennyson; but in building her case she disregards his extreme sensitiveness to criticism and the fact that his dread of critical onslaught was the primary cause for the period of silence (see above, pp. 33–36). In other notes I point out several weaknesses in her arguments and statistics; and that I by no means think the reviewers were alone responsible for Tennyson's development during the ten years' silence the present chapter makes clear. The Conclusion to this book should absolve me from any charge of accusing him of sycophancy or venality.

1. "Aspects of Tennyson, II," *Nineteenth Century*, January 1893, XXXIII, 173–174.

2. *Memoir*, I, 49.

3. Paden, *Tennyson in Egypt*, pp. 113–114. Tennyson went down in February (*Memoir*, I, 71).

4. Hallam mentioned the review in his letter to Hunt on January 11 (*Literary Anecdotes*, I, 24). Milnes, who was in Italy, received Monteith's letter in February (Reid, *Life . . . of . . . Milnes*, I, 106).

5. *Memoir*, I, 74–75; unpublished letter from Hallam to Emily Tennyson, January 25, 1833, in the Wellesley College Library.

6. *Materials*, I, 98. This part of the letter, dated Hastings, July 26, 1831, is not quoted in the *Memoir*, I, 81.

7. *Memoir*, I, 95, 96, 94, 122.

8. Garnett, *Life of W. J. Fox*, p. 284.

9. He also saw some foreign articles, for his son records (*Memoir*, I, 134) that his father "warmed to his work because there had been a favourable review of him lately published in far-off Calcutta." Tennyson is quoted (*Memoir*, I, 185n.) as saying, "Before the Penny Post [i.e., 1840] a wretched review from the Continent followed me all over England, and I had to pay one pound eight shillings for it." Tennyson may have been referring to a review simply in the sense of a periodical, but it seems likely that he meant

a periodical containing a review of his poems. Could this have been the critique in *Le Voleur*, December 1832, of which FitzGerald wrote (*Memoir*, I, 156), "You are called — guess what! — 'Jeune Enthousiaste de l'école gracieuse de *Thomas Moore*' — this I think will make you laugh and is worth postage"? Elizabeth Barrett Browning acted as an intermediary in forwarding a review published in an American newspaper in the early forties. See *Letters of Elizabeth Barrett Browning Addressed to Richard Hengist Horne*, I, 86–87.

10. The early biographers generally subscribed to this theory, which was strengthened by Lounsbury's confirmation of it (*Life*, pp. 333–336), despite his belief that the reviewers had no effect on the revisions and suppressions of the early poems. Sir Charles Tennyson lends family authority by writing (*The Devil and the Lady*, pp. vii–viii) that Tennyson's "extravagant sensibility to criticism . . . after the critical *vituperatio* of 1833 kept him silent for what should have been nine of the most fruitful years of his life." See also Charles Tennyson, *A. T.*, p. 152.

Recent scholars who have endorsed the belief that the reviewers caused the silence include: Walter Graham, "Some Infamous Tory Reviews," *SP*, XXII, 511; George L. Nesbitt, *Benthamite Reviewing*, p. 162; Edwin M. Everett, *The Party of Humanity: The Fortnightly Review and Its Contributors, 1865–1874*, p. 4; Henri Peyre, *Writers and Their Critics*, p. 42; Herbert J. C. Grierson and J. C. Smith, *A Critical History of English Poetry*, p. 403; and Alfred M. Terhune, *The Life of Edward FitzGerald*, p. 121.

11. *Trench*, I, 152.

12. Hallam Tennyson (*Memoir*, I, 138) says that in the spring of 1835, when urged to publish by his brother Frederick, "he would not and could not; his health since Hallam's death had been 'variable, and his spirits indifferent.'"

13. *William Bodham Donne and His Friends*, p. 16.

14. *Memoir*, I, 141.

15. *Materials*, I, 116.

16. *Memoir*, I, 97. Tennyson gives a poetic representation of this period of his life in the third stanza of "Merlin and the Gleam":

> Once at the croak of a Raven who crost it
> A barbarous people,
> Blind to the magic
> And deaf to the melody,
> Snarl'd at and cursed me.
> A demon vext me,
> The light retreated,
> The landskip darken'd,
> The melody deaden'd,
> The Master whisper'd,
> "Follow the Gleam."

See Gordon S. Haight, "Tennyson's Merlin," *SP*, XLIV (1947), 549–566. Charles Tennyson (*A. T.*, p. 517n.) believes that "the reference is to the family troubles which followed Dr. Tennyson's death in 1831, and the attempts made by the old man of the Wolds to divert Alfred from his determination to devote himself to poetry." But Hallam Tennyson, who was his father's constant companion when the poem was published and who would certainly know, says (*Materials*, I, 141), "The 'Raven croaked' ominously in the shape of the *Quarterly*."

17. *Memoir*, I, 96, 145.

18. *Memoir*, I, 157–160.

19. British Museum, Add. MSS. 34,621, fols. 70–71. Spedding's italics.

20. *Memoir*, I, 180.

21. *The Letters of Robert Browning and Elizabeth Barrett Barrett, 1845–1846*, I, 19–20.

22. June 1845, XXV, 536. Others who assert that Tennyson gave considerable heed to the reviewers in the correcting and suppression of the poems of his first two volumes are: Mary Gordon, *Christopher North: A Memoir of John Wilson*, II, 175–176; Henry Van Dyke, *The Poetry of Tennyson*, pp. 28–32, 36, 38–42; Henry Jennings, *Lord Tennyson*, p. 30; J. Cuming Walters, *Tennyson: Poet, Philosopher, Idealist*, p. 300; Andrew Lang, *The Life and Letters of John Gibson Lockhart*, II, 88; Stephen Gwynn, *Tennyson: A Critical Study*, pp. 31–32; Andrew Lang, *Alfred Tennyson*, pp. 22–23; Sir Alfred Lyall, *Tennyson*, pp. 15, 26; "The Centenary of 'The Quarterly Review,' " *Quarterly Review*, CCX (1909), 773–774; Aaron Watson, *Tennyson*, pp. 26, 33; Arthur Turnbull, *The Life and Writings of Alfred Lord Tennyson*, pp. 50, 58–59; Hugh Walker, *The Literature of the Victorian Era*, p. 297; Hugh I'Anson Fausset, *Tennyson: A Modern Portrait*, pp. 49, 56; F. L. Lucas, *Eight Victorian Poets*, p. 6. Nicolson (*Tennyson*, pp. 117–118), who attempts to follow Lounsbury, admits the file was applied more vigorously to the poems that had been most heavily censured. All these writers consider only North's review in *Blackwood's* and "Lockhart's" in the *Quarterly*.

23. *Memoir*, I, 122.

24. *Life*, p. 401.

25. In arriving at this figure I have counted any poem that received condemnation by any one reviewer. In most instances the reviewers were outspoken and there is no question. There are several borderline cases, however, where the reviewers were not quite explicit or where admission was made of some merit. Such were "A Dirge," "Claribel," and "Recollections of the Arabian Nights"; but I have included them, since it would be better to admit reasonable possibilities than to risk misrepresenting the evidence. In deciding these borderline cases the criterion has been whether the sum of a reviewer's comments indicates a serious disapproval or stricture. Accordingly, "Oriana," for instance, has not been included among the twenty-four, though Hunt commented that he thought the name, running through the poem, too often repeated.

26. "Love and Sorrow," condemned by the *Atlas*, is the only poem not censured by a review we know Tennyson saw. Hunt's comment (*Tatler*, February 26, 1831, II, 602), however, "The author must have been reading Donne, when he wrote it," may have affected the poet's judgment.

27. North, *Blackwood's*, XXXI, 740.

28. *Spectator*, III, 637–638; *Westminster*, XIV, 223; *Blackwood's*, XXXI, 740; *Athenaeum*, December 1, 1832, p. 770; *Literary Gazette*, December 8, 1832, p. 773; *Monthly Repository*, N.S., VII, 32–33.

29. See Tennyson's letter to S. E. Dawson (*Memoir*, I, 256–259). He was very resentful over Churton Collins's *Illustrations of Tennyson*. W. F. Rawnsley

records ("Personal Recollections of Tennyson — II," *Nineteenth Century and After*, XCVII [1925], 195), "Churton Collins he especially disliked. He complained to me: 'The critics won't allow me any imagination. They take a line like "Moaning of the homeless sea" and say "'Moaning,' Horace; 'homeless,' Shelley," and so on. Your friend Churton Collins makes me borrow expressions from men I never even heard of.' "

For charges of imitation, see *Spectator*, III, 638; *Tatler*, II, 601–602; *Athenaeum*, December 1, 1832, p. 770; *Literary Gazette*, December 8, 1832, p. 773; *New Monthly*, XXXVII, 69.

30. *New Monthly*, XXXVII, 70.

31. Knowles, "Aspects of Tennyson, II," p. 174; Knowles's italics. In addition, Hunt (*Tatler*, II, 601) had said of "Supposed Confessions": "It is such as Crashaw might have written in a moment of scepticism, had he possessed vigour enough. Or Andrew Marvel might have written it, when he was midway between his early opinions and his later."

32. Lounsbury (*Life*, p. 408) includes "Eleanore" and "Mariana in the South" in his list of poems attacked; but of these Croker (*Quarterly*, XLIX, 86) only said, "We pass by two — what shall we call them? — tales, or odes, or sketches, entitled 'Mariana in the South' and 'Eleanore,' of which we fear we could make no intelligible extract, so curiously are they run together into one dreamy tissue." With the exception of "Who can say," Croker attacked all of the thirteen poems generally criticized.

33. Hallam Tennyson records that his father regretted his lifelong suppression of "The Hesperides," and in consequence the son republished it in the *Memoir*. The suggestion seems all too obvious that originally Tennyson's judgment was strongly colored by the castigation of the reviewers.

34. My figures differ from Lounsbury's here, for his statements are based on the *Quarterly* alone. Besides, his computations are the result of comparing the lines quoted by the critic with the number of lines Tennyson reprinted. I have counted only the words and phrases or lines singled out by italics or special mention. Often the reviewers were forced to quote several lines to which they had no objection in order to make the thought of the passage understandable to the readers of their critiques.

35. See George H. Ford, *Keats and the Victorians*, pp. 43–45, and James F. A. Pyre, *The Formation of Tennyson's Style*, pp. 56–57. Pyre's undocumented reference to "Lockhart's" (Croker's) comment on several stanzas of "The Palace of Art" as "Keats turned imbecile" seems to be erroneous.

36. If Croker had nothing to say about "Rosalind" itself, some of his most scathing satire was directed at Tennyson's printing of thirty-two extra lines in a footnote. Originally intended to be part of the poem, they became "manifestly superfluous" even to the author; but he liked them and was unwilling to discard them entirely. Two similar footnotes appended to "The Palace of Art" were further fuel for Croker's fire, and Tennyson wisely deleted the notes when the poems were reprinted.

37. *Life*, p. 401.

38. *Memoir*, I, 96. Echoing Lounsbury, Miss Green (*PMLA*, LXVI, 663) says that soon after the 1833 volume appeared Tennyson "realised he had published prematurely, and large-scale revision was in any case inevitable if he ever wished to be taken seriously as an artist." But she documents the first

part of this statement with FitzGerald's remark, "Tennyson . . . regrets
that he has published at all yet," which occurs in a letter to Donne, dated
October 25, 1833 — six months after all the English reviews except Mill's
had appeared! And how "large-scale" and "inevitable" would Tennyson's
revisions and suppressions have been if he had not been castigated? Miss
Green (p. 679) further observes that "after 1833 . . . he had now become a
poet who aspired wholeheartedly to be taken seriously as a moralist and
thinker." Her belief that this aspiration governed his suppression of certain
poems seems plausible, and this same aspiration seems to have motivated a
number of the new poems in 1842 (see above, pp. 45–58). Yet Miss Green
refuses to acknowledge that the role of moralist and thinker was precisely
the one the critics were urging him to fulfill.

39. *Memoir*, I, 50n.

40. I have not included in my list poems cited in their entirety by the reviewers without any specific passages being condemned. Where there seems
to be a definite point of criticism concerned with each italicized word or
group of words, I have considered each a separate criticism. Where three or
four consecutive lines were cited with several italicized words or phrases, but
where the reviewer seemed to be pointing to the passage as a whole, I have
considered it one criticism. (Miss Green seems to me to distort her statistics
in Table B [*PMLA*, LXVI, 686–697] by counting each italicized word an
additional stricture.) Since the poems of 1830 were relatively short, the reviewers dealt with that volume mainly by complete poems, so that only
eleven passages were cited from them.

41. North (*Blackwood's*, XXXI, 731) charged Tennyson in the line, "Thou
art a mailéd warrior, in youth and strength complete," from "The Grass-
hopper," with absurdity and plagiarism from Wordsworth's conception of a
beetle as "A mailed angel on a battle day." Tennyson's whole poem hinged
upon the idea of the "mailéd warrior." The other passages in poems not
reprinted were in five short poems only. Eight lines of the sonnet "Buonaparte" were cited as unintelligible; all three stanzas of "O Darling Room"
were satirized; and there were six points singled out in "The Hesperides,"
eight in the sonnet "Mine be the Strength," and nine in "To ——" ("All good
things").

In Table B Miss Green ignores the censured poems not reprinted in 1842
and the passages singled out in them. By including among her tabulated
strictures poems censured as a whole that were republished and excluding
those that were not, she automatically weights her figures in favor of Tennyson's rejection of criticism.

42. In certain cases it may very well be that Tennyson's maturer judgment
coincided with the critics' objections and that his alterations were the result
of both influences. These cases cannot be clearly distinguished, but the admission weakens my position very little.

43. *Table Talk*, II, 164. Tennyson may have heard through Hallam or
Tennant of Coleridge's remark before *Table Talk* was published. In his old
age Tennyson explained that Coleridge's criticism probably stemmed from
an inability to scan his lines because he wrote his compounds without hyphens. Whether or not at the time he thought Coleridge's remarks the

product of misunderstanding, most of his new poems were written in a "well-defined metre," as the elder poet had suggested.

44. Pope-Hennessy, *Monckton Milnes*, p. 16.

45. *Formation of Tennyson's Style*, pp. 25–26.

46. Pyre, p. 26.

47. *Memoir*, I, 122.

48. See Pyre, pp. 40–57, 59–67, 85–93.

49. Pyre, pp. 58–59.

50. Pyre, pp. 26–27, 101–102.

51. *Memoir*, I, 188–189. Some of these poems were begun early in the period of silence; but, as Spedding (*Edinburgh Review*, LXXVII, 374) said of them, "though composed probably at various intervals during the ten intervening years, [they] have all, we presume, had the benefit of his latest correcting hand." Spedding, of course, as Tennyson's literary adviser, knew that such was actually the case.

52. North (*Blackwood's*, XXXI, 725–726) had deplored these — "National Song," "English War Song," and "We Are Free" — and wished that the young poet had written patriotic poems of real power.

53. In lectures on Victorian poetry at Harvard University.

54. *Memoir*, I, 60.

55. Ford (*Keats and the Victorians*, p. 34) says that in "The Poet's Mind" Tennyson "seems to be drawing . . . on the final scene in *Lamia*."

56. "The 'High-born Maiden' Symbol in Tennyson," *PMLA*, LXIII (1948), 236–238.

57. *Cambridge History of English Literature*, XIII, 40.

58. *Tennyson*, p. 25.

59. The very pertinent first sentence of this letter of 1830, quoted here from the *Materials*, I, 81–82, was deleted by Hallam Tennyson. The excised text appears in the *Memoir*, I, 68–69. Part of this letter is also published by Frances M. Brookfield, *Cambridge "Apostles,"* pp. 87–88.

60. Both letters to Donne appear in *Trench*, I, 52–53, 73.

61. *Life, Journals, and Letters of Henry Alford*, p. 103.

62. Hallam's letters are in *Memoir*, I, 501, 81.

63. *Unpublished Early Poems by Alfred Tennyson*, pp. 42–45.

64. The letters from Venables and Hallam Tennyson's remark appear in *Memoir*, I, 122, 123. The suggestions of James Spedding, who succeeded Arthur Hallam as Tennyson's literary adviser, must also have been of considerable influence, though but few of them are extant. For one instance, see letter dated September 19, 1834, *Memoir*, I, 139–140.

65. The reviews of Alford appeared in the *Athenaeum*, August 29, 1835, p. 661; *Literary Gazette*, September 5, 1835, p. 565; *Blackwood's*, May 1836, XXXIX, 577–593; and *Edinburgh Review*, January 1836, LXII, 297–318.

66. Milnes wrote to C. J. MacCarthy, November 11, 1835 (Reid, *Life . . . of . . . Milnes*, I, 159), "Trench's poems have reached a second edition, owing principally to a puff in *Blackwood*. He says he is afraid that it is the religious world that have bought them, not the poetical."

67. *Blackwood's*, September 1835, XXXVIII, 417.

68. *Quarterly Review*, June 1834, LI, 365–391.

69. *Philip van Artevelde*, pp. x–xiii.

70. *Memoir*, I, 141.

71. *Englishman's Magazine*, I, 619–621; *Writings of . . . Hallam*, pp. 188–191.

72. *Westminster Review*, XIV, 223–224.

73. *Blackwood's*, XXXI, 725.

74. *New Monthly Magazine*, XXXVII, 74. The italics are mine. Hallam (*Englishman's Magazine*, I, 621; *Writings*, p. 191) mentioned "the spirit of the age" in connection with Tennyson: "The author imitates nobody; we recognise the spirit of his age, but not the individual form of this or that writer. His thoughts bear no more resemblance to Byron or Scott, Shelley or Coleridge, than to Homer or Calderon, Ferdusi or Calidas." Clearly Hallam had reference to poetic tradition in speaking of "the spirit of the age" and not to the atmosphere of revolution, progress, and change with which the *New Monthly* was concerned.

75. *Monthly Repository*, N.S., VII, 40.

76. *London Review*, I, 422, 423. It is very likely that John Sullivan Dwight's lengthy and discriminating review published in America in the *Christian Examiner*, January 1838, XXIII, 305–327, would have been brought to Tennyson's attention by admirers in England or the United States. Dwight (pp. 324–327) thought Tennyson, though possessed of great excellences, "given too much to mere aesthetic enjoyment." "He has cultivated the ideal side of his nature to excess, and so almost forfeited his right to human society. Dearly he loves to look at things . . . but then all he cares to see is their shadows in the magic mirror that hangs before him . . . he will not turn around and shake hands with the reality." Dwight asked, "Does he commune with the *soul* of things? . . . Does he feel with the eternal *heart* of humanity, so that, when he speaks, it is as the echo of our own souls, 'deep calling unto deep'? Or is he but a butterfly flitting over the surface; all sense with neither feeling nor faith? What he speaks, is it true always, or only once? Does he utter what is in *all* men, or only the one mood of *one* man? Is he prophet-eyed? . . . Does he fulfill a poet's mission to his age, inspired and inspiring, cherishing in men's hearts the divine idea of man?"

77. *Materials*, I, 142. The italics are mine.

78. *Unpublished Early Poems*, pp. 75–76. The first stanza appears in the *Memoir*, I, 97, printed in the section which carries a running head of 1832; but the context in which it occurs is after the *Quarterly* review of April 1833.

79. *Unpublished Early Poems*, pp. 79–80.

CHAPTER III. THE CORNERSTONE OF FAME:
POEMS, 1842

1. Hallam Tennyson (*Memoir*, I, 166) gives two reasons for his father's decision to publish in 1842: "He must earn a livelihood on which to marry. . . . Another fact also began to dawn upon him, that if he never published again, even that which he had published 'would be taken out of its napkin and would be given to him who had published ten volumes.' " Lounsbury (*Life*, pp. 383–387) and Eidson (*Tennyson in America*, pp. xii, 33–35) assert that Tennyson was goaded into publishing by the threat of an American edition

of the unrevised poems. Terhune (*Life of Edward FitzGerald*, p. 121) maintains that FitzGerald was directly responsible for the poet's finally breaking his silence. It seems likely that all these circumstances combined to bring the poet to act. Although Wheeler's letter from America made Tennyson determine ("when I was wavering") to bring out his corrected poems, he had still not taken them to the printer a year after he had promised the American that he would do so. On March 2, 1842, FitzGerald finally "carried him off . . . with violence to Moxon: who is to call on him to-morrow, and settle the publishing of a new volume" (*Some New Letters of Edward FitzGerald*, p. 53). If other considerations, and especially the specter of an American edition, had not already been influencing the poet, however, his friend might not have carried the day, even with violence.

Merriam (*Edward Moxon*, p. 171) says that the volumes "came off the press early in July." Thomas J. Wise (*A Bibliography of the Writings of Alfred, Lord Tennyson*, I, 80) gives September as the month of publication. But Lounsbury's undocumented date is correct. *Poems* was first advertised as "just published" on Saturday, May 14, in *The Times*, p. 10; the *Morning Post*, p. 2; the *Morning Chronicle*, p. 8; the *Standard*, p. [1]; the *Examiner*, p. 320.

2. See *Poems*, I, 234.

3. Horton, *Alfred Tennyson*, p. 94; Turnbull, *Life . . . of . . . Tennyson*, p. 70.

4. *Memoir*, I, 188.

5. *Life*, pp. 417–419. The full discussion covers pp. 416–445.

6. Two of these ten reviews, the ones in *Tait's Edinburgh Magazine*, August 1842, and the *Cambridge University Magazine*, October 1842, Lounsbury apparently chose to ignore. They are mentioned briefly in the chapter on the American reception of *Poems* (*Life*, pp. 459–463). The other eight seem to have been unknown to him. Two of these, the reviews in the *Christian Remembrancer*, July 1842, and the *London University Magazine*, December 1842, are listed in *Bibliographies of Twelve Victorian Authors*, pp. 351–352. The remaining six have previously been unnoticed.

7. See Charles Mitchell, *The Newspaper Press Directory . . . 1846*, pp. 59–60, and Graham, *English Literary Periodicals*, p. 314. Elizabeth Barrett, before her marriage to Browning, wrote (*The Letters of Elizabeth Barrett Browning*, I, 199), "The 'Atlas' [is] the best newspaper for literary reviews, excepting always the 'Examiner.'"

8. Forster was the literary critic for the *Examiner* at the time, and it seems to have been understood that he wrote the review, for FitzGerald wrote to Frederick Tennyson (*Letters and Literary Remains of Edward FitzGerald*, I, 98), it "seemed so quiet that I scarce supposed it was by Forster."

9. *Life*, p. 419.

10. Mitchell, *Newspaper Press Directory . . . 1846*, p. 44.

11. For the *Sun's* higher opinion of Tennyson a few months later, see above, p. 72, and below, p. 200, n. 31.

12. See Mitchell, *Newspaper Press Directory . . . 1846*, p. 39. At this time the *Morning Post* was edited by C. E. Michele. See Wilfred H. Hindle, *The Morning Post, 1772–1937*, p. 247.

13. *Life*, pp. 420–423.

14. *Life*, p. 426.

15. The article was headed "New Editions," and Tennyson's *Poems* appeared second in a list of ten.

16. The whole article, running from p. 365 to p. 379, included remarks on *Josephine* by Francis M. Eaton and *Eva* by Sir Edward Lytton Bulwer.

17. The *Christian Remembrancer* was coedited by William Scott and Francis Garden, 1841–1844. See *The Cambridge Bibliography of English Literature*, III, 854.

18. The promise was carried out in the next issue, October 1842. See above, p. 73.

19. See Mitchell, *Newspaper Press Directory . . . 1846*, p. 38.

20. Lounsbury (*Life*, p. 463), when he mentions this review out of its proper context, says erroneously, as it will appear, "The only review of that period which gave full and unreserved utterance to the sentiment which was ultimately to prevail can be found in 'Tait's Edinburgh Magazine' of August, 1842."

21. *Life*, pp. 422–424.

22. W. Weir, "London Newspapers," p. 351.

23. On the *Weekly Dispatch* see Mitchell, *Newspaper Press Directory . . . 1846*, p. 56; Fox Bourne, *English Newspapers*, II, 101; Weir, "London Newspapers," p. 351.

24. *Memoir*, I, 212.

25. Letters from Spedding to Napier, January 28, 1842 (Napier Papers, British Museum, Add. MSS. 34,622, fol. 376), and November 10, 1842 (Add. MSS. 34,623, fol. 240ᵛ). See above, pp. 35–36, and James Spedding, *Reviews and Discussions*, p. 277.

26. *Edwin the Fair* was published in June 1842 and *The Lays of Ancient Rome* in October. Both were reviewed in the *Quarterly*, March 1843.

27. On September 11, 1841, Sterling had written to Trench (*Trench*, I, 262), "Lately I have been reading again some of Alfred Tennyson's second volume [*Poems*, 1833], and with profound admiration of his truly lyric and idyllic genius. There seems to me to have been more epic power in Keats — that fiery, beautiful meteor. But they are two most true and great poets." In a letter (now in the King's College Library, Cambridge, partly quoted for the first time with the kind permission of the Provost and Fellows of King's College) to John Stuart Mill, July 17, 1842, Sterling wrote of the newly published edition of 1842, "I have read Tennyson's poems with more pleasure even than I expected. There seems a doubt whether he could conceive various character but as a lyrical & especially a descriptive poet & writer of eclogues he stands quite in the first class of our countrymen."

28. Anne K. Tuell, *John Sterling: A Representative Victorian*, p. 147.

29. Tuell, p. 147. Caroline Fox (*Memories of Old Friends*, p. 325) reports Tennyson as saying that he only met Sterling twice. Nevertheless, from this letter to Mill, it is apparent that Sterling's review sprang from a desire to assist Tennyson and is to be ascribed to friendship. Although Sterling was of a slightly older generation at Cambridge, he was an Apostle. As noted in Chapter I, Tennyson played a part in his attempt to assist the Spanish Constitutionalists. The poet was also a member of the Sterling Club of London, founded in 1838 and named in honor of John Sterling. Sterling's cordial regard

for Tennyson is shown by a letter of October 1841, printed in the *Memoir*, I, 181.

30. The two letters are in Brightfield, *John Wilson Croker*, pp. 426–428.

31. *Observer*, September 18, 1842, p. [3]; *Sun*, September 21, 1842, p. [3]; *Inquirer*, September 24, 1842, p. 4. The *Sun* also indulged in the following observations: " 'Locksley Hall' — a production full of original beauty — displays much of that force of expression and fervor of emotion, which we find in some of the minor poems of Lord Byron. Mr. Tennyson has all the luxuriant imagery of Keates [*sic*], without any of his effeminate sensibility, and wilful caprice of rhyme. He feels strongly, and occasionally evinces much subtle power of thought; but he should beware of dabbling in metaphysics, which is the rock on which Coleridge split."

32. Lounsbury (*Life*, p. 433) admits that by contrast to the *Quarterly*'s previous attack its "grudging praise was accordingly exalted into panegyric." But he argues that the strictures on particular poems would make the most impression and concludes that "in spite of the praise lavished in a loose way upon the poet, it is doubtful if the article in question, if taken by itself, would have done as much towards extending Tennyson's reputation with the public as a whole, as it would towards detracting from it." This argument is hardly admissible, for from the point of view of a public who, we are told, were being sullenly opposed in their appreciation of Tennyson, Sterling's article was not an obstacle but a signal to advance. Whatever the comments of the reviewer, the extensive extracts from the poems could scarcely have failed to assist Tennyson's reputation.

33. As the *Inquirer* wrote of Milnes's article on October 15, 1842, p. 6, "It is chiefly made up of extracts well calculated to call forth curiosity and admiration among those who are still strangers to the volumes."

34. Hunt's authorship is established by a letter from Browning to Domett, November 8, 1843, *Robert Browning and Alfred Domett*, p. 97. See also p. 44.

35. *Sheffield Iris*, November 12, 1842, 2d part, p. [4].

36. As it was, Hunt managed to quote 110 out of the 462 lines of "The Two Voices."

37. In the collected volume for 1842 there is no indication of the month in which each issue appeared, and I have been unable to find an advertisement of the publication of No. 18, which contained the review of Tennyson. No. 16, however, was advertised in the *Athenaeum*, April 2, 1842, p. 284, and No. 19 in the same paper on December 31, 1842, p. 1142, to appear on January 2, 1843. If these numbers of the quarterly journal came out in April and January, it is most likely that Nos. 17 and 18 were issued in July and October, respectively. For the history and nature of the *Christian Teacher* and the *Prospective Review*, see Herbert McLachlan, *The Unitarian Movement in the Religious Life of England*, pp. 189–195.

38. *English Literary Periodicals*, p. 274.

39. Because of these remarks, Lounsbury (*Life*, p. 460), who resents the slightest adverse criticism of Tennyson, dismisses this critic as beneath comment and, taking a leaf from North's book, observes that no surprise can be occasioned by the early demise of the periodical.

40. Appreciation of Tennyson at Cambridge is also reflected by the demand for his volumes there. On August 16, 1842, FitzGerald wrote (*Letters and*

Literary Remains, I, 98), "Thompson . . . told me that very many copies had been sold at Cambridge." Tennyson's *Poems* took Oxford by storm. The Dean of Westminster is quoted in the *Memoir* (I, 205–206) as saying, "On my return to Oxford in October 1842 his name was on everyone's lips, his poems discussed, criticised, interpreted; portions of them repeatedly set for translation into Latin or Greek verse at schools and colleges; read and re-read so habitually that there were many of us who could repeat page after page from memory."

41. A contemporary opinion of this Journal is to be found in the *Inquirer*, December 10, 1842, p. 8: "This magazine, which has now reached its third number, is highly creditable to the talents and taste of the gentlemen, most of them, we believe, still pursuing their studies at the University of London, by whom it is conducted. Its contents are judiciously varied, and afford abundance of entertainment, and of what may be called light reading, as well as valuable information and subjects for serious thought.

"It has two great merits in reference to the prevailing practice of the present time. It is not chiefly or obtrusively a *political* magazine; and it is not specially devoted to the *humourous*."

42. Under "University Intelligence" William Arthur Case was listed as having taken an M.A. in Classics in the examinations of May 1842. See *London University Magazine*, I, 262.

43. See *Memoir*, I, 508–509.

44. *Life*, pp. 436–437.

45. See Spedding, *Reviews and Discussions*, p. 277.

46. *Life*, p. 417.

47. *Christian Remembrancer*, IV, 56; *Morning Post*, August 9, p. 6; *Church of England Quarterly Review*, XII, 371; *London University Magazine*, I, 292, 300; *Edinburgh Review*, LXXVII, 390.

48. *Life*, pp. 424–425, 429–430.

49. The *Christian Remembrancer* (IV, 43–44) believed Tennyson's changes to be "less prejudicial" than Wordsworth's and was not averse to the suppression of such "a fantastic disfigurement" as "more lovelier" in "Oenone," but the reviewer would have preferred a modification rather than the omission of certain stanzas in "The Palace of Art" and condemned two alterations in "The Lotos-Eaters." Chorley in the *Athenaeum* (p. 700) showed much the same attitude. He expressed "regret at certain changes, clippings, omissions, and additions" and would not agree with any of those in "The Miller's Daughter," although he sanctioned the suppression of "daffodilly" in "The Lady of Shalott."

50. The eight reviews approving the changes appeared in the *Examiner*, May 28, p. 340; *Monthly Review*, N.S., 1842 (II), 370; *Tait's Edinburgh Magazine*, N.S., IX, 508; *Weekly Dispatch*, August 21, p. 406; *Quarterly Review*, LXX, 395; *Cambridge University Magazine*, II, 631; *London University Magazine*, I, 310; *Edinburgh Review*, LXXVII, 377–379. The two accepting them as reasonable were the *Morning Post*, August 9, p. 6, and the *Westminster Review*, XXXVIII, 371.

51. In correcting one of Lounsbury's errors, Paden allows himself to slip into another. Of Lounsbury's statement (*Life*, p. 306), "Once and once only on the occasion of the publication of his first volume, his friends made an

effort to forestall the judgment of the public," he says ("Tennyson and the Reviewers," p. 29), "It would be correct to say this of the *Poems* of 1842, which were reviewed by Sterling in the *Quarterly*, by Spedding in *Blackwood's* [*sic*], and by Milnes in the *Westminster*."

52. The second edition was announced by *The Times* on June 12, 1843, p. 9. The third edition was published between April 28 and May 14, 1845 (*Publishers' Circular*, May 15, 1845, VIII, 148). The evidence concerning the fourth edition is confusing, but it seems certain that it was published in 1846. Browning wrote his future wife in a letter postmarked July 15, 1846 (*Letters of Robert Browning and Elizabeth Barrett Barrett*, II, 337), "Moxon tells me that he has sold fifteen hundred of Tennyson's Poems in a year — and is about to print another edition in consequence." Also, the title page of the fourth edition bears the date 1846. But the *Publishers' Circular* (November 15, 1847, X, 376) lists the fourth edition among the new works published between October 28 and November 13, 1847. This listing seems to be a mistake, no doubt caused by Moxon's advertising methods; for in the *Daily News*, December 14, 1847, in which he gave notice of the approaching publication of *The Princess*, he also advertised the fourth edition of *Poems* as "just published." The explanation may be that because of the continued demand, he printed the fourth edition in the summer of 1846 and, since it was selling so well, saw no need to advertise. By the autumn of 1847, he probably found himself with some of this edition still on hand and thought it wise to attempt to attract attention by describing the edition as "just published." There is a possibility that he thought such a notice might contribute to the demand for *The Princess*, when it appeared. The *Publishers' Circular* no doubt listed the fourth edition as published in the first two weeks of November through having seen an earlier advertisement than the one that I have discovered in the *Daily News*.

53. *A New Spirit of the Age* is listed as published between February 28 and March 13, 1844, in the *Publishers' Circular*, March 15, 1844, VII, 83. A second edition was brought out between July 13 and July 29, 1844. See the *Publishers' Circular*, August 1, 1844, VII, 235.

The essay on Tennyson opens the second volume (pp. 3–32). For Elizabeth Barrett's part in the authorship of this article, see *Literary Anecdotes*, I, 35–41.

54. March 23, 1844, pp. 270–271; April 6, pp. 318–319; April 20, pp. 357–358; April 27, pp. 381–383; and June 8, pp. 525–526. Since the volume for 1844 in the marked file of the *Athenaeum* is not annotated (see Marchand, *The Athenaeum*, p. ix), it is impossible to identify the writers of this correspondence.

55. The first number of the *British Quarterly Review* came out in January 1845 under the editorship of Robert Vaughan, the Congregationalist minister. Alexander Gordon in the *DNB* says, "During the twenty years of his editorship he [Vaughan] kept it at a high level of intelligence, and while retaining its nonconformist character and its theological conservatism, admitted on other topics a wide range of writers of different schools."

56. Published between December 29, 1845, and January 14, 1846 (*Publishers' Circular*, January 15, 1846, IX, 19).

57. Published between December 14 and December 30, 1846 (*Publishers' Circular*, January 1, 1847, X, 3). The chapter on Tennyson appears in *Homes and Haunts*, II, 452–470.

58. This article was reprinted in Gilfillan's *A Second Gallery of Literary*

Portraits, pp. 214–231. It is a rewritten version, though in a number of instances a verbatim one, of Gilfillan's essay that appeared in the *Dumfries-shire and Galloway Herald and Register*, October 16 and 23, 1845.

59. *New Spirit of the Age*, II, 4–5. These words about the progress of Tennyson's name were actually Elizabeth Barrett's. "Stony house" was the printer's misreading of "starry house" in her manuscript. See *Literary Anecdotes*, I, 37–38.

60. *The Speeches of Charles Dickens*, p. 93. I am indebted to Mr. Humphry House for calling this reference to my attention.

61. *Lectures Addressed Chiefly to the Working Classes*, I, 248–265.

62. *Homes and Haunts*, II, 455.

63. The above-quoted reviews of Bulwer appeared in the *Athenaeum*, March 14, 1846, pp. 263–264; *Eclectic Review*, April 1846, 4th Ser., XIX, 419; *Lowe's Edinburgh Magazine*, June 1846, I, 566–568; and *The Times*, June 5, 1846, p. 7.

64. See note 54, above. The quotations are from the March 23, April 6, and April 20 letters.

65. *Homes and Haunts*, II, 464.

66. *Monthly Repository*, N.S., VII, 40.

67. *Athenaeum*, April 6, 1844, p. 318.

68. *New Spirit of the Age*, II, 30–31.

69. *Chambers's Edinburgh Journal*, N.S., IV, 28–29.

70. *Robert Browning and Alfred Domett*, pp. 40–41.

71. He wrote to Gerald Massey in a letter of April 1, 1854 (*Memoir*, I, 405), "I am no reader of papers and Reviews."

72. Letters to Spedding and Moxon, *Memoir*, I, 218, 219. In November 1844 he wrote to Moxon (*Memoir*, I, 222–223) asking for a copy of Chambers's *Vestiges of Creation*, which he had seen advertised in the *Examiner*.

73. The quotations in this paragraph are from Wilfred P. Ward, *Aubrey de Vere: A Memoir*, pp. 71–72, 87. Tennyson's complaints in the April 17 entry referred to a review of Bon Gaultier's (William Edmondstoune Aytoun and Theodore Martin's) *The Book of Ballads* in *Fraser's*, April 1845, XXXI, 420, where the reviewer had introduced parodies of "Lilian" and "The May Queen" with the remark, "Here are next two right funny specimens of the absurd facility of Tennysonian verse." The "favourable review" mentioned in the July 16 entry was most probably the one published in *Chambers's Edinburgh Journal*, July 12, 1845.

74. The fourteen poems were:

Claribel	The Mermaid
Lilian	The Merman
Isabel	To J. M. K.
Song — The Owl	The Sisters
Second Song — To the Same	The Palace of Art
Recollections of the Arabian Nights	To — ("Clear-headed friend")
The Dying Swan	The Death of the Old Year

75. The thirteen poems were:

The Epic	Lady Clare
Walking to the Mail	Sir Launcelot and Queen Guinevere
St. Simeon Stylites	The Vision of Sin

The Two Voices   The Skipping Rope
Amphion   The Goose
Edward Gray   The Blackbird
Will Waterproof's Lyrical Monologue

76. *William Allingham: A Diary,* p. 150. Allingham gives substantially the same information again under date of October 16, 1881 (pp. 314–315). The testimony of Knowles is in "Aspects of Tennyson, II," pp. 181–182; that of Hallam Tennyson in the Eversley edition of *The Works of Tennyson,* III, 436.

77. *Memoir,* I, 194. See Pyre, *Formation of Tennyson's Style,* p. 162.

78. *Tennyson and His Friends,* ed. Hallam Tennyson, pp. 502–503.

79. The *Christian Teacher* (October 1842, N.S., IV, 415) was glad that Tennyson had not written a complete poem on the Arthurian cycle: "We like his fragments . . . better than we fancy we should have liked the complete and canto-divided poem. There is a vigour in these efforts, which, perhaps, would have flagged under continuance."

80. *Diary,* p. 314.

81. For instance, he wrote to Aubrey de Vere (*Memoir,* I, 283), "I don't know, but I feel quite sorry that Caroline (Standish) is married. She did so well unmarried, and looked so pure and maidenly that I feel it quite a pity she should have changed her state."

82. "Tennyson Papers, IV: The Making of 'The Princess,'" *Cornhill,* CLIII (1936), 672–673. Sir Charles (p. 673) interprets Hallam Tennyson's remark that "The Gardener's Daughter" was written while the poet was at Cambridge to mean that it was "actually completed at Cambridge," that is, in 1831. But Tennyson apparently was not ready to consider the task accomplished until 1833; for, as Miss Green (*PMLA,* LXVI, 670) points out, Arthur Hallam wrote in a letter of July 31, 1833, "I trust you finished the 'Gardener's Daughter'" (*Memoir,* I, 103). See *Memoir,* I, 248n., for the poet's talking the plan of *The Princess* over with his future wife.

83. *Edinburgh Review,* XV, 299–315.

84. See Nesbitt, *Benthamite Reviewing,* pp. 88–91, and Mineka, *Dissidence of Dissent,* pp. 284–296.

85. *Monthly Repository,* N.S., VII, 226.

86. Lounsbury (*Life,* p. 536) says, "Upon the part woman ought to play in life he had very definite opinions. In this as in many other of his speculations he was as much in advance of his age as to some of those whose cause he championed he would possibly seem behind now." Dawson, *A Study; with Critical and Explanatory Notes, of . . . The Princess,* p. 9.

87. *Athenaeum,* March 2, 1844, pp. 189–190; March 9, 1844, pp. 215–217.

88. The earliest reference I have found to Tennyson's working on *The Princess* at this time is April 18, 1845. Aubrey de Vere notes in his diary (Ward, *Aubrey de Vere,* p. 71) under that date, "Sat with Alfred Tennyson, who read MS. poetry to Tom Taylor and me. Walked with him to his lawyer's: came back and listened to the 'University of Women.'"

89. Charles Tennyson (*Cornhill,* CLIII, 677) writes, "There is no doubt that the addition and gradual expansion of the Prologue and Epilogue were intended to relate the poem more closely to the then present age, one of the chief problems of which it was meant to illustrate."

90. The prevailing thought on this point is expressed in a letter from

Bulwer to Coventry Patmore of July 27, 1844 (Basil Champneys, *Memoirs and Correspondence of Coventry Patmore*, I, 54–57). It might as well have been written to Tennyson, to whom its suggestions would have been equally applicable:

"DEAR SIR,

"Your little volume has reached me only within the last few days. . . .

"Your pages abound with unmistakable testimonials of no common genius . . . I honestly, and without compliment, think the promise you hold out to us — is perfectly startling, both from the luxuriance of your fancy, and the subtle and reflective inclinations of your intellect. It rests with yourself alone to fulfil that promise, — for no less honestly, I may say, tho' with respect, that I doubt if very large and material alterations in the faculty we call taste, are not essentially necessary to secure you the Wide Audience and the permanent Fame which must root themselves in the universal sympathies, and household affections of men. — As yet you seem to me to lean more towards that class of Poets who are Poets to Poets — not Poets to the Multitude. . . . In poetry as in life there must be something Practical kneaded up with the ideal — in order for our work to become solid. — However costly the materials for building, we cannot well dispense with cement. This practical power it is which the greatest Poets — (and those below the greatest who have been most popular, and cherished), eminently possess."

91. An interesting example of the feeling on this subject is to be found in a review of David L. Richardson's *Literary Leaves* in the *Calcutta Review*, July 1851, XVI, 289–320, in which the critic regretted that Richardson had "never taken a long flight." "No modern bard," he said, "may hope to live in the mind of posterity, unless he has enshrined his memory in some goodly monument, the work of his own genius. Even the flowing lyrics of Burns would scarce suffice to preserve the individuality of their author, unless aided by his 'Cottar's Saturday night.' "

92. *Memoir*, I, 166.

93. *Letters of Elizabeth Barrett Browning*, I, 361.

CHAPTER IV. ADVANCING REPUTATION:
THE PRINCESS

1. Elizabeth Barrett wrote to Browning in a letter postmarked January 31, 1846 (*Letters of Robert Browning and Elizabeth Barrett Barrett*, I, 444), "But the really bad news is of poor Tennyson. . . . He is seriously ill with an internal complaint and confined to his bed, as George has heard from a common friend. Which does not prevent his writing a new poem — he has finished the second book of it — and it is in blank verse and a fairy tale, and called the 'University,' the university-members being all females. If George has not diluted the scheme of it with some law from the Inner Temple, I don't know what to think — it makes me open my eyes. Now isn't the world too old and fond of steam, for blank verse poems, in ever so many books, to be written on the fairies?"

2. In a letter to Moxon dated 1847 (*Memoir*, I, 241). Tennyson wrote, "An Edinburgh paper mentions that I have a poem in the press. Confound the publicities and gabblements of the 19th century! "

3. *Memoir*, I, 240–241.

4. *Materials*, I, 319.

5. For the advertisements, see the following newspapers, December 14, 1847: *Morning Post*, p. 8; *Morning Herald*, p. [1]; *Morning Chronicle*, p. 8; *Daily News*, p. [1].

The *Critic*, December 25, 1847, N.S., VI, 415, included *The Princess* in its "List of New Books"; and the poem was advertised as "just published" in the *Examiner*, December 25, 1847, p. 832. It was again advertised as "just published" on Monday, December 27, on the front pages of the *Morning Post*, the *Morning Herald*, and the *Daily News*. Lounsbury (*Life*, p. 530) and Eidson (*Tennyson in America*, p. 57) give the date of publication correctly. Wise (*Bibliography*, I, 100), who lists November, is in error, as is Merriam (*Edward Moxon*, p. 178), who says that *The Princess* "was published probably in September."

6. See *Sheffield Times*, January 29, 1848, p. 2; *Metropolitan*, February 1848, LI, 220–221; *Lowe's Edinburgh Magazine*, February 1848, N.S., III, 245, 250; *Eclectic Review*, April 1848, 4th Ser., XXIII, 415; *Sharpe's London Magazine*, April 1848, VI, 140; *The Times*, October 12, 1848, p. 3; *Christian Remembrancer*, April 1849, XVII, 381–382; *Blackwood's Edinburgh Magazine*, April 1849, LXV, 467.

7. See references in note above except for *Lowe's Edinburgh Magazine*.

8. *Life*, pp. 543, 541, 540, 542. Lounsbury's impression seems to have been based on reviews in the *Athenaeum*, the *Spectator*, and the *Atlas*; but in discussing the opinions of these critics, he fails to give references. See undocumented quotations on p. 556 and his remarks on pp. 542–543.

9. For the identification of Marston's authorship, see Marchand, *The Athenaeum*, p. 277.

10. Mitchell (*Newspaper Press Directory . . . 1846*, p. 97) says of the *Guardian*, "It is a well-printed, large-sized journal; devoting ample space to the news of the week, with well-written criticisms on literature, music, and the arts, and able leading articles on most subjects which bear on the social reforms almost daily brought before the public." See also Fox Bourne, *English Newspapers*, II, 131.

11. The *London Journal* (I, 254) in 1845 said, "The literary-review department of this journal is conducted with much talent."

12. Lounsbury (*Life*, p. 544) says, "The article was almost certainly the work of Mary Howitt"; but this identification seems to be purely guesswork, and Mr. Carl R. Woodring, a thorough student of the Howitts, informs me that the notice is more likely by William Howitt. The style of the review, the remarks on Tennyson's feeling for the spirit of progress, and the discussion of woman's place in the social scheme bear out Mr. Woodring's opinion.

William Howitt and his wife Mary "sought in the pages of *Howitt's Journal*, in an attractive form, to urge the labouring classes, by means of temperance, self-education, and moral conduct, to be their own benefactors." The enterprise turned out to be "a pecuniary failure." See *Mary Howitt: An Autobiography*, II, 42–43.

By 1848 the Howitts were Tennyson's friends of several years' standing. It appears from the context of Mary Howitt's *Autobiography* (II, 27–28) that it was in the latter part of 1844 that Tennyson spent a night and a day with them at their house, The Elms, Lower Clapton. On this occasion they sat up until three in the morning talking and listening to Tennyson read his "exquisite poetry." On December 18, 1846, Mrs. Howitt wrote to her sister, "We have had Tennyson with us a good deal lately. We quite love him" (*Autobiography*, II, 41). See also Tennyson's cordial letters to Mrs. Howitt, *Memoir*, I, 237, 239, 261, 270–271.

13. See Mitchell, *Newspaper Press Directory . . . 1846*, p. 80, and Fox Bourne, *English Newspapers*, II, 131.

14. Probably the *Spectator*.

15. The *Sheffield Times* (January 15, p. 8), the *Leeds Times* (January 15, p. 6), and the *Manchester Guardian* (January 26, p. 2) printed "Tears, idle tears" in their columns of selected poetry. The following month the *Nottingham Review* (February 4, p. 2), the *Ayr Observer* (February 15, p. [2]), and the *Cambridge Chronicle* (February 26, p. [4]) republished the same lyric; and the *Nottingham Mercury* (February 11, p. 6) quoted thirty-seven lines from *The Princess*, beginning, "For woman's cause is man's."

16. The reprint of the *Athenaeum* review in the *Dumfries-shire and Galloway Herald* should be counted with the four unfavorable reviews. The seven favorable reviews were in the *Guardian*, the *Sun*, the *Examiner*, *Howitt's Journal*, the *Morning Post*, the *Manchester Examiner*, and the *Sheffield Times*. Lounsbury (*Life*, pp. 541, 543–544) admits that the *Examiner* and *Howitt's Journal* were favorable.

17. *Life*, p. 545.

18. *Letters of Elizabeth Barrett Browning*, I, 199; *Letters to William Allingham*, p. 41.

19. No exact information seems to be available on the circulation of the *Athenaeum*. Marchand (*The Athenaeum*, p. 45) believes that it probably attained a circulation of as much as 18,000 in 1831. There was some decline in the quality of the paper from 1846 to 1869, but what the number of its readers was in 1848 is impossible to guess. See Marchand, pp. 45, 76–79; also Fox Bourne, *English Newspapers*, II, 313.

20. See *London Journal*, I, 254, 431, 438, 200. I have been unable to discover information about the circulation of the *Guardian*, *Howitt's Journal*, the *Atlas*, and the *Britannia* at this time.

21. *Life*, p. 547.

22. *Athenaeum*, January 1, 1848, p. 7; *Spectator*, XXI, 41; *Atlas*, XXIII, 42.

23. In this case it seems correct to omit the *Dumfries-shire and Galloway Herald*, January 6, 1848, p. [4]. The seven instances in which the moral was mentioned were: *Athenaeum*, January 1, 1848, p. 8; *Sun*, January 8, 1848, p. [3]; *Examiner*, January 8, 1848, p. 21; *Howitt's Journal*, III, 28, 29; *Atlas*, XXIII, 42; *Morning Post*, January 22, 1848, p. 3; *Sheffield Times*, January 29, 1848, p. 2.

24. *Life*, pp. 547–548. In his discussion Lounsbury specifically cites only the reviews in the *Examiner*, *Howitt's Journal*, the *Eclectic Review*, the *Edinburgh Review*, and *Fraser's Magazine*. He comments on the critique in *Blackwood's* in another chapter, pp. 493–495.

25. This ratio was created by the addition of four favorable articles in the magazines for February to the ones already noticed (see the next paragraph). I have been unable to discover the exact dates on which these articles ap-

peared; but from the usual practice with the monthly magazines, it seems safe to assume that they came out about the first of February.

26. The *Dumfries and Galloway Standard and Advertiser*, February 16, 1848, p. [2], summarized the plot and took some of the extracts of *The Princess* from this review.

27. For the history, policy, and nature of the *Christian Reformer*, see McLachlan, *Unitarian Movement*, pp. 185–188, and Mineka, *Dissidence of Dissent*, p. 81.

28. This issue of the *Quarterly* actually appeared on the first day of April. It was announced as "published this day" in the *Athenaeum*, April 1, 1848, p. 331.

W. MacNeile Dixon (*A Primer of Tennyson*, p. 149) says that the review is "attributed to Sara Coleridge." Myron F. Brightfield ("Lockhart's *Quarterly* Contributors," *PMLA*, LIX [1944], 509) lists it as by "J. G. Lockhart (uncertain)."

29. In the light of recent developments, the unimaginative jibes in the *Quarterly* (LXXXII, 438) at the prophetic passages in "Locksley Hall" are worthy of notice: "We cannot but think that such a passage as this occurring in an ancient author would become a *locus vexatissimus*; and, after giving rise to a crowd of conjectures, would be dropped as hopelessly corrupt, with sighs of regret to think how fine it would be if it were but intelligible. For it would be gravely observed that 'pilots of the purple twilight' could not 'drop down with costly bales,' or stand in apposition to argosies with magic or any other kind of sails; that navies engaged in conflict to not '*rain* dew;' that the south wind can never be 'a world-wide whisper;' and that all this commotion of the elements, though it might be used metaphorically to *represent* great changes in the social machinery of the world, produces utter confusion when thus huddled in by the side of them, as if the two were homogeneous."

30. Mineka, *Dissidence of Dissent*, pp. 67–70; see also Graham, *English Literary Periodicals*, p. 239.

31. In the bound volume there is no indication of the monthly issues, but there is an advertisement of *Sharpe's* for April, listing its contents, in the *Athenaeum*, March 25, 1848, p. 325.

32. Graham (*English Literary Periodicals*, p. 256) says that the *North British Review* was an imitator of the *Edinburgh Review*. Patmore's authorship is identified by Frederick Page, *Courage in Politics and Other Essays, 1885–1896*, p. 204.

Patmore was a friend and zealous devotee of Tennyson's at this time. Champneys (*Memoirs . . . of . . . Patmore*, I, 60) thinks that their acquaintance began in 1846, although he is unable to discover any record of their meeting. "The acquaintance," he says, "soon ripened into intimacy: they met constantly, and used to take long walks together at night, often prolonging them into the early morning" (Champneys, I, 178). Tennyson's journal for May 1848 (*Materials*, I, 351) lists an engagement with Patmore on May 5, only a few days after his article in the *North British Review* had appeared; but Champneys (I, 182n.), referring to Patmore's reviews of Tennyson, says, "It appears certain that Tennyson never knew by whom these critiques were written."

33. This periodical was a continuation of the *British Critic*. See Mineka,

Dissidence of Dissent, pp. 51–53, for the history and policy of the *British Critic.*

34. The historians of *The Times* (*The History of The Times: II. The Tradition Established, 1841–1884,* p. 482) are unable to identify the author of this article from the records at their disposal, but Mr. Humphry House (*TLS,* November 4, 1949, p. 715) has shown that Manley Hopkins wrote either the review of *The Princess* or of *In Memoriam* for *The Times,* and possibly both of them.

35. On February 11, 1848, *The Times* sold 30,040 copies (*History of The Times,* p. 196).

36. Compare an ingenious exercise by Henry Sutton, entitled "The Poet's Mission," *Howitt's Journal,* III, 39–42, in which he makes a detailed interpretation of "The Lady of Shalott" as an allegory of a poet's life and the resultant death of his power to create true poetry if he surrenders to worldly fame and popularity.

37. Published between January 29, and February 14, 1848. See *Publishers' Circular,* February 15, 1848, XI, 72.

38. *Weekly Chronicle,* March 19, 1848, p. 3. According to the *London Journal* in 1845 (I, 397), "The WEEKLY CHRONICLE has all along been a consistent Whig. . . . The Literary Notices . . . are most impartially and judiciously executed; and publishers are in the habit of frequently quoting, in their advertisements of new books, passages from those reviews of the volumes so announced." The circulation was said to have been at that time "about 10,000."

39. See Strout, " 'Christopher North' on Tennyson," *RES,* XIV, 434n., and "William Henry Smith," *DNB.*

40. Of *Poems,* 1842, Lounsbury (*Life,* p. 418) writes, "There were some prepared to scoff and ready to prove that the light by which a few erring souls appeared to be dazzled was a mere meteoric exhalation which would speedily vanish from view. But it soon became apparent that the temper of the educated public was such as to make an action of this sort perilous." He calls this review in *Blackwood's* "on the whole very complimentary," adding, "In fact such was getting to be the temperament of the public that it was becoming a somewhat risky procedure for either reviewer or review to be otherwise" (*Life,* p. 493). Although Lounsbury certainly exaggerates, it must be said in fairness to him that a reviewer in the *Westminster Review* (July 1849, LI, 266), noticing the fifth edition of *Poems,* said "to dispraise [Tennyson] would show far more courage" than to express admiration of him.

41. For Tennyson's identification, in a letter to Aubrey de Vere, see below, p. 211, n. 57. Charles Peter Chretien was a fellow of Oriel College, Oxford. His *Lectures on the Study of Theology* was reviewed by the *Christian Remembrancer* (XXII, 252) in 1851.

42. De Vere writes that he first met Tennyson in 1841 or 1842. "Whenever we were both in London," he says, "I met him as often as I could" (*Memoir,* I, 207). Kingsley had been an admirer of Tennyson's poetry since the publication of *Poems,* 1842, which he described in a letter of June 8, 1842 (*The Life and Works of Charles Kingsley,* I, 74), as "the most beautiful poetry of the last fifteen years." He met the poet in December 1849 (*Life . . . of . . . Kingsley,* I, 233), and their acquaintance seems to have grown into a cordial

relationship. Early in 1850 Kingsley was on intimate enough terms to be cited as "strenuously" supporting Charles Tennyson Turner in urging the marriage of Tennyson and Emily Sellwood (*Materials*, II, 38). See also Tennyson's letter to Kingsley in 1853 printed in the *Memoir*, I, 366–367.

Eidson (*Tennyson in America*, pp. 68 and 223, n. 44), citing De Vere's and Kingsley's reviews, says, "The British critics had undoubtedly been swayed by public opinion." If there was any influence of public opinion upon De Vere's critique, it seems to have acted in the opposite direction. Where the author had written that Tennyson was a "great" poet, Empson, the editor, had changed the adjective to "true"; and De Vere writes (*Memoir*, I, 208), "He considered that the public would not tolerate so strong a eulogium."

In his reminiscences of Tennyson in the mid-forties De Vere writes (*Memoir*, I, 210), "Our many conversations, in those pleasant years, turned chiefly on Poetry, a subject on which Tennyson could say nothing that was not original." For De Vere's listening to Tennyson read the "University of Women," see Ward, *Aubrey de Vere*, pp. 71, 74.

De Vere's article in the *Edinburgh* also reviewed *The Poetical Works of Percy Bysshe Shelley*, ed. Mary Shelley (London, 1847), *Life, Letters, and Literary Remains, of John Keats*, ed. Richard Monckton Milnes (London, 1848).

43. *Memoir*, I, 260-261.

44. This review included remarks on *Poems, The Princess*, and *In Memoriam*.

45. The reviews are as follows:

Favorable	Unfavorable
Guardian	*Athenaeum*
Sun	*Dumfries-shire and Galloway Herald*
Examiner	*Spectator*
Manchester Examiner	*Atlas*
Howitt's Journal	*Britannia*
Morning Post	*Quarterly*
Sheffield Times	*Eclectic*
Gentleman's Magazine	*Sharpe's London Magazine*
Lowe's Edinburgh Magazine	*Dublin Evening Herald*
Metropolitan	*Literary Gazette*
Christian Reformer	*Tait's Edinburgh*
North British Review	*The Times*
English Review	*Blackwood's*
Fraser's Magazine	*Christian Remembrancer*
Edinburgh Review	
Christian Socialist	

46. *Examiner*, January 8, 1848, p. 20.

47. *Edinburgh Review*, XC, 406.

48. *Fraser's Magazine*, XLII, 250.

49. *North British Review*, IX, 61, 72.

50. *Athenaeum*, January 1, 1848, p. 6.

51. *Christian Remembrancer*, XVII, 382.

52. *Examiner*, January 8, 1848, p. 21. The second italics are mine.

53. *Sun*, January 8, 1848, p. [3].

54. The sixth edition of *Poems* was published between February 14 and 27; see *Publishers' Circular*, March 1, 1850, XIII, 92. The third edition of *The Princess* was published between January 29 and February 14, 1850; see *Publishers' Circular*, February 15, 1850, XIII, 77.

55. This remark occurred in a review of the fifth edition of *Poems*, in which the reviewer, who signed himself "Is. Is.," became ecstatic over "Locksley Hall," "Oenone," the political poems, "The Poet," "Ulysses," and "The Palace of Art." In a letter of January 9, 1850 (*Letters of Elizabeth Barrett Browning*, I, 431), Mrs. Browning wrote that Tennyson "stands already on a pedestal, and is recognised as a master spirit not by a coterie but by the great public."

The critic for *Lowe's Edinburgh Magazine* called him "*the* great poet of the day," and the writer of the notice in the *Manchester Examiner* said that he was already placed among "the Great Ones of Song."

56. *Memoir*, I, 256. Kingsley's critique in *Fraser's* (XLII, 245–255) is also included in this remark, but this article appeared after the publication of the third edition, in which the most extensive revisions are to be found. There was little in Kingsley's review that might have suggested alterations. For Tennyson's reaction to De Vere's article, see his letters to De Vere in the *Memoir* (I, 260–261, 281–283); see also above, pp. 132–138.

57. *The Poetic and Dramatic Works of Alfred Lord Tennyson*, p. 815, and *Memoir*, I, 280. In the letter to De Vere, Tennyson said, "The sea is my delight, tho' Mr. Chretien in the *Christian Examiner* says that I have no power upon him and represent him dead asleep." Although the poet wrote *Christian Examiner*, it is clear that he referred to the *Christian Remembrancer*, for the reviewer in that journal devoted the greater part of two pages to illustrating the tranquillity with which Tennyson reproduced the sea. "The same features characterise our author in dealing with nature," he commented, "as with man. One instance will suffice: let us observe how he treats the sea." And the reviewer went on to quote passages showing that the poet "confines himself to its gentler aspects." "These are pictures," he said, "undeniably; and true to nature; but still they are subdued. The waves roar like any nightingale; we see and hear as from a distance; there is a mistiness, a creaminess, a mellowness, a gleam of muffled moonlight . . . cast over all."

58. *Letters of Elizabeth Barrett Browning*, I, 361.

59. Although Wise is always unreliable, the original edition cannot have been much under his figure of 2,000 copies (*Bibliography*, I, 100); and a second edition was soon called for.

60. *Letters of Edward FitzGerald*, I, 237.

61. *Memoir*, I, 260.

62. *Memoir*, I, 282. From the context it is obvious that the letter was written not long after the publication of the third edition of *The Princess*, which appeared between January 29 and February 14, 1850. For documentation of this date, see below, p. 212, n. 63.

The review in the *Westminster* (July, 1849, LI, 265–290) was of the fifth edition of *Poems*.

63. While the third, fourth, and fifth editions appear to be editions in the accepted sense, bibliographical evidence indicates that except for the title gathering and a few minor alterations in the text, the second edition was

actually a reprint of the first. The dedication to Henry Lushington is dated January 1848. There is no reason to suppose that there was much delay in printing the second edition, so that even if January 1848 is the author's date (as it probably is), the book may well have been issued in late January or early February. At any rate, Patmore quoted a slightly altered passage from the second edition in his article in the *North British Review* for May 1848, which was announced for sale on April 29 in the *Athenaeum* of that date (p. 426). Lounsbury (*Life*, pp. 532–533) follows Wise in asserting that the second edition was published in September 1848.

The third edition is listed as published between January 29 and February 14, 1850, in the *Publishers' Circular*, February 15, 1850, XIII, 77.

The fourth edition is listed as published between March 29 and April 14, 1851, in the *Publishers' Circular*, April 15, XIV, 132.

The fifth edition does not appear in the *Publishers' Circular*, but it is given as published in February 1853 in Sampson Low's *A Catalogue of Books Published in the United Kingdom During the Year 1853*, p. 53, which is bound with the Bodleian copy of the *Publishers' Circular*, XVI (1853).

64. For example, the *Literary Gazette* (August 12, 1848, p. 531) cited the lines,

> and *light,*
> As flies the *shadow* of a bird, she fled,
>
> (1st ed., p. 51, lines 4–5)

as a "curious contradiction in mere terms." The *Britannia* (January 22, 1848, p. 61) remarked of the following passage, "Such an abominable collection of far-fetched prettiness was surely never heaped together before":

> Now while they spake, I saw my father's face
> Grow *long* and troubled LIKE *a rising-moon,*
> Inflamed with wrath: he started on his feet,
> Tore the King's letter, *snow'd it down,* and rent
> The wonder of the loom thro' warp and woof
> From skirt to skirt; and at the last he swore
> That he would send a hundred thousand men,
> And bring her in a whirlwind: then he chew'd
> The *thrice-turn'd* cud of wrath, and *cook'd his spleen,*
> Communing with his captains of the war.
>
> (1st ed., p. 15, lines 5–14; typography
> as printed in the *Britannia*)

A very interesting passage that Tennyson refused to change runs,

> Back started she, and turning round we saw
> The Lady Blanche's daughter where she stood,
> Melissa, with her hand upon the lock,
> A rosy blonde, and in a college gown
> That clad her like an April daffodilly
> (Her mother's colour) with her lips apart,

And all her thoughts as fair within her eyes,
As bottom agates seem to wave and float
In crystal currents of clear morning seas.

(1st ed., p. 39, lines 11–19)

The *Quarterly* (LXXXII, 445) complained, "What a pity to break this pretty picture by that harsh stroke about the mother's faded hue! — and daffodils are not April guests, but 'take the winds of *March* with beauty.' " In his first stricture the reviewer was obviously mistaken, for the parenthetical reference "Her mother's colour" is to the fact that all of Lady Blanche's pupils wore yellow gowns. Tennyson, who prided himself on the accuracy of his allusions to natural history might have acted on the second if his personal observation had not been to the contrary. He wrote to Rolfe (*Poetic . . . Works of . . . Tennyson*, p. 815), "Daffodils in the North of England belong as much to April as to March. I myself remember a man presenting me in the streets of Dublin the finest bunch of daffodils I almost ever saw on the 15th of April. It amused me at the time, for I had just been reading the Quarterly article." Rolfe adds to the poet's defense that "*ten days* of Shakespeare's *March* properly belonged to *April*, as we now reckon it."

65. The italics in this quotation and the one following are in the *Guardian*. "Fabled nothing fair" appeared in the third edition, p. 58, line 9.

66. Italics in the *Quarterly*.

67. It is possible that these passages were revised in Tennyson's general strengthening of the meter of the poem rather than as the result of the specific strictures cited here, but in either case their alteration seems to have resulted from adverse criticism.

68. *North British Review*, IX, 71.

69. *Formation of Tennyson's Style*, p. 171.

70. The *Morning Post* (January 22, 1848, p. 3) said that the second title, "A Medley," was "highly appropriate" and went "far towards disarming criticism"; for the poet had purposely made the poem a potpourri. It was "perfectly obvious" to the critic in the *English Review* (IX, 291) that "the poet designed from the first this charming combination of things old and new: this combination was his distinctive aim, and it is realized with a grace which probably none but himself could have attained. . . . it *is* all of one piece, and this wondrous unity in seeming discord is the distinctive charm of the work." De Vere asserted in the *Edinburgh* (XC, 390) that in being a medley the poem corresponded to the heterogeneous character of the age. Its narrative, he said, springs appropriately out of the situation described in the Prologue. In combining humor and solemnity, "the poem is in harmony with nature; who so intertwines the grave with the gay, in her passages of sadness or promise, that the colour of the web is dark or bright according to the humour of him who handles it." The *Christian Reformer* (N. S., IV, 112) and *Sharpe's London Magazine* (VI, 140) adopted the comparative method. Said the former, critics "will point out the inconsistency of modern science with 'tilt and tourney for a lady's hand,' with as much reason as if they were to object to the 'Christmas Carol,' that Scrooge the miser, a real personage, was inconsistent with a goblin in whose existence nobody believes." The latter maintained that if the action of *The Princess* was improbable, why so

also was that of *The Tempest*. But it should be recalled that Tennyson said he remembered adverse criticism only (see above, p. 38).

71. *Examiner*, January 8, 1848, p. 21.

72. *Athenaeum*, January 1, 1848, p. 7.

73. *Life*, pp. 535–536, 563.

74. *Memoir*, I, 253.

75. An early version of the lines that became the Interlude, without the simile of one who claps the hands to change the music, exists in a notebook in which Tennyson wrote short introductions, describing the narrator, for each of the parts of the poem. (See Charles Tennyson, *Cornhill*, CLIII, 678; Sir Charles kindly permitted me to examine this notebook.) Tennyson had abandoned this scheme before the poem appeared, and the influence of criticism upon his decision to refurbish and insert the introductory lines for part V as an Interlude is as significant as if he had written all of them entirely after the first publication of the poem.

76. *Athenaeum*, January 1, 1848, p. 7.

77. Patmore quoted this reading from the second edition in a footnote to his article in *North British Review* and remarked, "Mr. Tennyson has been taught, by the reception of his first edition, a little of the wisdom which is commonly the last at which great writers arrive, namely, that of giving the 'reading public' sufficient credit for obtuseness."

78. See *Britannia*, January 22, 1848, p. 61; *Literary Gazette*, August 12, 1848, p. 531; *Quarterly*, LXXXII, 450–451.

79. *Memoir*, I, 253–254.

80. *Memoir*, I, 247. Tennyson was by no means alone in seeking a compromise. As John Stuart Mill wrote on January 18, 1854 (*The Letters of John Stuart Mill*, II, 360–361), "In the present age the writers of reputation and influence are those who take something from both sides of the great controversies, and make out that neither extreme is right, nor wholly wrong. By some persons, and on some questions, this is done in the way of mere compromise; in some cases, again, by a deeper doctrine underlying both the contrary opinions; but done it is, in one or the other way, by all who gain access to the mind of the present age: and none but those who do it, or seem to do it, are now listened to."

81. *A Study . . . of . . . The Princess*, p. 49.

82. *Memoir*, I, 251.

83. Tennyson is quoted by his son (*Memoir*, I, 320) as writing, "A kind of waking trance I have frequently had, quite up from boyhood, when I have been all alone. This has generally come upon me thro' repeating my own name two or three times to myself silently, till all at once, as it were out of the intensity of the consciousness of individuality, the individuality itself seemed to dissolve and fade away into boundless being, and this not a confused state, but the clearest of the clearest, the surest of the surest, the weirdest of the weird, utterly beyond words, where death was an almost laughable impossibility, the loss of personality (if so it were) seeming no extinction but the only true life." He described this phenomenon in "The Ancient Sage," lines 229–239. Compare also the mystical experience recorded in *In Memoriam*, xcv. As Mr. Paull F. Baum (*Tennyson Sixty Years After*, p. 288n.) points out, however, the "weird seizures" are not mystical.

84. Lounsbury, *Life*, p. 535; Dawson, *A Study . . . of . . . The Princess*, p. 49.

85. See these passages in the fourth edition: Prince's seizure, p. 102, line 12 to p. 103, line 2; the joust, p. 131, line 12 to p. 134, line 4; and the mental condition of the Prince, p. 136, lines 1–3, and p. 159, lines 1–3.

86. The first letter is printed in the *Memoir*, I, 260, the second on pp. 281–282. Hallam Tennyson incorrectly dates the first letter 1847. Since the poet mentions De Vere's article in the *Edinburgh Review*, which appeared in the issue for October 1849, there can be no doubt that the new edition referred to is the third, published in 1850. Regarding the "dying and the dead," De Vere had actually said, "The combat takes place in the presence of both courts; and the Prince, with his two friends, after a terrible conflict, is left on the plain among the dying and the dead."

87. These animadversions specified in the *Edinburgh* may be summarized as follows: (1) the character of the Prince is not individualized enough; (2) classical allusions seem to be put into his mouth too frequently; (3) the diction is sometimes too colloquial; (4) a few periods occur which are lacking in compactness; (5) the Princess seems too metaphysical in her discourse with the Prince as they proceed on the afternoon excursion. There was definitely no reduction of the classical allusions or of the metaphysical content of the Princess's remarks. There are some indications that the poet made revisions in accordance with objections (1), (3), and (4), but the evidence is inconclusive.

88. The *Gentleman's Magazine* (N.S., XXIX, 131) said, "The incidents, rather than the characters, take our attention. We cannot sympathize with the Princess, because we cannot agree with her opinions, or approve her practice. She is to us a *frozen* woman throughout, and when she *thaws* at last, we should have liked a little more heat and more water." The *Quarterly* (LXXXXII, 443) commented, "The Princess is too soft to be terrible, and much too hard to be loveable."

89. Patmore (*North British Review*, IX, 70) observed the same point, saying of "Our enemies have fallen," "If we are to rest in the superficial meaning of the poem, this chant is a senseless impertinence."

90. *Memoir*, I, 254.

91. See *Athenaeum*, January 1, 1848, p. 8; *Examiner*, January 8, 1848, p. 20; *Manchester Examiner*, January 8, 1848, p. 3; *Atlas*, XXIII, 42; *Morning Post*, January 22, 1848, p. 3; *Sheffield Times*, January 29, 1848, p. 2; *Gentleman's Magazine*, N.S., XXIX, 120–121, 129; *Lowe's Edinburgh Magazine*, N.S., III, 254–256; *Quarterly*, LXXXII, 452; *Sharpe's London Magazine*, VI, 141; *Literary Gazette*, August 12, 1848, p. 531; *Edinburgh Review*, XC, 392–393, 396–397.

92. *The Correspondence of Thomas Carlyle and Ralph Waldo Emerson, 1834–1872*, II, 66.

CHAPTER V. THE PINNACLE OF SUCCESS: *IN MEMORIAM*

1. Tennyson printed a few copies and circulated them among his friends in the spring of 1850. Not long after the publication of the third edition of

The Princess in January 1850, he wrote in a letter to De Vere (*Memoir*, I, 282), "With respect to the 'Elegies,' I cannot say that I have turned my attention to them lately. I do not know whether I have done anything new in that quarter since you saw them, but I believe I am going to print them, and then I need not tell you that you will be perfectly welcome to a copy, on the condition that when the book is published, this avant-courier of it shall be either sent back to me, or die the death by fire in Curragh Chase. I shall print about twenty-five copies, and let them out among friends under the same condition of either return or cremation." William Michael Rossetti records in the "P R B Journal" (*Praeraphaelite Diaries and Letters*, p. 267) under date of March 21, 1850, "I went to Patmore's with the proof of his *Macbeth*. He has got one of some half-dozen copies of Tennyson's Elegies that have been printed strictly for private perusal."

In Memoriam may have been ready for distribution before June 1, for the *Publishers' Circular* (June 1, 1850, XIII, 190) listed it among the books published between May 14 and 29. But the actual day of publication seems to have been Saturday, June 1. In their issues of June 1, the *Athenaeum* (p. 583), the *Literary Gazette* (p. 380), and *John Bull* (p. 348), all listed *In Memoriam* in the column of new books; and Hallam Tennyson (*Materials*, II, 39n.) says that the poem was published on that date.

For estimates of the date of composition of various sections of *In Memoriam*, see A. C. Bradley, *A Commentary on Tennyson's In Memoriam*, pp. 11–19, and Eleanor B. Mattes, *In Memoriam: The Way of the Soul*, pp. 111–125. Although much of the poem was written in the early years, the letter to De Vere in 1850 quoted above shows that the poet continued to work on the "Elegies" until a very late date; and the proem was dated 1849 by the author.

2. See *Morning Post*, May 29, 1850, p. 8; *Spectator*, June 1, 1850, XXIII, 526.

3. Since this notice was very favorable, I see no reason to suspect that a joke was deliberately intended.

4. Hallam Tennyson (*Memoir*, I, 298) erroneously says, "At first the reviews of the volume were not on the whole sympathetic." Nicolson (*Tennyson*, p. 163), apparently enlarging upon this view, writes, "At first the reviewers were generally unfavourable, and it was only later, when the huge popularity of the book, not only with the general public, but also with the outstanding thinkers of the day, had been abundantly emphasised, that they altered their tone to one of deference." But Lounsbury (*Life*, p. 620) is substantially correct in saying, "From the very moment of its publication it was greeted with an almost unanimous chorus of approval by the critical press."

5. According to Mitchell (*The Newspaper Press Directory . . . for the Year 1851*, pp. 114–115), "The 'Leader' takes a bold aim. It aspires at being the organ of the religious and social reformers. . . . Some of the cleverest 'gentlemen of the Press' are connected with the 'Leader,' which is conducted in every department with great ability. . . . Literature forms a prominent feature in the 'Leader.' " For detailed information concerning the *Leader*, see Anna T. Kitchel, *George Lewes and George Eliot*, pp. 63–139. Lewes' marked file of the *Leader* is in the Yale University Library. I am indebted to Professor Gordon S. Haight for calling it to my attention.

6. In this comparison the reviewer referred only to the sonnet sequences of Shakespeare and Spenser.

7. I use throughout the numbers of the sections of the final text. Present section XXXIX was added in 1870 and section LIX in 1851.

8. Jerdan's connection with the paper ended on December 28, 1850. See "William Jerdan," *DNB*.

9. For identification of Marston's authorship, see Marchand, *The Athenaeum*, p. 278.

10. For information concerning the *Inquirer*, see McLachlan, *Unitarian Movement*, pp. 212–220.

11. See Mitchell, *Newspaper Press Directory . . . 1851*, p. 107.

12. *Autobiography of Henry Taylor*, II, 62. Miss Fenwick, a cousin of Taylor's stepmother, became a greatly revered friend and correspondent of his.

13. In this brief survey I do not attempt to mention all the reviews of *In Memoriam* which are cited in full in the List of Reviews, pp. 173–174 above. Varous sections of the poem, usually preceded by a short explanation of the nature of the work and a statement that it is addressed by Tennyson to Arthur Hallam, were printed in the following papers: *Scotsman* (Edinburgh), June 12, p. [3]; *Birmingham Journal*, June 15, p. 3; *Leeds Times*, June 15, p. 6, June 22, p. 6; *Bristol Mercury*, June 15, p. 6, June 22, p. 6; *Ayr Advertiser*, June 20, p. [2]; *Nottingham Mercury*, June 21, p. 6; *Belfast Protestant Journal*, June 22, p. [4]; *Perthshire Advertiser*, June 27, p. [4]. Further reprints from *In Memoriam* occurred in provincial papers during the remainder of 1850.

14. Champneys (*Memoirs . . . of . . . Patmore*, II, 303n.) identifies Franklin Lushington as the author of this review and quotes a letter to Patmore from Tennyson, written from the Lake District in 1850, "Will you get me a Tait? My wife wants to see the Review there of I. M." While Lushington seems to have been a genuine admirer of Tennyson's poetry, he could show exasperation with the poet's foibles. See his letter of February 8, 1852, to William Brookfield (Charles and Frances Brookfield, *Mrs. Brookfield and Her Circle*, II, 370).

15. Patmore's authorship is established by Frederick Page, *Courage in Politics*, p. 204.

16. Interestingly enough, William Michael Rossetti (*Praeraphaelite Diaries*, p. 282) under date of November 3, 1850, wrote, "Patmore does not believe we have any really great men living in the region of pure intellect; not even Tennyson, though he might have thought him such, had he not written."

17. Moxon advertised the second edition in the *Athenaeum*, July 13, 1850, p. 724. Lounsbury (*Life*, p. 623) says that the third edition "came out at the end of November"; and the *Morning Post*, August 31, and the *Eclectic Review* for September reviewed the second edition and not the third. But Sampson Low's *A Catalogue of Books Published in the United Kingdom During the Year 1850*, p. 23, gives the third edition as published in August. (This catalogue is bound with the *Publishers' Circular*, XIII [1850] in the Bodleian.)

18. *A. T.*, p. 247. Lounsbury (*Life*, p. 623), and Wise (*Bibliography*, I, 108) also say there were 5,000 copies in the first edition.

19. Tennyson thought the stanza was his own invention. "As for the metre of 'In Memoriam,'" he says (*Memoir*, I, 305–306), "I had no notion

until 1880 that Lord Herbert of Cherbury had written his occasional verses in the same metre. I believed myself the originator of the metre, until after 'In Memoriam' came out, when some one told me that Ben Jonson and Sir Philip Sidney had used it." Pyre (*Formation of Tennyson's Style*, p. 105) declares, "It was a natural product of his experiments."

20. The *North British Review* (XIII, 547) pointed out, however, that Tennyson was probably not the inventor.

21. The *Spectator* (XXIII, 546) was pleased with the "pictures of common landscape and of daily life." The *Inquirer* (IX, 389) declared, "The great charm . . . of the volume . . . lies in the exquisite description of simple and pastoral landscape." The *Morning Post* (August 31, 1850, p. 2) admired "the description of natural scenery, or the delineation of the domestic affections," which were both sources of inspiration and "comprehensive" and "delightful" subjects for the poet. The *Atlas* (XXV, 379) pointed out approvingly. "The images are all of the domestic type — the associations are redolent of the home and the household affections." The *Guardian* (June 26, 1850, p. 477), the *Britannia* (June 29, 1850, p. 410), and the *Court Journal* (August 10, 1850, p. 505) applauded Tennyson's observation and reproduction of nature; and Lushington in *Tait's* (N.S., XVII, 502) remarked upon the "power of accurate delineation of the charms of English landscape . . . visible everywhere through the volume." The *Westminster Review* (LIV, 99) rhapsodized, "Neither poet, nor poet-painter gives the beauty that belongs to English scenery as Tennyson does. Single lines, and solitary verses, forming home pictures of English life, giving the key to a world of rural beauty . . . press to the memory."

22. *Fraser's Magazine*, XLII, 255.

23. *Palladium*, I, 97–98.

24. Alfred Ainger ("Tennyson," *DNB*) says of *In Memoriam*, "The party theologians bitterly denounced it"; but this attack in the *English Review* is the only instance that I have found in print after an extensive search of religious periodicals.

25. *Essays Ancient and Modern*, p. 187.

26. *Standard of Freedom*, September 7, 1850, p. 12.

27. *English Review*, XIV, 68.

28. A letter from Mrs. Browning to Miss Mitford, December 13, 1850 (*Letters of Elizabeth Barrett Browning*, I, 472–473), expresses the same feeling as that of the *Eclectic*: "Indeed I do not wonder at the opinion which has reached us from various quarters that Tennyson stands higher through having written it [*In Memoriam*]. You see, what he appeared to want, according to the view of many, was an earnest personality and direct purpose. In this last book, though of course there is not room in it for that exercise of creative faculty which elsewhere established his fame, he appeals heart to heart, directly as from his own to the universal heart, and we all feel him nearer to us — I do — and so do others."

29. The *Inquirer* professed to be still a worshiper "at older shrines" than Tennyson.

30. The quotations in this paragraph are from the *Eclectic Review*, 4th Ser., XXVIII, 339; *Britannia*, June 29, 1850, p. 410; *Hogg's Instructor*, N.S., V, 367, 368; *Tait's Edinburgh Magazine*, N.S., XVII, 499. The *Inquirer* (IX,

390) was alone in saying, "Though the strain to which we have been listening will linger long in our memory, and recur at intervals amid the stir of life, yet we fear it is of too delicate structure to outlive our own age, and that it will — 'On the ear of Time,/Leave but a dying echo.' "

31. *Athenaeum*, June 1, 1850, p. 585, and June 22, p. 662; for Chorley's authorship, see Marchand, *The Athenaeum*, pp. 79 and 274, n. 101. Regarding Tennyson and Hunt, see *Leader*, June 8, 1850, I, 254; *Athenaeum*, April 27, 1850, p. 451, June 22, p. 662. Hunt discussed his own qualifications in *The Autobiography of Leigh Hunt* (III, 274–283), published on June 8.

32. P. W. Clayden, *Rogers and His Contemporaries*, II, 352, 353. Prince Albert himself wrote the letter to Rogers offering him the post. Since Prince Albert as Chancellor of Cambridge University had tried to get Rogers to accept an honorary degree, it is probable that the Prince was responsible for the proffer of the laureateship.

33. *The Letters of Queen Victoria . . . 1837–1861*, II, 266. Nicolson (*Tennyson*, p. 166) incorrectly reports that Leigh Hunt's name was one of the four submitted by the Prime Minister.

34. Clayden, *Rogers and His Contemporaries*, II, 354.

35. *Letters of Queen Victoria*, II, 272.

36. *Memoir*, I, 335. I am indebted to Miss Mary MacKenzie, Registrar of the Royal Archives at Windsor, for identifying Sir Charles Phipps's official position. Hallam Tennyson (*Memoir*, I, 334) says that the appointment was made "owing chiefly to Prince Albert's admiration for 'In Memoriam' "; but George G. Napier (*The Homes and Haunts of Alfred Lord Tennyson*, p. 89) asserts that "The Miller's Daughter" touched the Queen deeply and that "it was the recollection of this bucolic idyll which decided Her Majesty, in face of all opposition, to confer the much coveted wreath on its author." From Prince Albert's prominence in the correspondence with the Prime Minister, it appears that he was taking the lead about filling the office of laureate and that his judgment would most likely have been the deciding factor. Unfortunately, the Royal Archives throw no light on the matter.

The night before the letter arrived offering Tennyson the laureateship, he dreamed "that Prince Albert came and kissed him on the cheek, and that he said in his dream, 'Very kind, but very German.' " See *Memoir*, I, 335.

37. *Memoir*, I, 336, 334. Tennyson's letter of acceptance does not exist in the Royal Archives or the Public Record Office.

38. *Athenaeum*, November 23, 1850, p. 1218. Tennyson, of course, already held a Civil List pension.

39. *Leader*, November 23, 1850, I, 832–833.

40. *Leigh Hunt's Journal*, December 7, 1850, p. 16. Hunt had previously congratulated Tennyson personally in a letter of November 25 (*Materials*, II, 47–48).

41. *Letters of Elizabeth Barrett Browning*, I, 471.

42. *A Catalogue of Books Published in the United Kingdom During the Year 1851*, p. 27. (Bound with the *Publishers' Circular*, XIV [1851] in the Bodleian.)

43. *Correspondence of Henry Taylor*, p. 194. Taylor gives the "5,000 strong" figure.

44. Mr. House, who has shown (*TLS*, November 4, 1949, p. 715) that

Hopkins wrote either the review of *The Princess* or of *In Memoriam* in *The Times* — and possibly both of them — seems to think it more likely that he was the author of the latter. See above, p. 209, n. 34.

45. Knowles ("Aspects of Tennyson, II," p. 187) quotes Tennyson as saying, "If anybody thinks I ever called him 'dearest' in his life they are much mistaken, for I never even called him 'dear'" (I omit Knowles's italics). This remark indicates that the poet has seen the stricture in *The Times*.

46. The italics are in *The Times*.

47. "The 'Times' and the Poets," *Tait's Edinburgh Magazine*, January 1852, N.S., XIX, 18–21; *Two Lectures on the Influence of Poetry on the Working Classes*, pp. 26–34. The lectures were delivered in February 1852. *Tait's* attributed the belated animosity of *The Times* to political motives. The magazine asserted that *The Times* suspected Tennyson of "Liberal tendencies." The poetry of Browning and his wife had already become infected with "cosmopolite Liberalism."

"What [said *Tait's*] if the author of 'In Memoriam' should take to sympathising with the Italian Liberals? . . . Vague rumours have crossed us that Mr. Tennyson has lately voyaged to Italy. How do we know that he is not already in active correspondence with Mazzini? . . .

"So, lest Mr. Tennyson should do himself and the world some irreparable harm by a rash outburst of Republican melody, we, the *Times,* are minded to put him down privily."

48. *Memoir*, I, 297, 304.

49. "Aspects of Tennyson, II," p. 182 (I omit Knowles's italics).

50. As Mr. Eliot (*Essays Ancient and Modern*, p. 184) says, "This is not a question of insincerity: there is an amalgam of yielding and opposition below the level of consciousness."

51. *Tennyson Sixty Years After*, p. 125.

52. *Memoir*, I, 294.

53. Fourteen of the total number of twenty-five passages were singled out by *The Times*.

CHAPTER VI. CONCLUSION

1. *Essays Ancient and Modern*, p. 175.

2. Knowles, "Aspects of Tennyson, II," p. 170 (I omit Knowles's italics).

3. Ward, *Aubrey de Vere*, p. 74.

4. Tennyson is quoted by his son (*Materials*, II, 17n.) as complaining, "They are always speaking of me as if I were a writer of philosophical treatises."

5. *Letters of Robert Browning and Elizabeth Barrett Barrett*, I, 24.

INDEX